T5-CUP-106

^ATE ^

Library Instruction
and
Reference Services

Topics in *The Reference Librarian* series:

- Library Instruction & Reference Services
- Cataloging & Reference Services
- Evaluation of Reference Services
- Conflicts in Reference Services
- Personnel in Reference Services
- The Reference Interview

Published:

Reference Services in the 1980s, Numbers 1/2
Reference Services Administration and Management, Number 3
Ethics and Reference Services, Number 4
Video to Online: Reference Services and the New Technology, Numbers 5/6
Reference Services for Children and Young Adults, Numbers 7/8
Reference Services and Technical Services: Interactions in Library Practice, Number 9
Library Instruction and Reference Services, Number 10

Library Instruction and Reference Services

Edited by
Bill Katz and Ruth A. Fraley

School of Library & Information Science
State University of New York at Albany

The Haworth Press
New York

Library Instruction and Reference Services has also been published as *The Reference Librarian,* Number 10, Spring/Summer 1984.

The Haworth Press, Inc. 28 East 22 Street, New York, NY 10010

Library of Congress Cataloging in Publication Data
Main entry under title:

Library instruction and reference services.

    Published also as no. 10, spring/summer 1984, of the Reference librarian.
    Includes bibliographical references.
    1. Reference services (Libraries)—Addresses, essays, lectures. 2. Library orientation—Addresses, essays, lectures. 3. Bibliography—Methodology—Study and teaching—Addresses, essays, lectures. 4. Libraries and readers—Addresses, essays, lectures. I. Katz, William A., 1924-   . II. Fraley, Ruth A.
Z711.2.L732   1984   025.5'6   84-505
ISBN 0-86656-288-5

Library Instruction and Reference Services

The Reference Librarian
Number 10

CONTENTS

INTRODUCTION

An Overview   3
  Ruth Fraley

BI and Library Instruction: Some Observations   5
  Evan Ira Farber

Instructional Areas   6
The Reference Area   7
The Reference Desk   9
Working Space   11
The New Technology   11

Organizational Change: A Public Services Application 15
  John Lubans, Jr.

Step 1: Identifying the Problem   16
Step 2: Forming the Task Force   18
Step 3: Finding Out   18
Steps 1, 2 and 3 Applied   20

ANOTHER VIEW

Never Mind the Quality, Feel the Width   29
  Donald Davinson

Bibliographic Instruction and the Reference Desk:
A Symbiotic Relationship   39
  C. Paul Vincent

TECHNIQUES AND QUESTIONS

The "Compleat" Library Patron   51
  Robert Harris

The Reference Librarian Who Teaches: The Confessions
  of a Mother Hen   55
  John C. Swan

Training Reference Librarians Using Library Instruction
  Methods   67
  Anne F. Roberts

Library-Use Instruction With Individual Users: Should
  Instruction Be Included in the Reference Interview?   75
  James Rice

  Introduction   75
  An Argument for Library-Use Instruction in One-to-One
    Reference Service   77
  An Ethical Consideration   82
  Conclusion   82

Clues or Answers? Which Response to Library Users'
  Questions?   85
  Ray Lester

  Peripheral Factors   86
  Costs and Benefits   87
  However. . .   89

The Question of Questioning: On the Coexistence
  of Library Instruction and Reference   93
  John Budd

Reference/Technical Services Cooperation in Library
  Instruction   101
    Lois M. Pausch
    Carol B. Penka

Mental Maps and Metaphors in Academic Libraries   **109**
Raymond G. McInnis

The Concept of Mental Map   109
Mental Maps and Metaphors   110
Perception Studies   111
Referencing Behavior in Scholarly Articles   113
Mental Maps for Scholarly Articles and Other
    Modes of Scientific Communication   114
Conclusions   118

INSTRUCTION IN PUBLIC LIBRARIES

Library Instruction in Public Libraries: A Dream
Deferred, A Goal to Actualize   **123**
Patricia F. Beilke

Definitions   123
Need for Library Adult Education   124
Trends   125
Implications of Trends   126
Goals of Library Adult Education   127
Importance of Instructional Objectives   129
Evaluation Based on Objectives   129
Conclusion   130

Library Instruction Through the Reference Query   **135**
Jane A. Reilly

Structuring the Program of Library Instruction   137
Assisting the Patron to Gather Materials On-Site
    and Introducing Network and Supplementary Services   140
Sharing a Dream   144

Library Use Instruction in the Small and Medium Public
Library: A Review of the Literature   **149**
Jerry Carbone

Introduction   149

Trends   149
Definition of the Problem   150
The Literature   150
Philosophy of Library Instruction   151
Library Instruction: The Programs   152
The Attic Door Opened. . .   154
Conclusion   156

INSTRUCTION IN ACADEMIC LIBRARIES

**The Administrative Climate for Bibliographic Instruction
in Large Academic Libraries**   **161**
    Ron Blazek

Introduction   161
Review of the Literature   166
Methodology   168
Analysis of Data   171
Findings, Conclusions and Implications   176

**Library Instruction and Reference Service: Administration
of a Bibliographic Instruction Program in the Academic
Library**   **181**
    Maureen Pastine

Introduction   181
Administration of Bibliographic Instruction   182
Responsibility for a Bibliographic Instruction Program   183
Administration of Bibliographic Instruction Through
   Reference Departments   185
Summary   187

**Bibliographic Education and Reference Desk Service—
A Continuum**   **191**
    Mary Reichel

Library Instruction for Faculty Members   **199**
    Eric W. Johnson

The Student Orientation Class   200
Faculty Meetings   200
The Faculty Orientation Class   201

**Bibliographic Instruction in the Academic Library:
Looking at the Adult Student**   **205**
Mary Ellen Kennedy

**Library Instruction and Foreign Students: A Survey
of Opinions and Practices Among Selected Libraries**   **215**
Frank Wm. Goudy
Eugene Moushey

Methodology   217
Findings   218
Summation   224
Sources of Additional Ideas and Programs   225

No Royal Road   **227**
Melissa R. Watson

**Betwixt and Between: Some Thoughts on the Technical
Services Librarian Involved in Reference
and Bibliographic Instruction**   **233**
Amy Dykeman

**Library Instruction and the Advancement of Reference
Service**   **241**
Kathleen Coleman

Arguments Against Library Instruction   241
Theoretical Insights from Library Instruction   243
Practical Benefits of Library Instruction   246
Improving Reference Services   247
Conflicts in the Reference Department   248
The Future of Library Instruction and Reference Service   249

FORTHCOMING IN THE REFERENCE LIBRARIAN   **253**

Library Instruction
and
Reference Services

INTRODUCTION

An Overview

Ruth Fraley

Library instruction is most frequently discussed by academic librarians as part of public services in the academic library. The mission of colleges and universities that house these libraries is, after all, to educate, the primary activity to meet this mission is to teach, and the library is an important part of this system. The role of library instruction in the larger education system is not yet a firmly established tradition. There is room for change. However, the function of library instruction, regardless of the definition, is a factor in public services in all types of libraries. Public libraries have also had some form of orientation and/or education program in existence for some time, and the vision and perceived role of library instruction while it may differ from the academic setting, still affects the operation.

It is in higher education that the topic is discussed and dissected and at least two schools of thought have emerged. The first school is characterized by a firm belief in the value and importance of library instruction; there are no questions of legitimacy, instruction belongs, and indeed, is an essential part of library services. These individuals have moved from discussing the existence of the function to examining its attributes. The issues being examined include administration, adequate training for instruction librarians, technique, theoretic underpinnings, and proper place in the organizational structure of the library. Special instruction programs for identifiable groups of patrons, variations of techniques for differing intellectual preparation, and the relationship between service at the reference desk and the instruction program are topics of interest. The second school holds firm in its belief that library instruction is not needed as a separate library function, nor does it help the library fulfill its mission in this era of scarce resources. Some people think that instruction is doomed to failure by its very definitions, others consider it a shadow function, a poor imitation of teaching destined,

3

ultimately, to damage libraries and the profession of librarianship. Others of this school are not as vehement but consider instruction to be an integral part of reference service, so that division into a separate department is either wasteful and divisive, or detrimental to quality reference services.

There are also librarians who consider a modified version of the instruction program the only operable alternative, and there are shadings of perceptions and beliefs all along the continuum. It is one thing when library administrators give lip service to a positive role for instruction and to advocate its existence in the literature. The question of role, place, and direction will be answered in practice when instruction remains as a funded department as cutbacks are forced on total library operations.

Continued discussion will help define instruction for all types of libraries and will provide well-reasoned input for decision making.

BI and Library Instruction:
Some Observations

Evan Ira Farber

For the most part, academic library buildings have not been designed with bibliographic instruction (BI) in mind. One could say there are even some libraries that are highly regarded by architects, by library building consultants, perhaps even by library directors but which from the BI librarian's perspective are far from satisfactory. As a matter of fact, in most libraries, BI librarians have had to carve out space, or adapt space for instruction that was meant for other purposes. Some libraries were just lucky to have a classroom in the building which could be used for instruction or an audiovisual room which has worked out well. The reason for this lack of planning, I assume, is that BI as a regular part of the library program is a relatively recent development, and not too many libraries have been designed recently. Moreover, architects have not been familiar with the concept, and the books on library planning—those by Ellsworth, Metcalf, and the Cohens, for example—don't even mention BI. Even Ralph Ellsworth's piece in Lubans' *Educating the Library User,* a piece titled ''How Buildings Can Contribute'' (to educating library users, that is) speaks only about how the library can affect student attitudes towards studying and thus increase use of the library. His advice is good, to be sure, as far as it goes, but he doesn't seem to be at all aware of recent developments in BI. Thus, there has been no attention by designers or building consultants to either the impact of a building on a BI program or the impact of a BI program on the design of a building. This essay will focus on the latter, with some attention to the former.

My remarks will relate primarily to the use of a particular BI method—course-related, or course-integrated instruction. I am focusing on this method for two reasons: one, it is the method most

The author is a distinguished and early pioneer in the more imaginative efforts of bibliographic instruction. He is director of the Earlham College Library, Richmond, IN.

5

widely practiced and most frequently written about; second, it is the method which, in my opinion, is most effective.

INSTRUCTIONAL AREAS

Course-related instruction *can* take place in a class's regular classroom, but it's preferable, and thus more common, for the class to be brought to the library. And that's one reason for considering BI in designing a library. Now, within the library, the instruction may be given in one of several places—a room about the size of a classroom, a seminar room, or in the reference area itself—which one depends on several factors: the size of the class, the types of materials being used, and the instructional format (a lecture, a discussion, a tour, or a combination of these). First, let's talk about the classroom.

A matter that will arise immediately is: how close to the entrance should the classroom be? One doesn't want large classes traipsing through the library, but on the other hand one wants the classroom convenient to the reference area so materials can be brought in easily. Perhaps these two factors can be reconciled, but then one doesn't want to use prime space for classroom purposes.

Really, there is *no one* best location, and the factors to be considered will vary from library to library as will the weight given to each factor. A helpful listing of the factors can be found in the article "Structuring Services and Facilities for Library Instruction" by Tom Kirk, Nancy Van Zant and Jim Kennedy (*Library Trends,* Summer, 1980). They assume an existing classroom and in their discussion of whether to use that classroom, or the reference room, or the class's regular meeting place, they list various factors to be considered—convenience for the staff, the use of A-V facilities, size limitations, distraction to other users, etc. The listing by no means includes all the factors one needs to consider, but it should provide some guidance.

The desirable size and structure of the classroom will depend on the institutional context, but for most institutions, a classroom between 600 and 1,200 feet will suffice. This would be a room that holds about forty students comfortably. Classes that are much larger than this should be given instruction in their regular classrooms. In larger institutions, if the space is available, an even larger room that can be divided—with perfectly soundproof partitions—is very useful.

The rooms should be equipped so that a variety of audio-visual devices can be used: provide blackboards, a projection screen, adjustable lighting (adjustable from front to back, not side to side), multiple electrical outlets, and a telephone jack for demonstrating online searching. Seating should not be built-in and tables ought to be small and shaped so that they can be used in different configurations. The ability to accommodate a teaching situation is the objective. Finally, be sure that enough storage space for equipment is provided.

For instruction to very small groups, the reference area itself is not only appropriate, but desirable since it's so helpful to have the reference collection at hand. In these cases, a table in the reference area may be enough, but a small conference room in the reference area is even better since it will reduce the disturbance to others in the area.

Small conference rooms can be used well for instruction. They provide a feeling of intimacy and facilitate instruction. They're very useful in libraries, but in planning them, one should keep in mind possible acoustical problems.

THE REFERENCE AREA

Can the design of a reference area contribute to BI? I think it can, by encouraging users to follow a strategy. Design, after all, can contribute to the user's environment.

Every person who enters a library building in search of information must deal with the library's physical environment throughout the search process. This environment is the medium through which the user moves, and it is also a source of informational cues that he/she uses in making a series of wayfinding choices. Every user receives cues from the environment. Whether the environment will be an aid or an obstacle to the user depends on the extent to which the library acts to shape its environment as an instructional tool. (Informational Graphics and Sign Systems as Library Instruction Media, *Drexel Library Quarterly,* Jan., 1980, p. 54)

Suppose we think about designing the reference area so that its layout reinforces those things we teach in BI. We try to teach search strategy, and we ought to ask: can we reinforce that teaching with the layout of the reference collection? We try to break students of bad habits in searching for information. The typical student, in researching a term paper, will go immediately to the card catalog—the subject trays, probably—to get some books, any books, on the topic, and then will go to the periodical indexes (usually the *Readers' Guide,* of course) for a few articles. Now, even though students can and do find materials that way, we know that it's not the appropriate way to look for information, and what we try to teach students is a strategy that's appropriate for the particular subject or discipline. But the layout of our libraries doesn't encourage this—on the contrary. The card catalog *is* generally the first thing the library user encounters, and the *Readers' Guide is* usually the most accessible and prominent of all bibliographical tools. And there are good reasons for this—we've focused on convenience to users, and so the most frequently used tools, the card catalog and the *Readers' Guide* being the most obvious examples, are given the most convenient locations, and thus students are encouraged in their bad habits.

Should we think about locating materials so that the search strategy we teach will be reinforced? The only library I know of where this has been done to a significant degree is Earlham's science library, which was designed almost fifteen years ago. It is, to be sure, a small library—only 8,400 or so square feet and 35,000 volumes. But, it's a heavily used library, and one which Earlham students, in biology, chemistry and geology, especially are *taught* how to use and are *required* to use, from their introductory courses on. How does the plan work? The card catalog, for example, is not only divided, but physically separated. The author/title section is near the entrance, but the section containing the subject trays is at the back of the library. Students, then, encounter, in order, the encyclopedias and handbooks, next, the bibliographies, then the indexes and abstracts, and finally, the subject catalog. That is, of course, in general the order of reference tools we've tried to teach them.

Does it help? We think so, but can't really prove it. And because we think so we've talked about reorganizing the reference collection of the main library along the same lines, but couldn't for lack of space. But because we emphasize so strongly in our instruction the importance of beginning with encyclopedias or handbooks, and because there are so many little-known but extremely valuable specialized ones, we've pulled many of these out from the regular reference stacks and put them together in a much more accessible place.

My point really is that there are other criteria for planning the layout of a reference collection other than simply the convenience to users, or the convenience of the staff. Most libraries have periodical indexes out of call number order—shelved separately. It makes good sense, not only from the point of view of user convenience but because of the frequent additions. Perhaps the rationale of user instruction should also be considered, and the collection layout structured so that it helps reinforce the concepts we try to teach. It's not an easy matter, certainly, and it may be that difficulties outweigh the advantages, but if we really take bibliographic instruction seriously, then I think the design of the reference area ought to take it into consideration.

THE REFERENCE DESK

It's tempting to get into the subject of furniture design in general—it's such an interesting topic and so important to the workings of a library. But most of it has only a remote relationship to BI. The one aspect that has a close relationship to BI is the reference desk.

Some think of BI as a process that includes only the teaching of classes or groups of students, and perhaps the negotiation, planning and preparation that go along with that teaching. But the reference function is also a part of the BI process in several important ways. By watching for students who need help at the card catalog or in the reference area, and then approaching those students, reference librarians can often find out about assignments which require use of the library but for which no instruction has been given. It serves, then, as a means for soliciting instruction—and instruction for which there's been a *demonstrated* need, not just a possible need.

The reference function is also, of course, the means by which instruction is implemented or enhanced. That is, the instruction is given to a class, or a group, and in more or less general terms; the student applies the instruction to his or her own situation, and when running into a snag, approaches the reference librarian who can then show how to apply correctly the instruction or to go beyond it. It is one-on-one, effective education. The reference function, then, should be thought of as an important part of the BI process, and insofar as the reference desk helps or hinders that function, insofar as it is well placed or poorly placed, well designed or poorly designed, its placement and design are important to BI.

In his book, *Academic Library Buildings,* Ralph Ellsworth makes the usual points about the placement of the reference desk: it should be clearly visible from the entrance, and convenient to the card catalog, to the reference collection, and to the reference office. I would refine his points about placement in one regard: if at all possible the reference librarian ought to be able to see those working at the card catalog—not only so he or she is easily accessible to those who need help, but perhaps more importantly, so he or she can observe when users seem not to be using the catalog effectively and ask if they need help. In a large library, with many banks of catalogs, that's difficult to accomplish, but it ought to be attempted and in a smaller library there's no reason not to do it.

Ellsworth has nothing to say about the reference desk's design (and, indeed, that's not the purview of his book). Metcalf's only advice is that the reference librarian should be at "a counter rather than a desk" so that eye-level contact will approximate that of the user. "Sometimes," he says, "the librarian will want two desks, one with a sit-down and the other with a stand-up height."

The size, shape and height of the reference desk may seem a trivial concern, but if one grants the importance of the initial contact between user and reference librarian, then one need only look at the literature on office furniture design to see how those factors affect personal relationships.

In too many libraries I've seen, the reference librarian is situated behind counters or desks which are so imposing that, really, if they'd been placed on a Paris street in 1789, they might well have stopped the march on the Bastille in its tracks. Those fortresses, those bastions of expertise seem almost designed to *protect* the librarian from the student, rather than encouraging access. The ambience has been nicely described by Gyorgy Konrad in his novel, *The Case Worker.* Konrad had been a social worker in Budapest, and understands the relationship between bureaucrat and applicant, a relationship which might be parallel to that between a reference librarian and a timid student:

> The official has nothing to worry about. Impassive, draped in condescending superiority, he has the client—that frail, flustered being who wants something or is afraid of something— admitted . . . . The standard desk is no more than a yard

deep. But the two persons facing each other across it are as far apart as convict and jailer on opposite sides of the bars. There is no way around or across this desk; it stands between two faces, two enigmas, inert, but apportioning the roles as unmistakably as a whipping post or a guillotine.

WORKING SPACE

As for the work space in the reference area, the space needed for the day to day operation of the BI program, keep in mind that much of the process entails four kinds of office procedures that are not necessarily part of traditional reference service. I'm referring, of course, to the preparation and storage of materials of lectures and follow-up instruction—transparencies and handouts in particular. Obviously, space needs will vary from situation to situation, but consider what can be involved: a copier (one that can also make transparencies), word processing equipment, typewriters, plenty of counter space for cutting, pasting and collating, storage space for paper and supplies, and for files of materials. Keep in mind that a number of people may be working on one or several projects at the same time.

THE NEW TECHNOLOGY

All the above has concerned BI given by librarians; that is, librarians in person and instruction that deals mostly with printed materials. What about accommodating BI to the new technology? If libraries are going to change radically, if, in the new electronic library, users are going to use only keyboards and CRT's, and those items of equipment become more and more intelligent and friendly, why consider traditional, antiquated instruction in the plans for a new or renovated building?

The answer is that, yes, libraries are changing rapidly and 20 years from now will be very different. But for some time students will still be using many, perhaps mostly, traditional materials and will need to be instructed in their use. As for computer-assisted instruction, instruction in the use of traditional and/or electronic information sources, there's not much question that terminals can provide BI and can possibly provide it even on a more individualized basis, but that will be a while in coming, though one can read now reports of projects on computer-assisted instruction, much more sophisticated than that done at, say, the University of Denver in the early '70s. As users become more familiar with computers, and more importantly, as computers become more user-friendly, patrons doing their own searching may become the norm, and the kinds of instruction we give may be very different. But such developments will be a while in coming and for the time being—for the next decade or two, I think—students will need to be instructed in the more or less traditional methods of searching for information. These traditional methods will increasingly be augmented by computer-assisted instruction, particularly on the graduate school level and for more specialized subjects. Moreover, teaching the uses of online searching will be increasingly a part of BI.

What all this means for building planning, it seems to me, comes back to the quality of flexibility. Because we still don't know exactly how terminals will be used, or how many we'll need, or where the best locations for them are, or what is the potential of videodiscs, all we can plan on now is designing the building so that terminals can be placed almost anywhere. As one architect has written to me:

> Consideration should be given to providing centralized vertical shafts for installing future power and information wiring. A system of distribution of these utilities throughout an individual floor should also be planned. This may take the form of cable trays above the ceiling, cable ducts along exterior walls, conduits placed in the floor with outlets at planned locations . . ., a cellular floor system or a commitment to installing future conduits or cable trays as the need develops. Utilities placed above the ceiling will result in a need for holes in the floor above or ''power poles'' to the floor below as exact locations for the needed utilities are determined. Empty conduit runs in the structural columns for future utility access is another possibility.

That's good advice, and it's of much more general application than just to BI.

One could go on and on, I'm sure, relating BI to almost every aspect of building design, and every item of furniture and equipment, with the possible exception of pencil sharpeners and drinking fountains—and I suppose there are ways of relating to those. The important thing to keep in mind, however, is this: up to now, libraries have not been designed with BI as a major consideration, yet, at the same time, BI has become an important part of many library programs, and BI librarians have made enormous strides. That they have made such progress is admirable, a real testimonial to their dedication, energy and creativity. Imagine what could be done with better facilities!

Organizational Change:
A Public Services Application

John Lubans, Jr.

One frequently sees in the literature of management and, to some extent in librarianship, exemplars on how to bring about change or, in other words, formulas for introducing and managing new programs. One that I have developed and, unlike some statements more theoretically oriented, will attempt to apply in this chapter, is a composite from the organizational literature and my own experience. This general planning model (Figure 1) can be applied to user education, or to any other area considered for change.

This design, like others, consists of phases; these are to be identified in order that we can anticipate what will be needed; and, that we know the activities to take for achieving whatever goal we may have set up for ourselves. The figure describes a sequence of nine steps for use in the planning and implementing of innovative programs. Note that the detail in the steps appears fixed. It will in fact vary, depending on circumstances and especially on the amenability of administrators and librarians to the concept; in this case, of user education. Their interest may alleviate the stress on some of the early steps or make them particularly crucial. If people are eager to try out the idea, then there is less pressure on having to gain a group's commitment or allegiance.

These nine suggested phases create a working structure, a framework which is useful in developing a successful program and keeping it on course. In this article the first three steps are discussed and this is followed by an application and evaluation of these three steps.

The author is a leading expert on the subject of bibliographic instruction and has written many articles and books about the topic. He now edits a column on instruction in *RQ*. He is Assistant University Librarian for Public Services at the library at Duke University, Durham, NC 27706.

Appreciation is expressed to colleagues instrumental to this study: Jaia Barrett, Ron Butters, Mary Canada, Larry Kline, Ilene Nelson, Kitty Porter, Judy Quinlan.

Additional discussion of this topic can be found in, John Lubans, Jr. "Planning, Implementing and Evaluating" *Educating the Public Library User,* Chicago: ALA, 1983

FIGURE 1. The Planning Process: User Education

When	What	Who
1.	Identifying the problem	Manager, Librarians, Users, Other agencies
2.	Forming a task force	Managers, Librarians, Users
3.	Finding out	Task Force, Librarians, Users, Other agencies[*]
4.	Establishing objectives	Task Force[*]
5.	Planning the evaluation	Task Force[*]
6.	Choosing "solutions"	Task Force[*]
7.	Implementing the program	Task Force, Coordinator, Librarians, Other agencies
8.	Evaluating	Task Force, Users[*]
9.	Revising, Maintaining	Task Force, Coordinator, Librarians, Managers

Steps in Planning Process

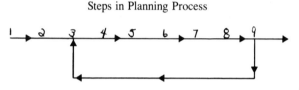

Feedback

*A consultant may be of benefit at this step.

STEP 1: IDENTIFYING THE PROBLEM

This is the reason behind considering a user education program. What factors are there that suggest that a problem may exist? This step is much the same as asking someone, retrospectively, what initially caused them to develop a user education program. Awareness that a problem exists will come from various sources; some examples:

—*User and marketing studies.* (Community analysis) A survey finds a large number of nonusers (or noncustomers) amidst the library's potential service population. A variety of programmed activities have had no or negligible effect on the proportions of users and nonusers. Nonuse is probably a result of multiple causes; one of these, perhaps the most significant, may be lack of any curricular need for using or awareness of information sources inside and outside the library.

—*User complaints.* A frequently heard complaint is that the library *never* has anything on the topics users want. The reference librarians counter this with the observation that a major share of this may be due to misuse of resources.

—*Redundant questions.* The reference librarian notices an increase in the frequency of questions of either a sophisticated or mundane nature. By keeping a record of representative questions it is observed that some research questions are often asked; possibly a teaching effort would be useful in providing an opportunity for users to get in-depth assistance on selected research topics.

—*Professional concern.* The literature alerts an administrator to developments in education that may influence library use. The College Board, and other national curriculum reform movements suggest information skills are indeed lacking among high school graduates and beginning undergraduates. A remedial program stressing *learning how to learn* may now be politically acceptable on campus; more so than the ''back-to-basics'' shibboleth may have been.

These situations may represent underlying problems or in the last case, a political opportunity directly to be acted upon in part through user education. However, if many believe there is *no* problem, the resistance to change will be strong. Likewise, if people believe that no program can effect improvement, there is further reason not to change.

While assuming widespread recognition of the need for user education, it is still necessary that an individual in a decision-making capacity be willing to champion the user education cause. This requires an organizational climate that encourages open discussion of new ideas and the willingness to consider implementing a new program. In most cases this person will be the library director, except for larger libraries with administrators in charge of the library's functional divisions.

Once the notion that a problem exists is accepted, the next step is to consider ways to do something about it through user education. Since more than a few people will likely be involved in educating and being educated it makes sense, both common and political, to gather insights from the people most likely to be participants.

STEP 2: FORMING THE TASK FORCE

Appointed and charged by the library administration, the task force is crucial to the overall user education program. The members should represent the views of the administration, the librarians and the users. The term "users" includes, besides individuals, outside agencies if they are part of the problem. For example, if a program is to be aimed at school age people, the advice of the students, teachers, school librarians or principals or all four will be necessary. Failure to have representation of those who are necessary to support or to participate in the program has weakened many programs in school and academic libraries. Yet the desire for representation should be tempered with concern about efficiency and manageability. The size of the task force should be limited. One way to do this is for the small committee to interview the representative group.

The committee or task force approach, flawed as it may be, is the best *potential* tool in countering resistance to change through the involvement of the people who may wield decisive influence. Just as any committee, the group may suffer from the ailments endemic to it, such as absenteeism, purposelessness and chronic discussion. The preventive cure is, of course, a clear charge with deadlines and a strong chairperson who can keep the task on course and interpret its recommendations to people on the outside, especially those in a decision-making capacity.

The first meeting of the group should be with the appointing individual so that questions can be asked and the charge clarified. In summary form, the task force will find out where the library is on the issue, where it wants to be and what it will need to do to get there.

STEP 3: FINDING OUT

Step three is different from the first one of problem identification. This step is meant to examine the alleged problem found in step one and to reveal and to seek out what additional information may be needed. The appointed group now focuses on *operationalizing* user education; to carry out this relatively nebulous assignment it will likely need to gather specific information to design an effective program. A series of fact finding efforts may be in order, such as asking users about their library experiences and whether they would be interested in use instruction. Such questions may reveal several potential target groups. Librarians not on the task force may also have insights and suggestions, as may teachers and librarians outside the library. If, prior to establishing objectives, the task force decides to do an in-depth analysis of library use and user education, employing a consultant might be a good idea. This person should have a background in user education *and* the making and doing of surveys, particularly those of the community analysis type.

Ignoring a measurement of what is happening *before* a proposed solution is carried out makes it difficult to reveal any improvement *after*. Baseline figures, as they are called, can be gathered, to a certain extent through response to a questionnaire or in the commonly maintained service statistics, for example, circulation, reference and user traffic. If an evaluation will be done it can be in the form of a "pre-test" of actual skills, attitudes or use patterns which can be then compared to a "post-test." An example would be the frequency of reference questions asked by the target group before and after instruction.

Another area of interest is a specific market analysis of instructional needs or the finding out what the user expects of the library, what services do they want, and what *they* are willing to do to better use a library. This type of questionnaire should list reasonable options the library is considering so that the user is faced with choices, e.g., of teaching/learning models instead of having to conjure forth unknowns. Including in this list of selections the category "Other; Please elaborate" allows for the respondents to give their own ideas should they wish to do so. Even here, the listing of the alternatives serves to focus the user's response. Note that the choices listed should be reasonable. Do not list marginal ideas that, while attractive, likely will not be funded or are not available, e.g., computer assisted instruction software and terminals.

This "finding out" step basically verifies that a problem exists and defines the shape of the underlying need and suggests ways of approaching the problem. In the event that the analysis shows little concern on anyone's part the project can be stopped or revised without the expense of providing a solution for a problem that does not exist. Such findings, however, should be considered with the background knowledge that for several reasons, largely the educational system, the user does not know what he or she is missing.

As mentioned earlier, the work of the task force might be facilitated through a consultant's expertise, particularly on questionnaire development and surveys. A trend worth noting in other fields is for the consultant to be more of a facilitator and less of a purveyor of a solution. As a facilitator the consultant encourages and actively includes the client in the development of a program. In something as complex as user education, this type of client-consultant relationship seems quite appealing. The traditional consultant as the dominant expert, while the committee stands-by, may lead to his or her riding their pet hobby horse with little applicability to the local program. While the consultant should not be viewed as above criticism there is something to be gained from viewing the consultant as an expert. His or her recommendations may become more influential than those made internally.

STEPS 1, 2, AND 3 APPLIED

This "change" model (Figure 1) has been used at a large academic library to investigate the receptivity of faculty to increased teaching activities by librarians.

Identifying the problem

That an intensified user education program was needed was generally agreed upon by this library's librarians and this was summarized during a discussion of user education needs. From *"Minutes"* of September 15 Public Services Librarians Meeting:

> A broad discussion followed concerning "User Education and Orientation" . . .
>
> 1. What are we doing?
>   a. Conducting tours for freshmen, graduate students and faculty . . .
>   b. Conducting subject seminars related to a specific class or discipline, such as art history, public policy, primary sources, ecology . . .
>   c. Giving bibliographic instruction to English I classes and summer students.
>   d. Providing tutorial instruction and term paper consultation . . .

2. What do/should students want us to do?
   a. Some upper classpersons realize too late that they would have liked to have known how to use the library sooner in their careers . . .
   b. Students need to learn "process," as well as content.
3. What does/should the faculty want us to do?
   a. Help with assignments which require use of the Library.
   b. *Some faculty want us to do nothing.*
4. What should we be doing?
   a. *Educate the faculty about the purpose of the library/librarians, its resources, and student needs.*
   b. *Let the faculty educate us about the needs of their classes, their own fields of research . . .*
   c. Work to change curriculum to incorporate learning the research process.
   d. Provide excellent reference service . . .

The Public Services Director will synthesize the concerns in the above and propose action steps for moving ahead . . .(emphasis added)

However, concern, as indicated in item 3b, was expressed about faculty reaction to librarian involvement in this activity. An earlier user education effort had been received somewhat chillingly by the faculty—some teachers allegedly stated: Librarians were to catalog; faculty would teach. The situation, even now four or five years later, still was perceived as sensitive.

Forming the task force

A committee was set up to conduct a survey of attitudes and opinions of the faculty on undergraduate student library skills and librarian involvement. Prior to the first meeting a rough draft questionnaire and announcement of the task force was sent to all participants in the Public Services discussion. From memo, of October 12 to all Public Services Librarians:

This follows our discussion about user education efforts during the September, Public Services meeting. In response to the expressed interest in the role of the faculty in our endeavors and *their* perception of what we are doing, I am proposing a survey of the faculty who teach undergraduates . . . Attached is a draft questionnaire for your consideration and response. An advisory committee has been formed to help me with the various aspects of the survey including question formulation and the analysis and interpretation of the response. The Faculty Survey Advisory Committee, which I will chair includes seven representatives from:

Public Documents (1)
English Department (1)
Reference (3)
Cataloging (1)
Chemistry Library (1)

Our first meeting will be scheduled shortly after your comments are received on the draft questionnaire . . .

As indicated, a member of the faculty was included on the eight member committee. Because of the potential sensitivity of the issue, considerable care was taken in developing the questions. The pilot study, after incorporation of revisions from public services librarians and the committee, consisted of the faculty and student members of the Library Council which is the advisory faculty group; and selected faculty Directors of Undergraduate Studies. An excerpt from the covering letter speaks for the care taken in this approach to the faculty.

Given the traditional rapport between librarians and the faculty we would like you to respond to the enclosed "Survey of Undergraduate Research Skills." With this questionnaire we are seeking an accurate and, if need be, an improved alignment of what we do in the library with what is done in the classroom about effecting intelligent library use. We seek to learn what the faculty expects of its students in using the library's resources and services. The reference questions students ask suggest that there is room for improvement in what we in the library do, especially in collaboration with the faculty.

Finding Out

The response of 266 questionnaires, 54%, has been, for some, surprisingly supportive of what could not but be perceived as increased library involvement in teaching. In fact, 62 individual faculty members signed up to take part in a workshop on undergraduate library skills and numerous others, over half, indicated they might be interested if the circumstances were right.

The survey results* have served several purposes, including:

1. To allay the misapprehension of some of the library staff about any potential rebuff from the faculty about librarians teaching information skills. In this regard several of the questions brought up the role of the librarian in the teaching process. For example Question 9 asked how they, in addition to their own advice, expected students learn to use the library; of the 5 categories, 98.4 percent checked "by asking a librarian." Question 10 specifically faced the issue head-on. It asked how "Instruction in library skills and techniques should be presented." Respondents were asked to priority rank six different ways of doing this. The four highest scoring arrangements follow:

	Total Score
1. within any class by the instructor	(314)
2. as a non-credit course taught by *librarians*	(301)
3. in a required mini-course taught by *librarians*	(232)
4. within any class by a *librarian* in collaboration with the instructor (emphasis added.)	(216)

Additionally, Question 12 asked for the faculty vote on ways of improving and increasing student's use of library resources. In the "yes" column, first place (90 percent) was given to *their* grading of term papers and projects to include bibliographic quality. Next, at 78 percent "yes," was formal instruction in library skills and techniques.

2. To confirm the impression that there is an obvious need for improvement in student information skills and that there are reasons why this should happen. This is evident in the faculty's expecting a wide variety of library tools be used by students, that they do assign projects requiring the use of library resources and that many have observed less than ideal student performance in this regard. The response to Question 1 on the faculty's rating student's overall ability to make use of library resources for research can be divided almost evenly between those assigning "excellent" (5.1%) and good

*A copy of the tallied questionnaire is available from the author; with the request send a self-addressed stamped envelope.

(46.5%) and those judging the ability at "poor" (6.1%) and "fair" (42.3%). Question 3 asks whether students "know and use reference tools" The response:

"Most do" at 25.6%
"Some do" at 56.2%
"Few do" at 12.9%
"Most do not" at 5.2%

may suggest a contradictory optimistic view; however, the "some do" category is not as strong as one might think. The computer analysis shows it includes 64% of the group judging student abilities at "poor" and "fair" in Question 1.

3. To raise faculty (and librarian) interest and awareness of the user education issue. Indicative of this are the 62 faculty who have signed up for a workshop to improve *their* teaching and that over half of the respondents indicated some interest in such a workshop *depending* on its value to them. Only 85 rejected the idea because of their belief they are already familiar with important library sources for undergraduates.

The reponse to a question on what criteria are used in evaluating a student paper's bibliography is particularly relevant since 60 percent said they *usually* look for a "demonstration of effective literature searching techniques," another 28% do this *occasionally*. However, a not insignificant 12% stated they *never* do this. The user advocate type librarian may conclude there is some missionary work to be done in these academic groves.

In brief, the survey results reveal high expectations by faculty in the students' abilities to find and use information in doing assignments; yet they believe there is considerable room for improvement in these same abilities. At the same time it is unclear how students are to acquire the necessary skills; but, by no means would librarians be unwelcome in helping students improve their abilities. If anything, the frequent positive response to questions suggesting a working-together between librarians and faculty speaks encouragingly for the continued evolution of a partnership. The next step, 8 months since the first, is for the committee to analyze the response and to make recommendations of objectives to the Library and the rest of the academic community. This would be followed by the other phases in planning model (Figure 1).

Did It Work?

The model as set forth appears to have been helpful for decision making in resource allocation. It has helped gather information which strongly suggests librarians have reason to continue and expand user education efforts at this library.

The process has moved us from a potential dispute over the "goodness" or "appropriateness" of user education to that of a considered rationale and *expressed* need for it from the most influential segment of the academic population.

What if it had gone the other way? Then, of course, the model provides that a re-consideration of the whole idea is in order. There is an advantage here in that an idea is exposed for evaluation prior to further investment of time and other resources. A negative response may provide clues that a service is not needed or that a modification is necessary before any implementation is made.

This type of planning process has important applications within the philosophy of an open organization that believes its employees are experts and that from them can come effective solutions to problems. This plan carries out the philosophy that problems can be best solved by those implementing the solution. If coalition and consensus are necessary, this process helps achieve them. Time however is a factor. In the example, over seven months have been spent on the first three steps of the nine step process. One can envision that a "decisive" administrator or prescriptive consultant could, in haste let fly with a grand user education scheme, or for that matter, a retrospective conversion project that hits the ground running or an automated circulation system to be installed next Tuesday, in lieu of the time-consuming process spelled out here.

The reader can decide which approach promotes organizational well-being, a staff's self-esteem, and in the long run, the development of superior programs in serving users.

ANOTHER VIEW

Never Mind the Quality, Feel the Width

Donald Davinson

Shooting foxes is one of the most heinous of social solecisms in British High Society amongst the huntin', fishin' and shootin' set. Of approximately the same order of magnitude amongst Librarians is venturing the opinion that User Education is a most disgraceful waste of library resources. It is one of the curiosities of the literature of librarianship that it is filled with success stories—'How we do it good in Oswaldtwistle, (Lancs.) or Totem Pole (Ark).'' Honest evaluation is not a strong point with librarians. Once they have set up some expensive activity or other, they are not at all keen to look at the facts. It must be a good thing, they argue, look at the resources it consumes. Jumping on passing bandwagons is what Librarians are best at, not planning where they are going and waiting for the right bus.

''One of the most burgeoning industries in Librarianship in recent years'' is one recent description of Library User Education.[1] Why has it become one of the most significant issues in Librarianship? Is it necessary? The answer to that question depends upon another— necessary for whom, the Library user or the Librarian? It would be pleasant to believe that Librarians had invented User Education because users needed it. Self interest is a powerful motivator and countless thousands of library users have been subjected to endless hours of the attentions of Librarian/Lecturers purely because it was a necessary function in the cause of Librarian self-aggrandisement.

In virtually all of the literature—and it is these days a massive literature—devoted to Library User Education there is no hint that Librarians think of the business as anything other than the best of ''good things.'' There is a large measure of self delusory belief that it is a good thing for library users but proof of the assertion, where attempted, usually amounts to self fulfilling prophecy if analysed.

In addition to being on *The Reference Librarian's* Editorial Board, the author is head of School of Librarianship, Leeds Polytechnic, Beckett Park, Leeds, LS63QS, England.

Assertion, it is said, is always easier to get right than fact. That there has been little serious effort to evaluate User Education in terms of either cost to benefit for student or cost to loss of other opportunities to Libraries themselves is evident from the literature. Without undertaking the, admittedly highly complex, research it is simply a further assertion to argue that User Education is too expensive and too low a return on investment for libraries to undertake. At least this further assertion does not cost anything! The cash cost of User Education is enormous. The opportunity cost is horrendous and, moreover, growing, for as cut-backs to library services take place it is rarely in the User Education field they occur. It is indeed possible to see that many libraries are actually increasing the proportion of their budgets spent on this most illusory activity.

Maintaining or increasing the size of the User Education cut of the budget in recessionary times is usually justified by overt and covert reasoning on the part of library managers. The overt reasoning—a kind of siren song to the Paymasters—is that as cut-backs take place the teaching departments suffer losses, often of their most experienced staff, and so to alter curricula to emphasize more student centred learning makes sense (it doesn't really but it *sounds* clever to say so).

If the Library, or so the argument goes, put on more formal instruction on how to find things and how to study (and study skills instruction are going to be the great new buzz words for the with-it Librarian of the mid 80s) then the College, University or Polytechnic will be able to manage with less academic staff resources. The covert reasoning is similar but with a slightly different focus. This is that the Library Managers know quite well that the Library is something of an expensive luxury in the eyes of many of your genuine academics and if it comes to the push of cutting or closing teaching department or a supporting or administrative service the academic establishment will choose the latter. This is especially true if the latter has personnel who are not protected by the, usually much stronger and vocal, Unions who look after teachers. ''Let us,'' say the Library Managers, ''lightly disguise ourselves as a teaching department by making a big fuss over our User Education programme. That way we hitch our wagon to the strongest gravy train on the railroads of academe.''

Hitching the wagon that way also has other inestimable benefits. For one thing it is then possible to pass oneself off as an academic. No longer is it necessary to face the acute embarrassment of having to admit to being a Librarian with all that the media mangling of that image connotes. A casual off-hand reference to teaching study skills at the local University, College or whatever sounds so much better than admitting to being a Librarian. Besides, and here is the clinching benefit, being a teacher—a real life genuine academic—pays better than being a mouldy Librarian. Much of the vast empire which is Library User Education has grown for no other reason than that such programmes are an entry point to a form of respectability of status for inferiority complex ridden librarians.

One of the primary incentives, perhaps *the* primary incentive, which librarians have in promoting User Education is that of securing for themselves status—what in the United States is termed "Faculty Status" and in the United Kingdom "Academic Status." A recent policy statement by one of the British Higher Education Teachers Unions actually states that only those librarians engaged in formal teaching of Library skills ought to be paid academically related salaries.[2] No finer invitation to librarians to waste their substance chasing moonbeams could be imagined.

Moonbeams chasing is what librarians who mess about in User Education are doing in terms of beneficial effects upon students. The process has, admittedly been rather more successful as a confidence trick pulled upon the employers to squeeze out better salaries and superior status. The practice of Higher Education these days creates conditions in which no matter how dedicated the User Education, the students hardly need to use the skills derived to cope with their course work. Librarians themselves have contributed to the irrelevance of much of their own instruction. Through encouraging lecturers and professors to supply the Library with copies of reading lists they issue to students, librarians have hit upon the wonderful notion of pulling off the open shelves the named texts and periodical articles and keeping them in a special collection adjacent to the issue counter—the "Reserved Collection," "Short Loan Collection" or "For use in the Library only" material. One recent survey of student use of a large academic library revealed that up to 75% of all use of the library was restricted to the material on lecturer's reading lists.[3]

The practice of lecturing staff in making assessments of student progress is another major contributing factor to the apprehension of students that the User Education programme is not central to their needs. It is not a common feature of the way the lecturer makes assessment of students that they reward enterprise. Wide reading

and carefully compiled bibliographies of references are either ig-
nored by lecturers or, at any rate, not conspicuously rewarded as
compared to unoriginal and unadventurous work by those who stick
to the plagiarization of a limited range of texts. Students soon learn
that this is the case and all but the most dedicated and highly motivated reduce their effort to the level of coping without too much
sweat. If this is considered too cynical an observation let the question be asked—how many User Education programmes are so integrated with the courses they ostensibly support that the Library staff
play an explicit part in the student assessment process? Add to this
another question. How many academics bother to find out from the
Library staff what their students have been reading? In the absence
of these two activities User Education is reduced almost to a non-
sense. The aspiration may be to create in every undergraduate student a reverence for information seeking which will lead to a life
time of creative library use and make them, each and every one, researchers on the farther frontiers of knowledge. The actuality is
considerably less impressive.

Perhaps the most bizarre manifestations of the User Education
obsession in Academic Libraries is that practised in some U.K. institutions where a special staff of Library User Education lecturers
are employed. They will be paid academic rates whilst the rest of the
library staff are less well rewarded. The Librarian/Lecturers teach,
or try to teach, students about the wonders of the world of information seeking. At best they raise in students expectations the library
can not satisfy. At worst they implicitly indicate to those same students that the library staff are a lesser race not in the business of providing anything more than a book portering service. Perhaps instead
of bizarre the word objectionable should be substituted, for unless
every member of a library staff is in the business of helping users
use libraries the very professionalism of librarians is called into
question.

The creation of a special grade of user education has other un-
desirable side effects. The Devil, it is somewhere said, makes work
for idle hands to do. The special lecturer/librarians have their peak
of activity when the Freshers are inducted. The rest of the year they
are available to think up all sorts of devilment. Their favourite is
producing audio-visual aids of an ever more exotic and expensive
nature. Beginning with the simple tape slide sequence, graduating
through twin screen, cross dissolve stereo sound productions they
ultimately emerge as creators of all singing, all dancing electronic

marvels of video recording. In these audio-visual affairs ends and means become gloriously confused. The initial motivation may well be to create artefacts capable of making the education imparted more effective, more interesting and more varied but it does not last. Very soon the producers become so absorbed in their mini-M.G.M. that they have less time to spend with students in the flesh but, never mind, the latest film or sequence is expected to solve all the problems the student might have. It also, and this is most important to the producers—gives them two further pieces of work to do. Firstly they can carry out experiments to "prove" the value of their production and then secondly they can write the whole success story up in the literature of librarianship and thus encourage others to follow suit.

In 1972 Hazel Meus was saying "the whole subject of audio-visual or mechanical aids to library instruction . . . is in that state of innovatory chaos out of which some order will presumably emerge in time."[4] It didn't. It just became more complicated and collapsed under the weight of its own irrelevance. Contemplating audio-visual instruction aids for library user education reminds one forcibly of the tryptych cartoon in a 1960s issue of *Punch.* Scene one is teacher talking to class. Scene two is tape recorder talking to class. Scene three is tape recorder talking to tape recorders. Audio visual aids have been produced in the pursuit of greater slickness, with-it trendiness and attempts to prove the virility of the librarians' claim to status which almost defy description so terrible they are. The co-operative series instituted by SCONUL (the Standing Conference of National & University Libraries) in the United Kingdom[5] illustrated how varied in quality library audio-visual aids are. Some items in that series are very good. They turn out usually to be the ones which were produced by competent media professionals working alongside librarians. Most are simply dull lack-lustre productions with an unclear focus and cloudy objectives produced by librarians themselves. A few are frankly dreadful apparently produced by myopic, adenoidal bullfrogs to judge from the sights and sounds displayed. All have, presumably been used in actual library situations. It is difficult to believe that they ever teach people much which sticks, though perhaps a couple of hundred thousand pounds (½ million dollars?) has been spent in recent years on 'proving' they do by the British Library. The idea that an itty-bitty tape-slide sequence shown to a class of freshers is an adequate surrogate for careful, sympathetic individual user assistance with a real problem in literature use is absurd. One of the most frequently advanced reasons for the need to employ surrogates is shortages of staff sufficient to do the individual job. It is true there is a shortage. Part of it arises out of the number of staff beavering away at the pilot projects for self-paced workbooks, tape-slide sequences or video films in places where library users can not disturb them!

Joseph Rosenblum's refreshingly contrary view to the usually received wisdom of user education that it could actually be counter productive is a rare one in the largely adulatory literature.[6] Rosenblum believes that half remembered library instruction may actually confuse such is the speed of change of literature structures. He may be wrong about that but only because he appears to believe library instruction will be "half remembered." It won't of course. It will be completely forgotten as if it had never happened. One proof of that might be that most Higher Education teachers are apparently incapable of using libraries effectively and, by definition, they are amongst the best of the student body of previous generations of instructed users.

Rosenblum's best point is that librarians are committed to the constant elaboration of their systems. He comments that they "come to regard themselves primarily as interpreters of there systems, they may come to require systems that need interpretation . . . they may come to view the simple index as a professional threat, the complex one as a professional ally."

Complexity is certainly the message dished up by the library user instructors for, as has been claimed earlier, they need to do so. As G.M. Smith has it[7] librarians do the job for the wrong reasons which he calls "status enhancement." Of course the user educators do not themselves admit to such motives. Not ever. To them (and they are probably seen at their starryeyed best in the *Journal of Academic Librarianship's* "Library Instruction: a column of opinion") it is all about such chimeric concepts as improving students' attitudes to the library and increasing their use of library resources through programmes of teaching, viewing the latest audio-visual aids and even sitting examinations.

The evaluations such starry-eyed self and other deluders indulge in is all closed system stuff and, surprise, surprise, always demonstrates staggering success calling for even higher input of resources. It is perhaps invidious to pick out any one of the many self congratulatory exercises with which the relevant literature is filled but a recent effort by Penelope Pearson and Virginia Tiefel[8] illustrates the problem the sceptic has in taking them seriously and believing their apparently objective altruism. The evaluation is of an obviously elaborate programme and the evaluation itself was labour intensive. The aim of the evaluation was to assess the effectiveness of the programme as mounted to determine what revisions might be needed in future. There is nothing wrong with that as far as it goes. This is, however, as far as most such evaluations go and it is not good enough. This is not the way evaluation of user education ought to be done but the alternative is not as easy and, worse still, might not produce the required results—proof of the efficacy of user education.

What would be both interesting and, indeed, invaluable for library managers and their paymasters would be a substantial study of the opportunity cost of user education. Such a study should attempt to determine what would be the effect of diverting the resources currently tied up in user education into other channels potentially providing outcomes similar to those ideals ostensibly embraced by the proponents of the business. It is true that at least some of the alternatives constitute heresy to the orthodox. Suppose, for example, one alternative evaluated was the reduction of the massive, complex and user daunting central libraries with large, ever changing and unrecognised staffs into a series of small cozy collections presided over by a small permanent and well known staff—small neighbourhood branch public libraries or academic teaching department libraries. Might it not be possible that the closer personal working relationships between users and librarians in these conditions would be a more effective means of improving library skills in users? True, the level of duplication of basic reference works might imply a lower overall quality of provision of material but would it matter? Nobody knows what the cost is of providing material in libraries which are never used but it is high and caused in part by being, to all intents and purposes ''lost'' in large libraries which it is impossible fully to realise the potential of. Librarians with small budgets and smallish resources work harder than fat cats who buy by the yard. The provision of library collections on the implicit proposition that everyone should be expected to need and use large research collections is not necessarily correct but is apparently a necessary ego trip for librarians to take. It is, after all, librarians who want the massive central libraries. The bulk of their users would prefer them smaller and cosier if anyone bothered to ask them.

Another evaluatory alternative might be to determine how far the money tied up in user educator librarians in Higher Education might stretch if applied to improving the quality of primary and secondary school libraries. If all library users going into Academic libraries and Public libraries had had a thorough grounding in library skills at school the need for expensive instruction at the tertiary level would be significantly diminished. Given the, usually, low quality of many school libraries it is not currently possible to expect Freshers in Higher Education to know their way around a library but perhaps they might if only a portion of the resources currently tied up in Academic libraries and the big Public Reference libraries was released to schools.

The simplest level of re-evaluation of the deployment of resources is that which might determine if greater cost-effectiveness might be obtained from resources employed in library provision by directing the effort put into user education back into "point of sale" service at the library issue counters and enquiry desks. Are there not too many instructional programme Chiefs and too few user serving Indians in many of our libraries. It is not, to at least one sceptic, entirely self evident that such a diversion would be insufficient to make a difference to direct user service. Maybe library staffs are not yet, like the iceberg, nine tenths submerged but they are working at it and to be fair, it is not only user educator librarians who need shooing up front in our libraries. Digging them all out could make a startling difference to the quality of public service.

Opportunity cost evaluation is not a strong suit amongst librarians. If it was all manner of gad-fly schemes designed more for ego inflation in librarians than for improved library service would never have happened. The proponents of user education in librarians use their evaluations to say "we know it's a good thing and even if we burst in the attempt we are going to prove it to ourselves and to you."

NOTES

1. Davinson, D.E. "Instruction in Library Use." *In Reference Service.* London: Clive Bingley, 1980, p. 178.

2. National Association of Teachers in Further & Higher Education. *College Library Policy Statement.* London: NATFHE, 1982.

3. Newcastle upon Tyne Polytechnic Library. *Book Availability Survey, Main Library.* Newcastle upon Tyne: The Polytechnic Library, 1982.

4. Mews, H. *Reader Instruction in Colleges & Universities.* London: Clive Bingley, 1972.

5. Hills, P.J. *Tape-slide Presentations & Teaching Packages for Library User Education.* London: SCONUL, 1977.

6. Rosenblum, J. *"Overdue: the Future Reference Service: Death by Complexity?"* *Wilson Library Bulletin* 52(4) December 1977, 300-301, 350.

7. Smith, G.M. *"Cause for concern."* *New Library World* 78(928) October 1977; 89-90.

8. Pearson, P. and Tiefel, V. "Evaluating Undergraduate Library Instruction at the Ohio State University." *Journal of Academic Librarianship* 7(6) January 1982, 351-357.

Bibliographic Instruction and the Reference Desk: A Symbiotic Relationship

C. Paul Vincent

A librarian should be much more than a keeper of books; he should be an educator . . . No . . . librarian is fit for his place unless he holds himself to some degree responsible for the library education of his students . . . Somehow I reproach myself if a student gets to the end of his course without learning how to use the library. All that is taught in college amounts to very little; but if we can send students out self-reliant in their investigations, we have accomplished very much.

Otis Hall Robinson[1]

At a time when bibliographic instruction has become a central concern of a profession which is witnessing the undiminished proliferation of both library materials and research complexities, the statement of Otis Hall Robinson will be viewed as little more than a truism. Much more intriguing is the fact that Robinson was speaking in 1876. As Frances Hopkins has pointed out, the concept of teaching library skills is as old as the concept of research-oriented graduate education; both date from the 1870s.[2] Moreover, the philosophy motivating such education was, as Robinson's statement suggests, comparable to that of many bibliographic instructors today. Library self-reliance was Robinson's goal, and it was a logical outgrowth of his reasonable belief that a college-educated individual should have the capacity to pursue independent research.

Robinson's goal was commendable. At a time when libraries were small (relatively speaking) and publishing, while beginning to blossom, was still minuscule, Robinson knew that library self-reliance was necessary and attainable. Unfortunately, his world was

---

C. Paul Vincent is Assistant Director for Public Services, Franklin and Marshall College, Lancaster, PA 17604.

monumentally different from ours. Robinson did not envision the revolutions which have transpired in specialization and technology in the twentieth century. Nor did he imagine the burgeoning accession of materials that has burdened libraries in post-World War II America.[3] As reference librarians involved in the education of our constituents, we are now confronted with a very serious question: can Robinson's goal of a self-reliant user withstand scrutiny in the 1980s, given the swelling of materials and the increasingly sophisticated nature of the typical academic library? We would be wise to contemplate this question at some length.

The simple yet neglected fact is that libraries have become too complex for even the librarians to maintain a thorough understanding of their convoluted nature. As the medieval historial might be hard-pressed to even haphazardly identify the significant details of the American Gilded Age, so too might the humanities librarian be confused by the intricacies of government documents while the science librarian may be incapable of using or even identifying *L'Année Philologique.* And such limited awareness does not necessarily indicate substandard training for either the historian or the librarian. Good reference service can be assured in this complex environment through the development of an interactive reference department as well as by an awareness of, and an ability to employ, online services. But the fact remains that graduate study in history and professional education in librarianship are both structured around the concept of specialization. While we may admire the renaissance man, we should also recognize him to be ''a thing of the past.''

Constance McCarthy has recently argued that reference librarians are prone to lament the manner in which students underestimate the complexity of libraries without acknowledging that they, as instructors, are often responsible for this attitude.[4] We must accept the fact that, when improperly pursued, bibliographic education can leave the student with the distorted notion that library research is simple. Unfortunately, even for the seasoned scholar, research is not a simple task because the complexity of our libraries has kept pace with the complexity of our society. If one rationally confronts the significance of such change, a major consideration is implied: how much should we, as librarians, expect our students to know? The answer to this question must be a product of the sophistication of the contemporary library, and a logical response to this age of specialized learning. While lower division undergraduates should acquire a knowledge of the "library process"—including an understanding of how to obtain materials of general interest—and graduating seniors should have the further capacity of doing basic research in their fields of concentration, it has become unreasonable to presume that bibliographic education is going to produce an independent, self-reliant library user. It is this presumption, however, which is the central motivating factor for many involved in library instruction. One significant and influential article advances the by no means unique proposal that bibliographic instruction is "intended to teach students to make intelligent, independent decisions about library use."[5] One can commend this statement as an ideal; however, the reality of libraries and the academic world precludes its attainment. As bibliographic instructors—particularly those of us who are involved in the liberal arts—we would be wise to instill in our students Goethe's dictum that "doubt grows with knowledge."[6] A discerning reference librarian has properly noted that too many of us are teaching students how to be librarians rather than fulfilling our more realistic function of using our training to aid students in their search for information.[7]

The disagreement over goals is, alas, not simply a theoretical dispute. The conviction that we are producing a self-reliant user is, I believe, potentially damaging to public service practice. If instructional programs are so sophisticated in their development, and so effective in their application, as to create self-sufficiency on the part of undergraduate students, then what is to become of reference service? While the answer to this question seems academic—no program of library instruction is capable of instilling self-sufficiency—many involved in library education have been confused by their own idealistic notions of its capabilities. As bibliographic instructors, we have apparently neglected to establish a *logical* rationale for our efforts. James Benson's necessary rejoinder that bibliographic instruction "seems to be perceived by many librarians as a self-evident social good, not needing an extensive rational or empirical evidence to substantiate its effectiveness" has been neglected by those who have the greatest illusions about the capabilities of bibliographic education.[8] The potential damage which can ensue from this neglect is evident in the forceful Keynote address of the 1981 ACRL Bibliographic Instruction Section Preconference. In this statement, Frances Hopkins points out that the academic reference desk was adopted from the public library model—that model specifically introduced in 1876 by Samuel Green at the Worcester

Public Library in Massachusetts.[9] As academic libraries gradually took their cue from public libraries and instituted reference service, bibliographic instruction vanished.

> Unlike BI, [however], reference service required no planning or lecturing, no direct involvement in the academic program, and little exposure to faculty scrutiny. To the average library school graduate, the role of reference librarian must have been more congenial than any attempt to emulate Justin Winsor as professor of bibliography.[10]

It appears that, in the late-nineteenth century, reference service and library instruction were regarded as roughly comparable, thus making illogical the simultaneous maintenance of both. But Hopkins seems to provide this historical background in order to support the premise that bibliographic instruction negates the need for academic reference service in the late-twentieth century.

> Public librarians appropriately established reference desks . . . Academic libraries, also appropriately, offered instruction to students in the use of library resources to answer questions that normally did arise from academic disciplines . . . The reference desk was designed for responding to specific questions and providing information, not for imparting an understanding of general research principles. Thus, it is hypothesized here that the reference desk, offering ad hoc information service, displaced BI so decisively as the focus and ideal of academic library service largely because few graduates of the clerically oriented library schools had the competence or status to teach research methods, however tenacious they often were in the search for information.[11]

While this disparagement of the reference process does not amount to a proposal for its actual elimination, Hopkins' hypothesis certainly implies the emasculation of current reference service by eliminating that portion of it which focuses on the instilling of research skills.

I have no argument with the aforementioned history of library instruction and the reference desk. It is impossible for me to assent, however, to the implication that, with the advent of sophisticated programs of bibliographic instruction, reference librarians need no longer concern themselves with more than "ad hoc information service" while at the reference desk. The conclusion that the academic reference desk—or, indeed, the public library reference desk—was designed for little more than the transfer of basic information may be warranted when viewed historically, but it does not do justice to the sophisticated reference-desk service which is offered at many institutions in the 1980s. Moreover, this is a perception which, if placed into practice, could result in significant harm.

There are, I believe, two fundamental reasons why sophisticated reference-desk service *must* be retained. In the first place, one can argue for combining reference service with library instruction for the simple reason that as bibliographic instruction increases so too does the demand for complementary reference service. There is a tendency to overlook the fact that bibliographic instructors are often speaking to some students who have never before used the library for the pursuit of research. Such students suddenly discover that libraries possess access to a wealth of information over which formerly they could only fantasize. The tangible result of this revelation is likely to be an increased and more sophisticated use of reference service. Such has certainly been the case with respect to the public services program at Franklin and Marshall College. During the 1979–80 academic year, librarians met with 18 courses in a total of 46 classroom sessions. The total number of reference questions (not including simple directional questions) for the same year was 4,928. By 1981–82, the instructional totals had increased to 48 courses and 76 classroom sessions, while the number of reference questions (again, not including directional questions) had jumped to 8,868.[12] Furthermore, the quality of reference-desk inquiry increased along with the advancement of library education. In 1979–80, the reference department did not include research inquiries as a separate category of question; this oversight was corrected, however, in June 1980. During 1980–81, 198 of 6,805 questions were of a research nature. In the following year, this figure had risen to 653 of 8,868 questions.[13]

The conclusion which one should draw from such statistics is clear: regardless of library instruction, it remains impossible for a librarian involved in a "one-shot" lecture to cover every tool that might be useful for the unique research needs of each individual student.[14] Professional reference librarians should remember that they prepared themselves for public service by taking quarter/semester courses in Basic Reference, Advanced Reference, and a variety of subject bibliographies. This training has been supplemented, moreover, by hours (years?) of hands-on experience. A session of bibliographic instruction can do little more than touch the surface when it comes to informing a student about the tools available in the reference department, or the sometimes convoluted processes required to do research on an esoteric subject. Whereas a simple search strategy can be taught, and an *understanding* of finding tools (catalogs, bibliographies, and indexes) can be disseminated, the multitude of indexing titles and factual sources (for biographies, dates, definitions, statistics, *ad infinitum*) available to the student, and the eccentricities associated with researching any number of topics, will never be related through a one-hour library instruction session. One-on-one reference service, of a sophisticated nature, remains absolutely essential.

There is a second, and more tangible, reason for maintaining a high level of reference service. Have those who may be contemplating the diminution of reference-desk service, due to the establishment of programs of bibliographic instruction, remained cognizant of the fact that not all of our patrons are experiencing such instruction? Even if we postulate that library-use education is capable of creating an independent library user, we can not assume that everyone who needs to do research has experienced such instruction. Not only do our libraries serve transfer students, students involved in continuing education courses, and faculty and administrators; they generally also maintain a position as publicly-accessible institutions. If our resources are available to anyone, then we retain an obligation to help people make intelligent use of these resources. This can only be guaranteed through the maintenance of traditional, high grade reference service. It would be a narrow and elitist attitude indeed if a librarian were to deny a patron the benefit of his/her skill because that skill could only be accessed through bibliographic instruction.

As a reference librarian involved in bibliographic instruction, I hold a certain vested interest in the continued existence of both forms of public service. I would venture to guess that this is an interest shared by my readers. In this period of financial retrenchment, public service librarians should be far more circumspect regarding the manner in which they portray reference service. While the cynic might say "aha, Vincent is only attempting to maintain his job," the realist will certainly recognize that there is more than a job at stake. If administrators are given what appears to be a choice of functions, we could conceivably witness the absurd support of library instruction at the expense of reference service. Not only does efficient public service require both functions, but many of our professional positions rest upon the understanding that both functions are *skillfully* performed. As devotees of the liberal arts process, our aim to advance that process need not conflict with our pragmatic dependence upon its continued existence. We would do well to move away from the distraction of debate and acknowledge the fact that the aims of bibliographic instruction and reference service are symbiotic.[15] Perhaps our attention should now be devoted to the development of a sophisticated program which logically combines bibliographic instruction, online searching, and reference-desk service. In any case, we must be reminded of Constance McCarthy's argument that there is "no such thing as *sufficient* library instruction . . . We must still be sure to leave our students with the wish to know more, rather than the mistaken notion that they have been given the key that will open all bibliographic doors."[16]

It is unfortunate that McCarthy's philosophy needs reemphasis not because librarians are refusing to instruct their students, but because some very capable reference librarians are assuming that their task begins and ends in the classroom. In evangelic prose, Anne Roberts has argued that libraries should "shape the environment through programs of library instruction."[17] It is this kind of head-in-the-clouds approach that is causing librarians to dismiss bibliographic instructors as "the moral majority of the library profession."[18] Roberts continues by claiming that it is "the main goal of the library" to help transform students into independent learners through library instruction. Quoting Stephen Bailey's poignant observation that our nation is "in woefully short supply of people equipped to look at problems as a whole, at life as a whole, at the earth as a whole," Roberts optimistically responds that library instructors have begun the process of national renewal "by becoming mediator, communicator, and instructor."[19] Acceptance of this quasi-omnipotent role is tantamount to suggesting that bibliographic instructors hold the keys to the nation's intellectual salvation.

While bibliographic instruction is a necessary response to the information explosion, we delude ourselves when we believe that we can do more in the classroom than introduce students to the magnificent storehouse of knowledge which is our libraries. Jeremy Sayles helps bring us back to reality by pointing out that the "reservoir of experience" which we possess as reference librarians "cannot be taught in the form of library instruction. This life experience cannot be transferred in an instant to students, yet they need its fruits desperately—in prompt service.''[20] No more dramatic declaration for the maintenance of quality reference service can be made. It should be imprinted on our minds that we are, and we must remain, service librarians.

REFERENCES

1. Quoted in Millicent D. Abell, "The Changing Role of the Academic Librarian: Drift and Mastery," *College and Research Libraries* 40 (March 1979): 155-156. I should like to acknowledge the assistance provided by Nancy Grey, Bill Katz, and David W. Lewis in polishing this article. While responsibility for the opinions expressed is my own, the manner of expression benefitted from their suggestions.

2. Frances Hopkins, "A Century of Bibliographic Instruction: The Historical Claim to Professional and Academic Legitimacy," *College and Research Libraries* 43 (May 1982): 193.

3. The change in the Harvard College library collection can serve as a significant indicator of the transformation which has occurred since the era of Robinson. In 1877, Harvard possessed a remarkably large collection of 164,000 volumes. Today the Harvard libraries house more than 10 million volumes. See *Encyclopedia of Library and Information Service,* 33 vols. (New York: Marcel Dekker, 1968-82), X, 336; and *American Library Directory,* 35th ed. (New York: R.R. Bowker, 1982), p. 625.

4. Constance McCarthy, "Library Instruction: Observations from the Reference Desk," *RQ* 22 (Fall 1982): 36.

5. "Think Tank Recommendations for Bibliographic Instruction," *College and Research Libraries News* 42 (Dec. 1981): 394-398.

6. From *Sprueche in Prosa (Proverbs in Prose);* quoted in John Bartlett, *Familiar Quotations* (Boston: Little, Brown and Co., 1980), p. 397.

7. Jeremy W. Sayles, "Ideas, Concepts, and Practices," *Southeastern Librarian* 30 (Winter 1980): 198-201.

8. James Benson, "Bibliographic Education: A Radical Assessment," *Proceedings from the Second Southeastern Conference on Approaches to Bibliographic Instruction* (Charleston, S.C., 1979), p. 55.

9. Rewritten as "A Century of Bibliographic Instruction," 192-198.

10. *Ibid.,* 194.

11. *Ibid.,* 196.

12. See David W. Lewis, comp., "Reference Department: Annual Report, 1979-80," and "Public Services Department: Annual Report, 1981-82," Fackenthal Library, Franklin and Marshall College.

13. See *Ibid.,* and "Public Services Department: Annual Report, 1980-81." Research questions were defined as those reference queries requiring more than three minutes of research time.

14. The paradigm of the "one-shot" instructional session is being employed only because this is the approach *most commonly* utilized. Even an instructional approach which incorporates three or four sessions in a semester, however, is not going to create the user who can function independently of the reference desk.

15. The clearest example of this debate is the recent symposium "Reactions to the Think Tank Recommendations," *The Journal of Academic Librarianship* 9(March 1983): 4-14. While the core of this symposium is negative reaction to a somewhat polemical—and, thus, misunderstood—piece which I coauthored on "The Think Tank Recommendations for

Bibliographic Instruction,'' *College and Research Libraries News* 42(December 1981): 394-98, I should like to refer readers to the useful rejoinder of Janice T. Koyama, ''Bibliographic Instruction and the Role of the Academic Librarian,'' 12-13.

16. McCarthy, ''Library Instruction: Observations from the Reference Desk,'' 37.

17. Anne Roberts, ''The Changing Role of the Academic Instruction Librarian,'' *Catholic Library World* 51 (Feb. 1980): 283.

18. Quoted in John Lubans, Jr., ''Library Literacy,'' *RO* 22 (Fall 1982): 14.

19. Roberts, ''The Changing Role,'' 285.

20. Sayles, ''Ideas, Concepts, and Practices,'' 199.

TECHNIQUES
AND QUESTIONS

The "Compleat" Library Patron

Robert Harris

Several years ago during a discussion of the bibliographic instruction program at our library, a friend informed me that "if you give a man a fish you feed him for a day, but if you teach a man to fish you feed him for a lifetime." He seemed to think that this maxim applied not only to the question of public welfare but also to bibliographic instruction. The use of this maxim for the latter purpose implies two things: (1) that it is possible and desirable to teach a library patron to be an independent or self-reliant user of libraries and (2) that the same library patron is going to need those library skills throughout his life. Although there is very little evidence to support either of these assumptions, at present a number of BI librarians are forcefully asserting their validity.

"Think Tank Recommendations for Bibliographic Instruction," published in the December, 1981 issue of *College & Research Libraries News,* includes the following two declarations: (1) "Bibliographic instruction is intended to teach students to make intelligent, independent decisions about library use. To be able to use the card catalog, reference sources, or computer terminals to retrieve information on very specialized topics, or to recognize that libraries are classification systems to organize the materials, are fundamental skills that each student should possess."[1] (2) "Competency in library research should be a fundamental goal of education. Effective bibliographic instruction contributes to students' understanding of the nature of learning and scholarship, directly supports their coursework and helps prepare them for self-directed life-long learning."[2] In another recent article on the same subject, Brian Nielsen affirms that the advocacy of self-reliance on the part of library patrons is a key point in the debate.[3] At an informal meeting of BI librarians in San Antonio this past January, statements

---

The author is the Chief Reference Librarian at Southwest Texas State University, San Marcos, TX 78666.

51

were made to the effect that "this is an information age. We are an information based society. Most of what students learn today in college will be out of date in 15 years and they must know how to keep up."

Before going any further, it should be acknowledged that there are some excellent reasons for offering bibliographic instruction. Two librarians at Southwest Texas State University recently prepared a slide-tape presentation on *Psychological Abstracts* which we think will have a real impact on several hundred psychology students each year. The case for bibliographic instruction has been stated very succinctly by Mary Reichel. Ms. Reichel affirms that "Literature searching, the process of knowing about library resources and finding information, can be seen logically as going from the general to the specific." At the general end bibliographic instruction is appropriate and at the specific end assistance from a reference librarian will often be necessary.[4] However, the claims being made on behalf of patron self-reliance and the universality of the need for library skills simply cannot be supported.

In a recent issue of *RQ,* Constance McCarthy argues persuasively that patrons who have been encouraged to believe that they have been prepared "to use any library unaided, for any purpose, for the rest of their lives" are in fact very poorly equipped to deal with a complex, rapidly changing library world. If instead BI librarians instill in patrons a healthy respect for the complexity of bibliographic research, they will not fall into the trap of believing that one outline or formula "can encapsulate good research strategy for all disciplines." Ms. McCarthy concludes that in the absence of standard codes and conventions the proliferation of online databases and catalogs actually makes the possibility of patron self-reliance more remote than ever before.[5]

In a brief paper in the *Journal of Academic Librarianship,* Joseph Rosenblum emphasizes a point which Ms. McCarthy just touches upon. He asserts that within a short time after a student graduates from college "his or her knowledge of biology and of a library will be of a piece—outmoded.'"[6] This is a very important point in this debate because some BI librarians seem to be claiming for library skills a timeless quality which is evidently not to be found anywhere else in the sciences, social sciences, or humanities.

The recent literature dealing with online catalogs seems to support Ms. McCarthy's comment on that subject. Marshall Clinton, in describing Phoenix, states that because most users learn best from individual instruction the library has had to form an "instructional corps" to work in the catalog area. He points out that people who can't type or are poor spellers are at a particular disadvantage in using Phoenix.[7] Anne Godzins Lipow states that in her judgment "as online catalogs become more sophisticated we'll see that in person instruction is more necessary than ever, not less."[8]

Occasionally a BI advocate will commend self-reliance for patrons because he alleges that the unobtrusive study of reference service has shown it to be so inadequate.[9] Eleven years of reference experience in an academic library convinces me that such research is probably not relevant to most academic reference situations where the vast majority of questions tend to be routine in that the librarian has answered either the same question or a very similar question many times during a semester and during previous semesters. With respect to public libraries, the library use studies surveyed by Michael H. Harris and James Sodt do not support the bleak conclusions drawn by some of the exponents of unobtrusive research. For example, in 1978 Gallup found that only 5% of library visitors were dissatisfied with the ability of librarians to answer reference questions.[10] Even if we conclude that library patrons at public libraries do not know poor reference service when they see it and that reference service in public libraries is inadequate, the obvious answer would seem to be to provide several thousand more good reference librarians—not to try to train 200+ million people to be their own reference librarians.

The claim that in an information age everyone needs to have library skills is not as easy to refute as the claim for the desirability of user self-reliance. Our society may be information based and we may be in an information age. These terms do have a certain social scientific ring to them. Still, no published research has ever shown that one needs to have library skills in order to cope successfully in modern society. Michael Harris and James Sodt conclude that "a majority of American adults are in reality nonusers of libraries."[11] In a 1976 survey of library use in New Jersey, 87% of New Jersey adults thought that it was "very important that all communities have public libraries," but only 27% of New Jersey adults said that "it would make a great deal of difference to them personally if a public library were not available to them." The most frequently mentioned reasons for believing the public library to be important were (1) education and children and (2) reading. Reference services came in a distant third.[12] In a recent article in *Library Journal,* W. Theodore

Bolton comments on how few people look to the library as a source for "everyday coping information."[13]

In conclusion, there is no proof and very little evidence that teaching every college student a general search strategy and some facts about libraries is going to turn any significant number of students into self-reliant life-long library users. Some BI librarians may wish that these things were true and some may think that some day they will be true. However, wishing does not make it so, and we must be careful that we do not confuse wishful thinking with vision. For the present, all BI librarians know that an effective BI program requires a broad base of faculty support. Intellectual clarity is the specialty, the stock in trade you might say, of the higher education community. With such a clientele, we are not going to advance the cause of bibliographic instruction by making claims for our program which cannot be substantiated.

REFERENCES

1. "Think Tank Recommendations for Bibliographic Instruction," *College and Research Libraries News* 42 (December 1981): 395.

2. "Think Tank Recommendations," p. 397.

3. Brian Nielsen. "Teacher or Intermediary: Alternative Professional Models in the Information Age," *College and Research Libraries* 43 (May 1982): 185.

4. Mary Reichel. "Bibliographic Instruction and the Reference Desk," *Journal of Academic Librarianship* 9(March 1983): 10. This brief article was published as part of "Reactions to the Think Tank Recommendations: A Symposium."

5. Constance McCarthy. "Library Instruction: Observations from the Reference Desk," *RQ* 22 (Fall 1982): 36-41.

6. Joseph Rosenblum. "The Shifty Shoals of Bibliographic Instruction," *Journal of Academic Librarianship* 9 (March 1983): 8-9. This brief article was published as part of "Reactions to the Think Tank Recommendations: A Symposium."

7. Marshall Clinton. "Phoenix: An Online System for a Library Catalogue," *Database* 5 (February 1982): 65.

8. Anne Grodzins Lipow. "Practical Considerations of the Current Capabilities of Subject Access in Online Public Catalogs," *Library Resources and Technical Services* 27 (January/March 1983): 86.

9. Brian Nielsen, p. 186.

10. Michael H. Harris and James Sodt. "Libraries, Users, and Librarians: Continuing Efforts to Define the Nature and Extent of Public Library Use," *Advances in Librarianship* 11 (1981): 120.

11. Michael H. Harris and James Sodt, p. 132.

12. Gallup Organization. "Use of and Attitudes Toward Libraries in New Jersey (abstract)," *Unabashed Librarian* no. 39 (1981): 22-32.

13. W. Theodore Bolton. "Life Style Research: An Aid to Promoting Public Libraries," *Library Journal* 107 (May 15, 1982): 963.

The Reference Librarian Who Teaches:
The Confessions of a Mother Hen

John C. Swan

This is in many respects an elaborate defense of the simple and time-worn practice of taking a library patron in hand and walking and working through the search process with that person. More than that, this is an assertion that this homely activity, conducted in the right spirit, can be the foundation for truly effective library instruction. Since the arguments concerning such instruction which follow may seem an odd mixture of the reactionary and the enthusiastic, I had better make it clear that they are conditioned by experience in a specific context. In many libraries, especially small, very active academic libraries in which professional versatility is a necessity even when it is not an unalloyed virtue, the reference librarian (in the singular) is also in charge of teaching others how to use reference tools, and by extension, the rest of the library. The performance of this dual role of reference and teaching encourages much overlapping of (and some conflict between) the two activities; it also brings one to see the deep connections between them—connections which transcend this small-college environment.

In his invaluable "Library Literacy" column in a recent *RQ*, John Lubans quoted an accusation from one of the disgruntled that serves here to sound the reactionary note: "BI—The moral majority of the library profession."[1] Jeremy Sayles amplifies this charge: "There is a continuous commotion about the evils of spoon-feeding, of dispensing information. We librarians are supposed to feel guilty if we *give* information to students. Yet, this is what we are prepared for: indeed, this is our function."[2] This reaction to the "library instruction juggernaut" is very understandable, even from one who, like Mr. Sayles, believes strongly in "a program of basic research skills to complement the traditional reference service."[3] But then,

---

John C. Swan is Reference Librarian, Lilly Library, Wabash College, Crawfordsville, IN 47933.

55

the juggernaut itself is understandable, considering the resistance, the hostility, and the inertia of librarians and faculty (not to mention students) which BI missionaries have had, and still have, to overcome. But even taking the passions of the struggle into account, there remains a basic disagreement about priorities. On the one hand, referring again to Sayles, "Library instruction, at best, is merely the overture to traditional reference service. It does not replace it; it complements and strengthens it."[4] Or, in a more recent statement, a response by two librarians to the controversial ACRL Bibliographic Instruction Section "Think Tank Recommendations," "Such instruction is not designed—nor should it be designed—to make the student user independent of the reference department. We need not make every student a reference librarian, though we can certainly make them more knowledgeable."[5]

On the other hand, the "Think Tank" itself provided the most assertive claim for the pride of place of BI in their rejection of "the notion of bibliographic instruction as a secondary activity of library reference departments, instead viewing it "as the very heart of the reference process."[6] As one who has been to the Mountain (Earlham) and communed with the Truth (Evan Farber's annual workshop) in this matter, I feel the force of the "Think Tank" claim. Indeed, armed with the appropriate clay tablets, we at Wabash have begun to put into effect, with modifications to suit our circumstances, a number of Earlham techniques for moving library research methodologies closer to the center of the students'—and faculty's and librarians'—consciousness. The innovations have begun to add considerably to our thriving program of one-shot course and assignment-related library tours. Working with faculty to develop assignments that require the students to create annotated bibliographies in a sequence of phases, and also working cooperatively to develop research assignments that encourage specific and intelligent use of reference tools, have begun to take us beyond what is possible in the one-shot program.

It is no reflection upon my experience in the Earlham workshop (although I eagerly and futilely looked for substantial flaws that would let me out of this painful change in life) that I still find myself among those who cannot jump into the Think Tank. (I ought to make clear that Earlham was not literally represented in the Think Tank group, although it has long been one of the most successful examples of an instruction-centered library.) BI just isn't the "very heart of the reference process," either for the librarian or the patron. The essence of the process is obviously the search itself, the use of the investigative skills in interplay with thought and experience, not the mere acquisition of those skills. For all the considerable good in them, the ACRL recommendations, at least the most overreaching of them, present the danger of separating the learning process from the using process. It is true enough that it is necessary to focus upon educational techniques and program planning,[7] but if BI is treated as an end in itself, a discipline for students to master, rather than a path to the mastery of real disciplines, then the vital link between searching and learning can be broken. The relentless earnestness and simplified abstractness of many BI exercises, especially those only tenuously related to real course needs, based on regimented preparation conducted, often, away from the points of use, can turn the searching adventure into the sterile pursuit of a flow-charted answer.

Constance McCarthy has provided an illuminating analysis of the way in which some users of the library are led to "underestimate the complexity of library systems" by "library instruction that stresses details and permits easy success at the expense of realistic experience with library research."[8] This kind of misunderstanding can lead to patron guilt and frustration when the application of dutifully learned simple procedures doesn't pay off, but more seriously, it fosters the belief that the search for information is nothing more than obediently following the schematics set forth by the librarians and their guides. The assumption that the truth lies at the other end of a string of keywords and cross-references does yield results in many cases—there is never a shortage of simplified questions with simplified answers—but it also carries the danger of a flat and uncreative relationship with information and ideas. This is especially true for the many who find the library a rather foreign place to begin with, for whom any quick and easy pathway to an answer or to a paper topic is likely to be the end, rather than the beginning, of inquiry.

To be fair, it must be said that the Think Tank recommendations envision a much richer and more fully developed instructional process, although the language they choose to describe this vision is not always reassuring. "All sound instruction is based on the imparting of the basic tenets of a body of knowledge; all instruction should be conceptually based."[9] Fine words, supported by the collective wisdom of countless educators who have chosen to address students' capacity to understand in preference to their capacity to memorize.

But what do they mean in light of the statement under the heading, "The Importance of Research:"

> Bibliographic instruction should be based on knowledge of the social and intellectual characteristics of the academic disciplines which give rise to their different patterns of scholarly, bibliographic, and encyclopedic literature . . . . Instruction librarians should make explicit (and thus teachable) the tacit knowledge of experienced researchers and determine the concepts and techniques which should be taught.[10]

If this means we should master and then impart "sociology of knowledge," research networks, "deep structure" and metaphors of reference rather than, or even antecedant to, actual research skills, it could well lead to the alienating abstraction of one of the few learning activities that can be both concrete and conceptually stimulating at the same time.

For all their moments of insight and their structural elegance, the attempts so far to do this conceptual structuring, the ghostly paradigms cast up by McInnis[11] and Nitecki[12] (for instance) fail to put weapons for enlightenment into the hands of this teaching librarian. Even more chilling, but just as much in line with the Think Tank thought, is Keresztesi's argument that librarians should not seek "the solution in the acquisition of degrees in practice-oriented subject disciplines, but by preserving proudly our generalist posture, we should cultivate our own garden."[13] By "generalist" he does not mean the pseudo-polymaths that most of us in reference gradually become ("wizard" was Daniel Gore's term, I believe), with our efficient, reassuring and superficial acquaintance with vast, bleeding chunks of the world of organized knowledge. No, he means something more exalted and severe, the mastery of a real discipline, a "science of bibliography" in which we learn and teach the "topography" of the disciplines, each suitably arranged into multi-categorized "dimensions."[14] It is undeniable that there is a discipline of bibliography, just as there are several thriving varieties of information science, citation analysis, operations research, and sociologies of inquiry. It may well be that this "meta-librarianship" fits well into this world. But just as BI is not for the purpose of transforming the unsuspecting patron into a reference librarian, it is similarly irrelevant to turning out information scientists (although it should be a good start for both procedures, come to think of it). The metaphorical approach certainly can't provide the sense of the activities of research and inquiry that actual experience in subject disciplines can; it has yet to demonstrate its conceptual usefulness to the reference librarian who would also gladly teach.

Reference librarians are, the stereotype to the contrary, quite often eager to be helpful. Not only is that what we are paid for, but the "sitting duck" nature of the reference desk instills in many of its occupants the urge to demonstrate in public that they can be useful, even expert. Producing the requested information quickly, accomplishing this without letting the patron in on the false starts and dead ends, often effects a wonderful transformation of image: Sitting Duck becomes Eagle Eye. To befowl the image one more time, it must be confessed that the same motivation plays a role in the mother hen impulse. It is satisfying to watch the look of gratitude supplant that of anxiety as I lead the patron to the right places, clucking concernedly all the while. It must also be admitted that the "reference interview" that goes with this style is not always successful—just as mother hens can get in the way of their own offspring.

These confessions are not meant to deny the value of the mother hen approach, but to make it clear that, despite its efficacy, it has its dangers. In fact, the mother hen quality is extremely useful for both fulfilling the immediate needs of the patron and establishing a relationship of trust—always devoutly to be sought, of course, but especially necessary in a small college situation, where there is a particularly direct connection between this trust and the amount of business that comes the way of the reference desk.

Most relevant here, this nurturing behavior of the reference librarian has a direct impact upon the instructional role. The pedagogy of the connection rests on simple grounds, one of which is well expressed by Joanne Euster: "Bibliographic instruction at its most elemental level is simply one-on-one reference assistance."[15] This is the most compelling reason that the joining of reference and BI ought to be much more than the shotgun wedding it often seems to be. One-on-one instruction is only practical when there are time, resources, and staff for it, a less-than-common conjunction these days. However, it is my experience and my basic argument that the more that one-on-one approach can be carried over into group instruction (and even herd instruction, as some institutions conduct it), the more effective is the teaching.

Having made the claim that mother henning has something to do with teaching, I am obliged to put it into the context of the "information versus instruction'' question; after all, mother hens of the reference species seem to be firmly on the "information" side of this debate. In his stimulating discussion of "alternative professional models," Brian Nielsen refers to the performance of reference work in sociological terms as a "core professional task":

> First of all, reference is a librarian role that involves a "professional-client" relationship, unlike other task areas such as cataloging, book selection, and administration, where the contact with library users is not often direct . . . . Reference work is also a specialty area in which the "application of special and esoteric knowledge," that criterion so important to achieving professional status, is patent: the public perception of the all-knowing reference librarian (which coexists with other, less flattering images) is testimony to this . . . Still other qualities of reference work that give weight to its "core task" nature are that the work is not reducible to rules, it is difficult to measure, and its practice relies on intuition, hunches, and bits and pieces of information that only long experience and a retentive mind—not a textbook—can develop.[16]

The consequence of this professional identification has been to emphasize what Nielsen calls the "intermediary" aspect of reference, the librarian enhancing his status (*re* the Eagle Eye) by mediating between his resources and the patron, rather than providing the person with the skills to use those tools independently. The professional is encouraged in this practice by the fact that he/she really does, or ought to, know the ropes better than they can be taught within the constraints of bibliographic instruction. And the patron is usually there in the library for information rather than training, anyway. Nielsen argues well that the intermediary role is essentially limiting and, if used alone, is finally doomed to serve only an elite who can afford the services of the staff trained in that role:

> If librarians truly wish to work toward the best interests of their users, it is absurd to continue to advocate the old classic professionalism, which places users in a dependency relationship with librarians. Such a relationship does a disservice to users and ultimately retards the development of library services, of librarians, and of much library technology.[17]

The argument is convincing, but it does not foreclose the very important possibility that modified versions of the "old classic professionalism" can be combined with the teaching of library skills. Indeed, the most effective teachers, at least in terms of intimacy with the subject to be taught, ought to come from the ranks of these "intermediaries," reference librarians who have a working sense of what Elizabeth Frick has called a "basic art"[18] in our complex world of information, the art of literature searching. The force of that word "art" may not apply to the search in its expressive sense, but as an evocation of the thought, creativity, and reflection that goes into the best searching, it will do just fine.

In order to understand how a clearly intermediary approach to reference can also partake of the teacher's role, it is necessary to move beyond Nielsen's alternatives—and more is implied here than merely that reference librarians can also be instruction librarians. Janice Koyama, supporting Nielsen, has emphasized that:

> Extremists on either side are better directed to forge a new alternative role . . . and to accept reference desk activity and bibliographic instruction as interrelated, compatible, and necessary for the future growth and continuing existence of both.[19]

This acceptance of the alternatives echoes the stance which Katz has taken, a position which has behind it a good deal of scepticism about the claims that have been made for BI. He believes that:

> the library user, and nonuser, should be given a choice. It is important to stress "given a choice." The user should have the option either (1) to learn how to use the library or any of its parts, or (2) not to learn how and still to expect a full, complete, and total answer to his or her question(s) from the reference librarian.[20]

It is important for the establishment of trust between the librarian and his patron that the latter feel that he does indeed have a choice. More than once I have seen a student withdraw that trust when his question evoked a lesson rather than an answer or a specific path to an answer.

Koyama's "new alternative role," I could argue, ought to be a rethought version of the old mother hen role; however, the alternatives of which it is made only partly express the notion of mother hen as teacher. In practice, this is not so much a set of alternating roles as a simultaneous combination. And this is not to construct a paradox, but to describe a teacher. Like the good teacher, the reference librarian who would teach something of his trade even as he connects questioner with answer must have a richer self-conception than that of information dispenser. He must be a role model.

Every good teacher is to some degree a role model, but this does not mean a model for teaching (except perhaps for those students who will themselves teach, and even bad teachers have served that function for generations of bad teachers after them). The teacher who succeeds in communicating with his students does present himself as a source of learned skills and knowledge, to be sure, but that role would have little communicative impact if the teacher did not also reveal the thinker and learner inside that teacher role, using, testing, applying the education and experience which he seeks to convey. In other words, the teacher who manages to make a difference is a role model as a learner for the students who learn from—or more precisely with—him.

This is hardly a fresh insight, but it is also hardly a guiding principle among librarians who find themselves attempting to communicate some portion of their research skills to single or multiple students. Not that it prevails among teachers themselves—Ivan Illich's well-known condemnation of the educational system could, with very little alteration, apply both to hard-nosed reference librarians and the most righteous of the BI crusaders:

> Schools are designed on the assumption that there is a secret to everything in life; that the quality of life depends on knowing that secret, that secrets can be known only in orderly succession; and that only teachers can properly reveal those secrets.[21]

Librarians often conceive of their professional role in essentially clerical and externally manipulative terms: they are paid for mastering systems of storage and retrieval according to outward descriptions and codes, but the actual content of what they manipulate is beyond their purview. Therefore, that which they seek to teach they also present in terms of these externals. Even on a one-to-one basis, this presents a formidable challenge to anyone who seeks to make this into an enlivening educational experience (not even considering the countless librarians and teachers of librarians who have been perfectly content with memorization of index titles and coverages). It just may be that the necessary life-giving principles will emerge from the aforementioned efforts of McInnis, Nitecki, Keresztesi, and the like. However, since these theoretical plumbings are more likely to lead to greater abstraction instead, it might prove more useful to learn from the success of those reference/instruction librarians who are not hampered by an outsider's relationship to the world of content. These include reference librarians who insist on remaining in touch, however superficially, with the literature which lies at the other end of their indexes. And they include mother hens who draw sustenance not only from their mothering but from the substance within the knowledge structures through which they guide their charges.

Pauline Wilson has drawn the distinction between the roles of the teacher and the librarian upon this external/internal basis:

> The teacher must have a good understanding of the content of that portion of the graphic record which he or she is charged with disseminating . . . . The librarian, on the other hand, must have a different understanding . . . an in-depth understanding of the graphic record as a structure, an entity . . . . The librarian does not disseminate content and does not disseminate by teaching but by means of library processes.[22]

It is possible for the reference librarian who also teaches research skills to accept this distinction simply by alternating between the two roles ("librarians sometimes teach").[23] However, it is much more liberating (potentially), and much closer to the complex reality of the librarian's actual research process if we discard this categorization and admit that content is very much in the librarian's domain.

We should teach the research process as an activity which does indeed offer the fascination and complexity that we ought to recognize in a "basic art." To do this we must draw upon the questions and the issues themselves; we can't stop at keywords and cross-references. This is not an argumentation for unnecessary complexity or mystification (no mother hen could ever mystify, except maybe with prose); there really are simple, straightforward questions and answers, and they are surely necessary in beginning BI. But the teacher's truth holds even from the start: To give a student or a class of students a genuine sense of the search, show them a searcher in action, grappling with content as well as index terms, ideas as well as citations. The reference librarian in particular has the excellent opportunity to serve as the role model, the expert learner demonstrating for the novice learner. This, by the way, is an opportunity that will be lost if conflict and specialization eventually put bibliographic instruction exclusively in the hands of library instructors who are responsible only for teaching and therefore develop their teaching routines at the expense of their own knowledge.

The reference librarian who consciously fulfills the function of the role model both as reference guide and as teacher must confront his research challenges, not as an expert in the content of the matter he searches, but as one skilled in the discovery and quick evaluation of that content. Very importantly, this requires the willingness to be vulnerable, *not* concealing those false starts and dead ends, being honest about what one understands and what one doesn't (sometimes especially difficult for wizards).

One of the basic sources of resistance to the belief that librarians must deal with content as well as structure is the clear impossibility of becoming a real wizard, of learning in any depth at all the content of the subject matter to which we provide access. But how many "real" teachers have in-depth knowledge of even their own fields in the modern age of information, except in cases of extreme specialization? Mastery of content is not the point, either for the reference librarian or, nearly always, for the persons for whom, with whom, the reference process is accomplished. What is relevant? Engaging the content in a meaningful way, an act which must be preceded by similarly meaningful search.

The unique pedagogical advantage of mother henning relates directly to this business of making the search meaningful. One of Carl Rogers' most creative (over)statements is to the point: "I have come to feel that the only learning which significantly influences behavior is self-discovered, self-appropriated learning."[24] In the light of this passage, the mother hen has a distinct advantage over the prescriptive instructor, Illich's teacher of "secrets." No one would deny that young chickens and young humans learn most naturally from role models; there is no reason this should not apply to library instruction. We who concernedly shepherd the patron through every step of the research course, sharing, sympathizing, worrying, have stepped at least part of the way out of the prescriptive role; we encourage the student's learning by self-discovery because we must go through it ourselves. We cannot deny that there are always the dangers of smothering or infantilizing our charges, but that means we must ply our trade with a healthy awareness—and mother henning is not the kind of role that excludes all other styles and approaches in those who adopt it, although it does serve as an excellent base of operations.

Despite the image and the natural dynamics of this approach, it is not an exclusively individual mode of instruction—most mother hens have a fair number of offspring exploring at the same time. The basic attitude of openness, the personal concern, and the sense of discovery may be difficult to maintain all the time, but a nourishing attitude is usually itself rewarded with nourishment. It is not difficult to adapt the attitude to classes of BI students, and its effects linger even when major logistical compromises are necessary. In my experience, it has been possible to use the individual approach with a group, using questions and research problems arising from the group, with more success than the canned demonstration, in spite of the preordained success and efficiency of the latter. However it is applied, against whatever obstacles of numbers, time, and resources, the mother hen style should have value in any library teaching context. When the spirit is right, it bears the seeds of trust, shared experience, and real library education.

NOTES

1. Lubans, John, Jr. "Library Literacy," *RQ*, Fall 1982, p. 14.

2. Sayles, Jeremy W., "An Opinion about Library Instruction," *Southeastern Librarian*, Winter 1980, p. 199.

3. *ibid.*, p. 198.

4. *ibid.*, p. 200.

5. Lewis, David W., and C. Paul Vincent, "Reactions to the Think Tank Recommendations: A Symposium: An Initial Response," *Journal of Academic Librarianship*, March 1983, p. 5.

6. "Think Tank Recommendations for Bibliographic Instruction," *College and Research Libraries News*, December 1981, p. 395.

7. For a humane and practical view of the planning side, see Keith M. Cottam, "Avoiding Failure: Planning User Education," *RQ*, Summer 1982, pp. 331-33.

8. McCarthy, Constance, "Library Instruction: Observations from the Reference Desk," *RQ*, Fall 1982, p. 36.

9. Think Tank Recommendations, *op. cit.*, p. 396.

10. *ibid.*

11. McInnis, Raymond, "Do Metaphors Make Good Sense in Teaching Research Strategy?" in Cerise Oberman and Katina Strauch, *Theories of Bibliographic Education: Designs for Teaching* (New York: Bowker, 1982), pp. 45-74.

12. Nitecki, Joseph Z., "An Idea of Librarianship: An Outline for a Root-Metaphor Theory in Library Science," *Journal of Library History*, Winter 1981, pp. 106-120.

13. Keresztesi, Michael, "The Science of Bibliography: Theoretical Implications for Bibliographic Instruction," in Oberman and Strauch, *op. cit.* p. 26.

14. *ibid.,* pp. 21-24.

15. Euster, Joanne, "Reactions to the Think Tank Recommendations: A Symposium: 'Full of Sound and Fury, Signifying' What?" *Journal of Academic Librarianship,* March 1983, p. 14.

16. Nielsen, Brian, "Teacher or Intermediary: Alternative Professional Models in the Information Age," *College and Research Libraries,* May 1982, p. 185.

17. *ibid.,* p. 188.

18. Frick, Elizabeth, "Teaching Information Structure: Turning Dependent Researchers into Self-Teachers" in Oberman and Strauch, *op. cit.,* p. 193.

19. Koyama, Janice T., "Reactions to the Think Tank Recommendations: A Symposium: Bibliographic Instruction and the Role of the Academic Librarian," *Journal of Academic Librarianship,* March 1983, p. 13.

20. Katz, William A., *Introduction to Reference Work,* Volume II: *Reference Services and Reference Processes,* Third Edition (New York: McGraw-Hill, 1978), p. 261.

21. Illich, Ivan, *New York Review of Books,* 1971, quoted in *Morrow's International Dictionary of Contemporary Quotations,* Compiled by Jonathon Green (New York: Morrow, 1982), p. 360.

22. Wilson, Pauline, "Librarians as Teachers: The Study of an Organization Fiction," *Library Quarterly,* Volume 49, No. 2 (1979), p. 155.

23. *ibid.*

24. Rogers, Carl R., "Personal Thoughts on Teaching and Learning," in William F. O'Neill, *Selected Educational Heresies* (Glenview, Illinois: Scott, Foresman, 1969), p. 210.

Training Reference Librarians Using Library Instruction Methods

Anne F. Roberts

A myth may be defined as an unproved belief that is accepted uncritically and is used to justify a social institution. One such myth that prevails in librarianship is that the certification of our profession makes the graduate an instant expert in all areas of the field. A professional librarian who has recently graduated with an MLS degree in hand, having taken courses in many different areas, is suddenly expected to perform at a high level on the job. It is assumed that librarians, once they have mastered knowledge of their field, can work effectively in whatever part of the library they choose. Later, it is supposed that librarians can move into other sections of the library and execute their duties well. The reality is something else.

It is strange that in a service profession such as librarianship no prominence is given to reference or library instruction training for pre-professionals. Other professions, such as law and medicine, have resident internships where trainees are under the tutelage of senior practitioners. Some pre-professional training has been introduced recently in the area of online computerized searching, but even here it is hardly a well-developed training program.

There is not even much professional literature written about reference training, either in relation to internships or staff development workshops. What little is available in the literature often gets tied in with the policies and procedures of the level and type of reference services offered by the individual library, but not formal training procedures.

The question that must be asked is "at what stage is the professional reference librarian able to face users with confidence and handle their inquiries with skill?" A "professional reference librar-

Ms. Roberts is the author of *Library Instruction for Librarians* (1982) and a well known expert in the field. She is a librarian at the State University of New York at Albany, Albany, NY 12222.

67

ian'' can mean anyone from a newly minted MLS degree holder to an experienced librarian recently transferred to the reference department, or even an experienced reference librarian coming from a reference department in another library. All the above categories of professional reference librarians need new training. And that training should be both of sufficient quality and of adequate duration suited to the specific needs of the institution, and aimed at reaching the goals of the library within the institution. What many call reference training programs currently are no more than sessions of orientation, which are fine for what they are, but do not go far enough.

There are several types of existing reference training programs. One popular form which is commonly used is having the new reference librarian work closely under the supervision of an experienced reference librarian. A training program may be the only time in the career of a librarian when supervision occurs, and therefore this period is of crucial importance. The experienced reference librarian may not have had good training, may not be well-versed in current reference tools and methods, or the new technology, and may have incurred bad habits over the years. These bad habits may be passed on to the new reference librarian. Even experienced reference librarians may not know the environment of a different library, for each library has different services and different user populations.

Most library administrators do admit that reference training is important, but that it is too costly in terms of staff and time. Special libraries have patrons who demand expertise and hold staff individually accountable. They appear to be the only libraries really concerned with high quality staff training for reference librarians. They very often have the resources and investments of the collections to develop good staff training programs.

British librarians seem to favor training programs for all types of inservice librarianship, including reference. Isaacs, in the article on inservice training for reference work, states that under no circumstances can any librarian face users without a six month training program at the very least. In this program, all reference questions are recorded and used as the basis for training; these actual questions form the heart of the course. From these questions, the new reference librarian gets a sample of how complex and varied the questions asked at a reference desk are, and what a wide range of topics is covered. No answers are required to answer the questions by the trainee, but the source for the answer is cited, and some clues are given by the trainee. The experienced reference librarian and the trainee go over the sources, answers, and clues together while the questions are still fresh in the new reference librarian trainee's mind. By doing this, a practical sense of the sources and a greater sense of realism are achieved, according to Isaacs.

The Canadians also favor inservice methods for librarianship, and McGill University has an extensive training program. This inservice project for reference covers: one week of orientation sessions; three months of structured observation at the reference desk with a senior librarian (the trainee is not permitted to answer any questions); five hours of training in reference methods used to answer the most frequently asked type of questions; five hours of training in the card catalogue pointing out its idiosyncracies; ten hours browsing in the reference collection itself; and seven hours reviewing the telephone queries received by the reference desk.

The Brooklyn Public Library is one American institution known for its excellent training program for all professional librarians. The reference training emphasizes the card catalogue as a way to answer reference questions, and this methodology is highlighted for new librarians. Brooklyn Public Library's program, like all good training programs, is structured, lengthy in duration, extensive in subject coverage and methodology, well thought-out and tested, and based on the realities of reference work at one institution. One cannot help but contrast these reference training programs with the reference courses in the schools of library science which are inconsistent. Professional education for librarianship stresses theory over practice in most instances. Whatever practical assignments are given tend to have abstract questions which relate to generalities rather than to specific situations.

Galvin, in his article, sees the new reference librarian as providing information at a high level in order for librarians to keep their status. He is vague on exactly how this is to be done and how the service is to be upgraded. He notes the lack of standards of quality in reference service and stresses that standards are needed in order to improve the level of performance of reference librarians. Standards can only be improved by implementing a rigorous training procedure which will, by implication, lead to higher levels of reference service being performed by the new reference librarian.

Like the dearth of professional literature for training reference librarians, similar circumstances exist for training instruction librarians. There is an excess of materials written for the profession on how to perform library instruction for users, and many articles telling library schools what to teach and how to teach it in the area of bibliographic instruction. This is mainly because the field of library instruction was developed in libraries by practicing librarians and was not part of the regular library school curriculum as was reference. The library instruction movement crested in the 1970s, and most libraries promoted the idea of library instruction, user education, or library orientation in some form. Naturally, different librarians had different ideas of how users should "learn the library," and made claims for the success of their particular method. But again, little or no professional literature has appeared describing a training program for instruction librarians. One of the reasons for this might be another myth: anyone can teach.

Another difficulty has been the changing roles of reference librarians. Reference librarians have moved from conservators, collectors, custodians, and caretakers to counselors, mediators, facilitators, and educators. The nature of reference service itself has changed, from information to instruction. As Schiller points out in her article, the definitions of reference service have usually included both instruction and information, but with differing degrees of emphasis. Reference service consists of personal assistance to users in pursuit of information, and also provides guidance and direction in the pursuit of information rather than giving users the information itself. Often information and instruction have been at cross purposes with each other since each term has been joined with a conflicting view as to the amount of assistance to be offered in each case. Information has been associated with giving the greatest amount of service, while instruction limited the service to pointing the way for users. Since libraries are viewed as educational institutions they automatically perform a teaching role. But teaching in a different sense: to inform users of the types of information and materials available so they can make good decisions and judgments in answering their needs.

If all of this confuses reference and instruction librarians, it certainly confuses the users. Users want answers, not instruction. Library instruction and reference service are seen as a continuum since both are part of an overall process geared to guiding users to effectively and efficiently employ the materials and resources of libraries. Librarians strengthen their understanding and expertise by doing library instruction and reference service; the users' needs are also served well since both types of service are important to users and complement each other.

One way to determine what the components of a good staff training program for reference librarians might be is to look at the performance functions a reference librarian is required to attain. The University Libraries, State University of New York at Albany, under the Reference Services Unit Coordinator, William Young, developed informal guidelines for evaluating the effectiveness of librarians serving at the reference desk which outline some of the functions reference librarians perform. They include: *knowledge of reference sources* (new titles, indexes and bibliographies which provide bibliographic control over documents and law collections); *reference technique capability* (ability to find reference sources to successfully answer questions through using the card catalogue, bibliographies); *knowledge of the libraries' general collections* (awareness of locations and contents of subject strengths); *knowledge of other services relevant to reference service* (online searching, archives, special collections, microforms); *ability to communicate effectively with patrons* (display courtesy, patience, a demeanor which encourages patrons to approach reference desk, conduct a successful reference interview); *ability to make use of computerized systems as they relate to reference service effectively* (circulation system, cataloging system, online quick searching); *ability and willingness to instruct patrons in the use of reference sources; ability and willingness to communicate effectively on a professional level with other library colleagues; promptness, reliability and cooperation in fulfilling reference desk and reference service responsibilities.*

As the functions demonstrate, there is a wide variety of skills upon which to design and plan a reference staff training program. I would like to suggest one method based upon my observations and experiences in library instruction for a reference staff training initial program using videotaping. Just as those in the teaching profession need to see themselves and hear themselves as others do, so reference librarians need to see and hear themselves interacting with their users and patrons in the context of their job. Videotaping reference desk interviews and interactions can be a useful way to analyze reference librarians' ability to communicate effectively by observing the level and intonation of speech, body gestures, and stance and posture.

For the first time "performer" videotaping can be overwhelming; the cameras, lights, crew, and microphones all add to the present tension of being "on stage." A warmup exercise is suggested to help alleviate any stress or fears of the videotaping. In this exercise reference librarians are asked to explain how something works or to describe a simple object to a friend for no more than five minutes. All librarians participate, so the atmosphere is non-threatening and relaxing. After everyone has been taped, the librarians view themselves and comment on what transpired—how they felt, what they noticed, what they looked like, and what they sounded like. With this initial experience of videotaping accomplished, the next exercise, that of being videotaped at the reference desk, is less threatening. Videotaping sessions can be extremely helpful in illuminating communication interactions. Some common problems reference librarians seem to have in interactions that are highlighted by videotaping are: not establishing eye contact; speaking too rapidly; giving out too much information at once; pausing infrequently to allow for questions; using excessive hand or foot gestures; not involving the other person in the conversation; and not listening attentively to the other person. After these videotaping sessions at the reference desk it is useful to allow some time to pass, perhaps an hour or more, before viewing the tape. This is so the reference librarians can distance themselves from their performing in order to view themselves more objectively. One method which works effectively is for the whole group to view the tape in its entirety first, and then to go over the tape segment by segment to analyze more closely the individual performance. Most often the individual spots certain characteristics or elements of the performance that need improving, but peers in the group can also offer useful suggestions. If videotaping is used long enough, real changes in reference librarians' behavior at the reference desk during interactions with users will occur. Most people want to improve their communication skills, and the use of videotaping reveals to them all too clearly those habits they wish to alter.

Videotaping reference librarians at the reference desk is only one component in a reference staff training program and only addresses the *ability to communicate effectively* function. There are other reference functions which also need addressing in a training program: *knowledge of reference sources* can be given coverage through the use of exercises designed by instruction librarians for users to learn about the various types of reference books; *reference technique capability* can be covered in the same way, with card catalogue exercises designed by instruction librarians for their bibliographic education sessions; *ability to make use of computerized systems* can be addressed similarly by using exercises designed for user education purposes; *ability and willingness to instruct patrons in the use of reference sources* can be accomplished by having the reference librarian trainees actually teach users how to employ those materials, for the way to learn something is to teach others; and *ability and willingness to communicate effectively on a professional level with other library colleagues* can be covered by having the new reference librarian trainees give a presentation to their library colleagues on professional resources or methods. All of these methods and more are in the catalogue of tools, techniques, and tactics used by instruction librarians and have proven themselves effective.

Reference librarians in the present and future already have the image of technologist and information specialist as well as intermediary and instructor. Reference librarians will undoubtedly continue to act as intermediaries between users and whatever systems libraries employ. They will have to act as instructors by providing access to those systems. Most library users will be relatively sophisticated and self-reliant when it comes to computerized systems and electronic means. What they will want to know is information on how these systems work with particular attention paid to their unique features and procedures on how to use them.

As in any profession, training should be an ongoing activity. This is especially true in a field that is as fast-changing as the library world and the profession of librarianship. No individual can keep up with everything, but individuals can contribute their expertise and knowledge in specialized areas. Instruction librarians have been using a variety of methods that can be readily adapted for a reference training program. Any training program fits into an overall staff development program and can be an integral part of an ongoing sequence. Since library instruction methods already exist and the literature about them is prolific, it makes sense to use them where they work. Reference librarians are key professionals in libraries; they should be trained so that they can perform their functions on a high level. Library instruction methods offer a solution to training reference librarians.

REFERENCES

Budd, John. "Librarians are Teachers." *Library Journal,* (October 15, 1982): 1944-1946.
Bunge, Charles A. "Strategies for Updating Knowledge of Reference Resources and Techniques." *RQ,* (Spring 1982): 228-232.
Galvin, Thomas J. "The Education of the New Reference Librarian." *Library Journal,* (April 15, 1975): 727-730.

Isaacs, J. M. "In-service Training for Reference Work." *Library Association Record,* (October 1969): 301-302.

Nielsen, Brian. "Teacher or Intermediary: Alternative Professional Models in the Information Age." *College and Research Libraries,* (May 1982): 183-191.

Rider, Lillian M. "Training Program for Reference Desk Staff." ED 175 486.

Roberts, Anne. "The Changing Role of the Academic Instruction Librarian." *Catholic Library World,* (February 1980): 283-285.

Roberts, Anne F. *Library Instruction for Librarians.* Littleton: CO, 1982. Libraries Unlimited, Inc. (Library Science Text Series).

Rosenblum, Joseph. "The Future of Reference Service: Death by Complexity." *Wilson Library Bulletin,* (December 1977): 300-301.

Schiller, Anita R. "Reference Service: Instruction or Information?" *The Library Quarterly,* (January 1965): 52-60.

Turner, S. W. "Relevant Reference Training." *Pacific Northwest Library Association Quarterly,* (April 1976): 15-17.

Vuturo, Robert. "Beyond the Library Tour: Those Who Can, Must Teach." *Wilson Library Bulletin,* (May 1977): 736-740.

Wilson, Pauline. "Librarians as Teachers: The Study of an Organization Fiction." *Library Trends,* (April 1979): 146-162.

Young, Arthur P. "And Gladly Teach: Bibliographic Instruction and the Library." *Advances in Librarianship,* (1980): 63-98.

Library-Use Instruction
With Individual Users:
Should Instruction Be Included
in the Reference Interview?

James Rice

INTRODUCTION

The literature which deals with the topic of library-use instruction has grown exponentially. The programs implemented to provide this instruction have grown as well. Despite this two-fold growth rate, a debate continues to rage as to whether library-use instruction is a legitimate part of ongoing reference service, especially the reference interview.

Schiller, for example proposes that there is an antithetical relationship between the role of teaching and that of providing information. She goes on to conclude that the direct provision of information is the first priority for reference service and the teaching aspect is not necessarily a reference function.[1]

Wilson states that librarians cannot justifiably claim to be teachers and that they may do harm to the profession if they try. She considers the idea of librarians as teachers to be an "organization fiction." This means that librarians have wrongly adopted the role of teacher to increase their self-image and buttress the status of our profession.[2]

Neither Wilson nor Schiller provide any documentation or data to support their claims. While both of these ideas might be developed into worthy research hypotheses, there is little evidence that either argument is well-founded.

In fact, even a perfunctory look at the literature will reveal many

James Rice is Assistant Professor, School of Library Science, 3076 Library, The University of Iowa, Iowa City, IA 52242.

documented cases of successful library-use instruction efforts. In one example, university librarians enjoy faculty status as teachers and the president publicizes a complete commitment to the role of the library and the teaching of library-use integrated into all library service as well as the total curriculum.[3]

As early as 1943, Anne Morris Boyd stated that "the teaching function of reference work is as important in all libraries as the information-giving function, if we believe in the library as an educational institution."[4] Library-use instruction has been included in reference service policy statements for at least ten years.[5] Teaching has been included in the ALA standards for reference service for some time.[6]

Research also has indicated the benefits of library instruction in reference service to individual users. For example, Howell and Willigen have found a relationship between patron satisfaction with reference service and the library-use instruction they received during the service. The findings of this research suggest "that reference librarians can assist patrons more effectively when they consciously cultivate a teaching role as opposed to acting more passively (and perhaps more impersonally) as information source."[7]

At the foundation of the arguments presented by both Wilson and Schiller is the question of whether the basic reference function should include teaching. Part of the problem, according to authors such as Wynar, Vavrek, Whittaker and Rettig is the lack of an adequate theory of reference work.[8]

Another aspect of this problem, according to Robert Wagers, is the misunderstanding of the role of instruction in meeting information needs. An assumption that instructive elements of reference services might detract from maximum information service is not based on any empirical findings. In fact, the instructive function *may be* one of the forces necessary for effective reference service. We must transcend the notion that information is the total end product of reference service.[9]

A third reason for all of the confusion is simply a semantic one. Some people are erroneously convinced that providing information is incompatible with teaching. They argue that teaching is, by definition, a separate activity from that of meeting a specific information need.

If we consult the Oxford English Dictionary we find that the word "teach" means to show, present, point out the way (guide), to show by way of information or instruction, to impart or convey the knowledge of, to make known, deliver (a message), to communicate or inform.[10] Certainly it is a complex word. That any reference librarian can deny any pedagogical aspect to reference service is very difficult to understand. From a linguistic point of view, it could be argued that the two activities are essentially the same thing.

However, a major distinction that must be understood in these arguments is the difference between classroom teaching and one-to-one teaching of individual patrons. In any formal coursework, students have a choice in whether to participate or not. Even if library-use instruction is a required component of a curriculum, the ultimate choice is the student's.

But in the immediacy of one-to-one reference service, individual library-use instruction may be an imposition on the user. This would be particularly true if such instruction was attempted without users being given a choice. Some librarians argue that it is wrong to impose instruction on a user when he or she really only wants the answer to an information need.[11]

Certainly, this is a very legitimate question to raise and one that deserves much more attention than it has received from our profession so far. It has two elements. The first is the question of whether attempted instruction is an infringement on the rights of the user. The second element is the question of whether attempted instruction detracts from the effectiveness of the librarian in fulfilling the information need.

This article will attempt to deal with this two-fold question.

AN ARGUMENT FOR LIBRARY-USE INSTRUCTION IN ONE-TO-ONE REFERENCE SERVICE

In order to understand the effects of instruction on individual reference work, we must consider the issue in the context of the reference interview. This is where the actual information need is determined.

The nature of a good reference interview is expertly and thoroughly discussed in sources which are readily available to readers.[12] The techniques involved include such things as speaking and listening skills, warmth, approachability, open-ended questions, non-verbal communication, personal appearance, directing full attention to a user, and effective summarizing skills.

The body of theory and knowledge in the area of interpersonal communication is quite extensive. Any reference librarian should be familiar with the Shannon and Weaver communication model developed in 1949.[13] Various refinements and additions to this body of theory have been developed by DeFleur, Osgood, Schramm, Dance, and others.[14]

While this area has evolved in sophistication and understanding, the initial basic contribution of Shannon and Weaver has generally remained unquestioned. (See Figure 1) Put in simple narrative language, this includes the need for absolute clarity in communication, the presence of potential noise or distortion in communication and the two-part responsibility of sender (message encoder) and destination (message interpreter) in the success of the process. We can think of the reference librarian and the user as the sender or destination (depending on the direction of messages) and the questions and discussions during the interview are messages or signals which we transmit and receive continuously. Noise is anything which might disrupt or distort clear communication. It might be audible noise, a scornful expression, or even a distracting thought.

Some authors, notably Rettig, have taken one or more communication models and applied them to the reference process in an attempt to formulate a definitive theory of reference work.[15] It can be very useful to view the reference interview as an exercise or even a ritual in interpersonal communication.

For example when a librarian appears to be in a hurry, when he or she uses the word "obviously," or when he or she smiles smugly, an interview may be irrevocably lost in noise. A thorough discussion of such nuances of human interaction is far beyond the scope of this article. But a very entertaining and superb discussion of them may be found in a book by Erving Goffman.[16]

But where does teaching and instruction fit into this?

Just as scholars have formulated reference theories on the basis of communications models, education or teaching theories have also evolved using the same models. Educators such as Davis, Alexander, Yelon, Levi and many others have thoughtfully developed total instructional design systems around such models.[17] Notably Gale has proposed a teaching and learning model which is derived specifically from the Shannon and Weaver Model (See Figure 2).[18]

When the reference process and the teaching process are viewed in this light, it can be seen that, at the most fundamental level of both activities, they really aren't very different. To successfully teach anything to anyone we must employ the same techniques as we do in

Figure 1.   THE SHANNON AND WEAVER MODEL (1949)

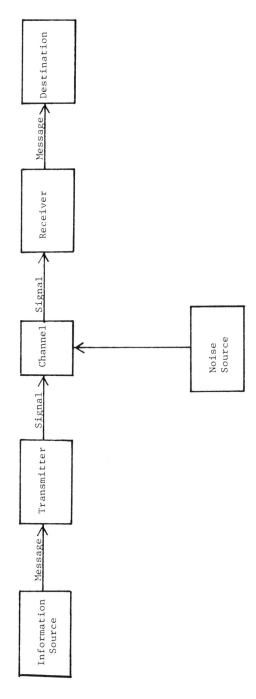

Figure 2. THE COMMUNICATION MODEL AND THE INSTRUCTIONAL
PROCESS (Gale, 1975)

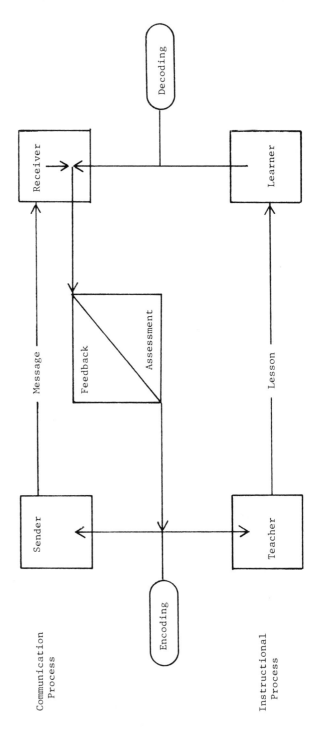

reference interviews. As any good teacher knows, clear articulation, listening skills, receptivity, summarizing skills, concentration and coherence are all indispensible in the classroom. Both teaching and interviewing are forms of interpersonal communication and the differences between the two activities are (on a theoretical level) actually cosmetic. The most basic skills employed in either activity are employed in both.

In teaching, as well as reference work, questions of ethics and effectiveness constantly emerge. Far too often, a teacher's personal opinion passes for factual information in the classroom, schools of thought are not properly or equitably represented in a discipline, and students are subjected to unprepared effusive rambling. Mindless memorization is still employed as a technique for learning principles and concepts. Students are tested on information which was never taught.

Clearly the questions of ethics and effectiveness also involve the question of whether users or students are given a choice in how the communication process proceeds. Current teaching theory increasingly employs the practice of setting objectives and learning outcomes prior to instruction. This is done *with input from the students* in the spirit of mutual agreement on where the instruction is leading. Good teaching relies on open and clear communication to support the concerted efforts of all parties involved. The accountability for success rests just as much with the teacher as it does with each student (each of them being both senders and receivers in a communication process).

In the reference interview, both the user and the librarian are responsible for the effectiveness and success of the process. It should be very easy for librarians to ask questions and clarify the objectives of an information need. This clarification should include giving users a choice regarding library-use instruction. Consider the following examples:

1. Would you like to learn how to look up this type of information or would you simply like me to look up the answer for you?
2. I can try to find the answer to that for you or I could show you some sources which you could use yourself. Which would you prefer?
3. I'll be glad to introduce you to the use of that index or I can just look up that citation, whichever you wish.
4. If you're in a hurry today, I can just get you the answer. Or if

you have a few minutes I could teach you how to use the service so you can poke around yourself. What's your pleasure?

AN ETHICAL CONSIDERATION

In this writer's experience, there are a number of library users for whom privacy is a major consideration. They are reluctant to seek help from a reference librarian because they don't want to discuss their information need with anyone. Perhaps it is a medical or legal problem. Perhaps it is a personal problem involving mental discord or psychological disturbance. For whatever reason, these patrons might seek out instructional reference service rather than direct information. In this way their real need would not be revealed and they could be more self-sufficient in finding the information they need.

From an ethical standpoint this writer contends that we have an obligation to provide the instructional avenue of service to patrons. How can we meet the privacy needs of certain people if we have only one approach: determine the question and find the answer? It is, in fact, most ethical of us to broaden the scope of individual reference work to include the availability of instruction. Patrons will then, indeed, have a choice and may be more likely to seek out the service of a reference librarian.

Some users would rather look things up, scan citations, browse through indexes, and generally seek information on their own. Others might wish only answers. The proportions of patrons on either side might vary depending on the type of library. In a special library or information center, library-use instruction may have nearly no place at all. In an academic environment, it may be involved in the bulk of information needs. Research would help to reveal the proportion of various user groups who need instruction or simply information. In any case, it is through the communication process that we should reveal the users needs for both information or instruction or both.

CONCLUSION

Writers on this issue often refer to the importance of having the broadest and most effective possible reference service in meeting information needs.[19] It is undeniable that at least some patrons want library-use instruction as part of reference service. Given a choice, these users will opt for any learning which increases their self-sufficiency in libraries. Research supports a claim that there is a relationship between library-use instruction (included in individual reference work) and patron satisfaction.[20] It is through an open communication process combined with a broad scope of service that ethics and effectiveness are served.

If we do not make library-use instruction available to those patrons who want or need it, then we are not giving them a choice. Therefore, this writer contends that the fullest and most effective possible reference service to individuals should include the availability of instruction in library use. This recognizes that specific information needs may well include the desire for instruction about the access to that information. In this way, the widest possible scope of information needs will be met in a free and effective communication process.

REFERENCES

1. Anita R. Schiller. "Reference Service: Instruction or Information," *Library Quarterly* 35(January, 1965) p. 60.

2. Pauline Wilson. "Librarians as Teachers: The Study of an Organization Fiction," *Library Quarterly* 49(April 1979) pp. 146-62.

3. Robert C. Spencer. "The Teaching Library," *Library Journal* 103(May 15, 1978) pp. 1021-4.

4. Anne Morris Boyd. "Personnel and Training for Reference Work," in *The Reference Function of The Library*, ed. Pierce Butler (Chicago: University of Chicago Press, 1943), p. 254.

5. Mary Jo Lynch. "Academic Library Reference Policy Statements," *RQ* 11(Spring 1972) pp. 222-226.

6. Hannelor B. Rader. "Reference Services as a Teaching Function," *Library Trends* 29(Summer 1980) p. 95.

7. Benita J. Howell et. al. "Fleeting Encounters – A Role Analysis of Reference Librarian – Patron Interaction," *RQ* 16(Winter 1976) p. 127.

8. Bohdan Wynar. "Reference Theory: Situation Hopeless But Not Impossible," *College and Research Libraries* 28(September 1967) pp. 337-42. Bernard Vavrek. "A Theory of Reference Service," *College and Research Libraries* 29(November 1968) pp. 508-10. Ken Whittaker. "Toward a Theory for Reference and Information Service," *Journal of Librarianship* 9(January 1977) pp. 49-63. James Rettig. "A Theoretical Model and Definition of the Reference Process," *RQ* 18(Fall 1978) pp. 19-29.

9. Robert Wagers. "American Reference Theory and the Information Dogma," *Journal of Library History* 13(Summer 1978) pp. 265-79.

10. *Oxford English Dictionary* V. 11 (Oxford: The Clarendon Press, 1933) pp. 126-8.

11. William A. Katz. *Introduction to Reference Work, V.II Reference Services and Reference Processes* (New York: McGraw HIll, 1982) pp. 60-1.

12. For just two examples, readers may consult: Katz. *Introduction to Reference Work V. II* pp. 41-61 and Gerald Jahoda, *The Librarian and Reference Queries: A Systematic Approach* (New York: Academic Press, 1980) pp. 85-141.

13. C. Shannon and W. Weaver. *The Mathematical Theory of Communication* (Urbana:University of Illinois Press, 1949).

14. For a good summation, see Denis McQuail and Sven Windahl. *Communication Models* (New York: Longman House, 1981) pp. 10-36.

15. Rettig "A Theoretical Model . . . ."

16. Erving Goffman. *Interaction Ritual: Essays in Face-to-Face Behavior* (Chicago: Aldine Publishing Company, 1967).

17. See Robert Davis et. al. *Learning Systems Design, An Approach to the Improvement of Instruction* (New York: McGraw Hill, 1974). Also see H. Levi. *The Nature of Persuasive Communication,* Instructional Systems Technology Division Student Handout, Indiana University. Bloomington, Indiana.

18. Fred Gale. *Determining the Requirements for the Design of Learner-Based Instruction* (Columbus Ohio: Charles E. Merril Publishing, 1975) p. 16.

19. Katz V. II p. 60. Rader pp. 98-99. Schiller p. 60. Wager p. 77-79.

20. Howell p. 127.

Clues or Answers?
Which Response
to Library Users' Questions?

Ray Lester

Let us imagine someone coming into your library and asking a member of your library staff: "I need information on the toxicity of 1*H*-indole-3-butanoic acid." Does the staff member say: "Come back in half an hour and I will have the answer?" Or does she take the enquirer to Sax's "Dangerous Properties of Industrial Materials' and similar volumes; and then if necessary on to "Toxicology Abstracts," or even "Chemical Abstracts," showing him how each works; but then leaving him to find exactly the information he needs. (For simplicity, I am assuming that the librarian is female, the enquirer male.)

Or someone asks: "I need some good references on Philip Larkin's poetry." Does your librarian say: "Come back this afternoon—or tomorrow if you would like the references nicely typed." Or is the reader taken to MLA Bibliography, the Annual Bibliography of English Language and Literature, Abstracts of English Studies, British Humanities Index, Journal of Modern Literature (many readers will know better than I which tools are best to use); and then left to hunt for and pick some good references himself.

"I am doing a comprehensive review of the effect of monetarist policies on the rate of inflation. Could you do me a full bibliography?" Would the answer be: "Yes, come back in four weeks." Or is the reader taken to a whole host of tools, no doubt starting with guides such as John Fletcher's "The Use of Economics Literature."

Dr. Ray Lester is Librarian, London Business School Library, Sussex Place, Regent's Park, London NW1 4SA, UK.

In these and similar examples the first course of action we can call giving *answers,* the second giving *clues:*

> *Clue* "Fact or principle that serves as guide, or suggests line of enquiry in problem or investigation." (Concise Oxford English Dictionary)

In this paper we discuss whether librarians should aim to give "answers" or "clues" when responding to users' questions. I write from the viewpoint of an academic librarian, though much of this discussion is applicable to all types of library.

PERIPHERAL FACTORS

In trying to focus on the factors that should influence whether we give clues or answers to our users, we need first to mention a number of factors that in practice influence that decision, but usually should not.

When Is the Question Asked?

If our libraries were open and fully staffed for twenty-four hours of every day, it would not matter when questions were asked. In practice such a level of service is not considered appropriate; and we justify something less. Thus at best we provide a patchy professional service. We try to make sure our service is at least tailored to user demand, hoping that that demand reflects real need. But one crucial research question answered late one summer evening may be worth more for humanity than answering a hundred questions asked merely out of curiosity. A set of volumes being bound can scupper the most carefully organized reference and information service. However, for our purposes here let us assume that we are providing an optimum level of professional service.

How Is the Question Asked?

So often a rude manner from the user, even if an answer could have been provided, will get at most a clue, and a pretty obscure clue at that: such as the time honoured response "Have you tried the catalogue?" when the user only wanted to sharpen his pencil. Again, let us assume that all our librarians are tactful and helpful.

Where Is the Question Asked?

This is more problematic. It is extraordinarily difficult getting the user to ask his question at the point where he will get the best answer. So often, even with the most obscure questions, non-professional staff will be tried first; and if they fail to produce a good response the user will not persevere. Again, let us assume that our user asks or is referred to the librarian most appropriately qualified to produce a response to his question.

Why Is the Question Being Asked?

We also assume for the purposes here that the user's question is related to the research and teaching of the (academic) library's parent institution; and is not being asked in some other connection. If it is not related, the succeeding discussion is hardly pertinent, in the sense that the library has little incentive to work towards a more cost/beneficial operation. It may indeed be the case, for instance, that my first question was asked because the enquirer was worried because he had spilt some of the chemical in his cup of coffee whilst gardening: the chemical being the active ingredient of "root powder." But let us assume not.

What Is the Question?

The problem we are discussing arises with virtually any question. Even the seemingly most innocuous question can lead into problems. It is inevitable that the questions librarians are asked have some uncertainty about their nature or their answer, given the academic environment, and the fact that they are being asked at all (otherwise the users would have found out the answers themselves).

COSTS AND BENEFITS

Given those assumptions, what we must focus on is "who is asking the question?" and "who is trying to respond to the question?" What we have to try to assess is whether, given the costs of the system with which we are concerned, there is in general more benefit if the librarian goes away and produces *answers;* or more benefit if she "merely" provides *clues.*

To make a little progress, in this difficult area, I suggest that we conceptualize one particular institution with one specific user and one specific librarian. Is it then more beneficial in general for questions existing in the mind of the user to be given answers or clues? We are looking for some general guidelines to operating our academic libraries. Clearly, there are a range of both costs and benefits that might respectively be incurred and gained by both librarian and enquirer. Let us assume, for the moment, that the end result of the search for information is the same, irrespective of who carries out the search. We might then consider how long it takes for the user or librarian to answer the enquiry, and assess the value of each's time. To begin to be rigorous we would need to look at what the user or librarian would have been doing if they had not been answering an enquiry—using the economist's notion of "opportunity cost." In the librarian's case, if she was not answering the user's question, she could well have been preparing some guide to using the library which might well have proved of direct assistance when our user came to answer the question himself.

But, surely, the crucial point is that my assumption of a moment ago is just not true. In fact, other than for simple questions, it is rarely possible for a librarian to produce overall the same end result as that of an enquirer. Even if the librarian fully grasps the nature of the question being asked (and I submit that for most research questions this would be the exception rather than the rule), in answering that question she would be unable to communicate the same benefit to the user as the user would have acquired had he answered the question himself. It is in the very process of answering a question, that we perceive what is the real question we are asking. This is why there is such a vast literature for the reference librarian on such matters as "question negotiation" and the importance of the "reference interview" and "feedback."

In his fascinating book "Two kinds of power," Patrick Wilson contrasts:

- *Exploitive power*—the power to procure the best textual means to a given end. To have that power it is necessary to evaluate the literature—to make value judgements.
- *Descriptive power*—the power to produce writing satisfying some evaluatively neutral description. To have that power it is not necessary to evaluate the literature.[1]

As Wilson says: "no one who could have exploitive control would want descriptive control." No one who could be given the six best documents for his purpose would want sixty that were potentially relevant (and within which the six best were somewhere to be found). Librarians generally do not have "exploitive power" because they are not able to evaluate the worth of the material they process in answering users' enquiries. Indeed, librarians normally positively refuse professionally to comment on the worth or not of the literature they read. In passing we might note that this is perhaps the main reason for the failure of the librarian to achieve true professional status.[2] The true professional prescribes, and subjects his decisions on what he prescribes only to the review of his professional colleagues. He demands an autonomy of judgement, seeking the exclusive right to name and judge the successes or mistakes of colleagues. Professionals "profess" to know better than their clients what aids them or their affairs. The librarian, on the other hand, insists that she is not prepared to tell people what they should read. Her role is to facilitate unrestricted access for all persons to all information and ideas subject to no judgement as to the value, appropriateness or even potential harm to the patron. To use my earlier example, we still provide information on the toxicity of root powder to our user even if we know he is concerned not that he may have got some into his own coffee, but whether he might usefully put it into someone else's coffee!

To return to our main theme, I would submit that the academic user should answer his own question rather than the librarian because:

a. Only he really understands what he needs.
b. Answering, with its refinement of the question, is an integral part of the research process.
c. Only he can judge the value of the material he retrieves—can sort the wheat from the chaff. There is never any shortage of material to read; the problem is finding the best to read in the limited time we have available.

HOWEVER . . . .

However, despite all this theory, it is a fact that:

a. Most users remain abysmally inefficient in their use of libraries.
b. Most users cannot or will not be educated in the use of libraries.[3]

We can argue, as I have done here, that our users should acquire sophisticated literature handling skills; and of course many of the best researchers do just that. But what about the rest—the silent majority? Should we persist in trying to persuade those users to use the full range of literature themselves, because in the end that will be best? Or, faced with user apathy, should we take the matter into our own hands, and provide the answers users need, or more precisely the answers that we imagine that they need, ourselves?

The latter approach has gained much momentum in recent years, but it has taken two quite different forms. In the first approach, particularly associated with the public library sector, librarians—not understanding exactly what information the user needs—have decided to give the user as much information as they can find, in the hope that somewhere within will be the actual information that is needed. "All information must be available to all people in all formats purveyed through all communication channels and delivered through all levels of comprehension" (American Library Association statement). The best comment I have seen on that proposal comes from Karl Weintraub: "Does the ALA promise to teach calculus in two easy TV lessons? And will it provide, at easily accessible news stands, and in Spanish, Swahili, Armenian or Korean, an analysis of Kant's 'Critique of Pure Reason' for IQs of 60?"[4]

The alternative approach, particularly associated with the academic library sector, is to suggest that our librarians should take the initiative in specific areas and enter fully into the user's decision making process. For example, Swanson[5] has suggested that our role should be:

a. To identify and understand the important problems libraries should solve.
b. In this light to examine critically present solutions.
c. To discover obstacles that stand in the way of improvement.
d. To invent, test and evaluate new solutions.

Brittain,[6] in a valuable review of the social science area, has suggested that the idea of a passive role for librarians and information specialists is no longer tenable. They have obligations to all social scientists who are prepared to enter into communication, to ensure a fair and balanced information system for the common benefit.

But if librarians are to take this latter approach, which has much to commend it, clearly they would need a detailed knowledge of the subject areas wherein lie the problems that need solving. Librarians would need to become what Patrick Wilson[1] calls "bibliographical consultants," rather than simply "bibliographical aids." But most of us as librarians, I submit, do not have anything approaching the detailed knowledge of the subject area that would be needed to take the sorts of initiative suggested by Swanson and Brittain.

It is precisely this lack of detailed subject knowledge (at least in many of the subject areas in which we have to operate) which convinces me that as a librarian I will provide overall the most cost beneficial service to my users if I limit myself, in general, to providing "clues" rather than "answers." The ideal then would be able to stand by while my users actually choose and use the bibliographical and other tools that I have indicated might be of value. We come close to achieving this ideal when we act as intermediaries in online computer searches. With non-computer systems, we can hardly hide under the table or behind the curtain, ready to pop out the moment the user starts going wrong in his research strategy. All we can do is to tell him what to look in, and how to look in it; and of course to beseech him to come back if he has any problems at all.

Other reference and information librarians, perhaps most, do not have my inhibitions. Denis Grogan[7] in his book "Practical Reference Work," deals in cavalier fashion with those who doubt the librarian's ability to answer any question that might arise. And he seems to revel in the fact, as he sees it, that the mastery of the bibliographical and reference tools necessary to exploit a library's potential to the full is beyond the reach of those without a full training in systematic bibliography. He feels that it is just not possible to train most users to answer their questions properly. So, as librarians, we must answer those questions for them.

As an academic librarian, my conclusion is different. In a nutshell, I may have the greatest knowledge on earth of what bibliographical tools are available and how to use them. But all this knowledge is to nought if I am neither sure exactly what information the user needs, nor when I have found it.

REFERENCES

1. Wilson, P. *Two kinds of power: an essay on bibliographical control* Berkeley, University of California Press, 1968.

2. Asheim, L. "Librarians or professionals," *Library Trends, 27* (Winter) 1978, p. 225-257.

3. Lester, R. "Why educate the library user?" *Aslib Proceedings, 31* (8) 1979, p. 366-380.

4. Weintraub, K. J. "The humanistic scholar and the library," *Library Quarterly, 50* (1), 1980, p. 22-39.

5. Swanson, D. R. "Libraries and the growth of knowledge," *Library Quarterly, 49* (1), 1979, p. 3-25.

6. Brittain, J. M. "Information services and the structure of knowledge in the social sciences," *International Social Science Journal, 31* (4), 1979, p. 711-728.

7. Grogan, D. *Practical reference work,* London, Bingley, 1979.

The Question of Questioning:
On the Coexistence
of Library Instruction and Reference

John Budd

There is a definite relation between library instruction and the reference function. Too often, however, it is an implicit, sometimes even a tacit, relationship. There is an unfortunate tendency to emphasize differences and distinctions of the two—emphasis which is heightened by current practice in both areas. For instance, Frances L. Hopkins urges the establishment of bibliographic instruction as a separate function in libraries, and suggests that librarians engaging in such activities look upon themselves as bibliographic instruction specialists.[1] Such a view seems to impose a gulf between two library services which frequently have identical goals.

Examination of the relationship between library instruction and reference services requires some effort at determining the characteristics and aims of both functions, which is not a simple task since there are nearly as many theories as theorists. In general, reference service involves providing needed information to users. At a glance one can recognize that this is a gross understatement of reference practices. There are actually several levels of reference service, as many writers have noted. The higher levels may involve some instruction, not only in the use of certain materials, but in research techniques and possibly even particular subject areas. The key to a definition of the reference function is that it (most often) involves service to individuals rather than to groups. Because of this, reference services can be, at various times, extremely efficient or extremely inefficient. The function is most efficient when it involves assisting individuals' unique research endeavors and is most inef-

John Budd is an experienced reference librarian now at 320 Craige Hall, University of North Carolina at Chapel Hill, Chapel Hill, NC 27514, where he is in the doctoral program in library science. He normally will be found at Southeastern Louisiana University, Hammond, LA.

ficient when it involves the repetitive provision of information to members of a group or class.

The first difficulty encountered in examining library instruction is understanding and keeping separate the terminology used by different authors. James Rice, for instance, enumerates distinctions between "library instruction" and "bibliographic instruction." The former involves instruction in the use of specific library materials, such as indexes, bibliographic tools, and others; the latter, Rice claims, represents a more advanced level of instruction incorporating research methods and practices and the study of bibliography.[2] While the levels of instruction are recognized here, the remainder of this paper will make no formal discrimination between the two terms, but will use them interchangeably.

Regarding the purposes of library instruction, the Think Tank on bibliographic instruction, which met in 1981, formulated a statement on what such instruction should seek to achieve.

> Bibliographic instruction is intended to teach students to make intelligent, independent decisions about library use. To be able to use the card catalog, reference sources, or computer terminals to retrieve information on very specialized topics, or to recognize that libraries are classification systems to organize the materials, are fundamental skills that each student should possess.[3]

The statement seems reasonable, but there is a rather insidious side to it. It is not realistic to expect all library users to make *independent* decisions about the wealth of materials the library can provide. If such a goal could be met, the need for the reference function would disappear. Anyone who has worked as a reference librarian will acknowledge not only the futility but also the undesirability of attempting to make all library users (students and faculty) experts in the intricacies of the library. The result could well be a very high level of user frustration.

The above statements are not meant to imply that there is no place in the library for formal instruction programs. Quite the contrary is true. A well-conceived program of instruction can instill greater interest in students and can serve to integrate the totality of library services into students' curricula. There are conditions affecting the success of these programs, though, and also limits to their practicality. Such factors should not prohibit the initiation or continuation of instruction programs in libraries. The situation which is most bene-ficial to users is an amalgamation of instruction and reference ser-vices, with the former providing an introduction and the latter seek-ing to meet in-depth needs of users. It should be remembered that neither instruction nor reference services exist for librarians; they share the goal of facilitating use of materials by those who have need of the materials.

While the two functions may share altruistic goals, practice in each of the areas may sometimes be less than altruistic. Some ref-erence departments or individual reference librarians may seek to foster a mystique surrounding the reference function. The individual or collective efforts can create an image of the librarian as "keeper of knowledge" and can encourage in users the belief that unanswer-able requests are their fault. Library instruction programs, at their worst, are concerned with their own legitimation. The Think Tank recommendations (to politicize the function as a movement within librarianship, to assume primacy as *the* most important reference activity, to advance the view of bibliographic instruction librarians as watchdogs over publishing in subject disciplines) can be seen as integral to such efforts at legitimation. Library instruction for the sake of the librarians involved in it is contrary to the basic goal stated above. Unfortunately, the recommendations of the Think Tank are overwhelmingly slanted toward librarians and con-spicuously ignore the recipients of library instruction.

One problem plaguing librarians in public services (reference and bibliographic instruction included) is what Jon Lindgren sees as the myth (which needs exploding) that libraries are easy to use.[4] This belief is shared by students and faculty and, in fact, according to Thomas G. Kirk, students' attitudes that they know how to use the library may be due to their teachers.[5] Constance McCarthy points out some bad effects of library instruction which result in or contri-bute to the attitudinal problem: some may feel guilty because they think library instruction should have taught them how to be indepen-dent library users; some are overconfident and believe that when they are unable to find information they seek, the library is failing; some feel indignation because they have been led to believe that all information is accessible.[6] Reference librarians may also be culpable of perpetrating the "easy to use" myth. Lindgren writes:

> Reference librarians appear to function mechanically much of the time, as conduits between users and their required re-

sources, and do not always take time (or have the time to take) with each user to weave a reference response into the flimsiest fabric of instruction.[7]

Of course this paper is not meant to be simply an indictment of all the ills of poorly-constructed library instruction and reference programs. The two functions have the potential to prevent or eliminate the aforementioned problem of attitude. Avoidance of the problem depends upon cooperation between the two services and the recognition that libraries are complex and rich systems and that few (if any) individuals are cognizant of all their intricacies. No person should be told that libraries are simple, or even that libraries are absolutely logical. (Library of Congress Subject Headings contradict such a supposition.) Not only are libraries complex at present, but they are evolving as knowledge grows and technology advances. The changes that libraries undergo should also occur with the realization that libraries are systems, so that they are not made unduly complex.

The complexity of libraries is the major reason why neither reference nor bibliographic instruction should attempt to stand alone. They are correlated services; neither is in an ascendant position. Anita Schiller recognizes the importance of a library instruction program and says, "To make available, and even to require, instruction for groups or individuals on a formal basis seems a more efficient utilization of resources than to repeat the same process endlessly with individuals in an informal and haphazard way."[8] Certain elements are basic to library use, regardless of subject discipline, so these elements can be presented in a formal manner as an introduction to use of the library. Other elements are basic to particular disciplines and can be presented formally at a more advanced level. There comes a point, however, when individual needs or interests negate the effectiveness of formal, organized attempts at instructing users. Regarding the limitations of the usefulness of library instruction, William Katz states, "To assume that library education can equip an individual to everything he or she needs is to short-change the user."[9]

The purposes of both bibliographic instruction and the reference process should be examined in greater detail at this point. First, it must be reiterated that library instruction does not exist for its own sake—no function of the library does. Next, library instruction and reference do not exist in a vacuum. Both functions are, or should be, designed to assist with the overall education of the students and with the research of the students and faculty. Students and faculty tend to take a pragmatic view of the library; it is present in order to meet their needs. Because of such a view, library instruction ideally should supplement the subject instruction received by the students. Colin Harris is of the opinion that library instruction and subject instruction are inseparable. He writes:

> Information is seen by librarians as being disembodied from the study of subjects, something that can be stored and retrieved. But the information of a subject *is* the subject. To study a subject is to handle the information of the subject. The study of the subject is the proper place for education about the structure of the subject's information system, about access to the system and about the evaluation and use of the information. User education is therefore the proper province of the subject teacher.[10]

Harris's comments are indeed provocative. He acknowledges the library's dependence on those without to define the services offered, but he seems to place a chasm between teacher and librarian. His point is a bit more applicable to reference services, which depend on user initiation and, so, more directly on users' immediate needs. He states further, "Even with a librarian expert in a subject, there is not the same relationship as between teacher and student. The librarian does not define the task or determine the reward."[11] Harris ignores the place of library instruction, possibly allied to subject instruction, in which the librarian does define the task and determine the reward. Cooperation is needed between librarians and teachers for the full value of library instruction and reference services to be realized.

Keith J. Stanger echoes Harris's observation on the faculty as instigators of library use:

> Classroom instructors are the key individuals who possess the greatest ability to make changes in the use of libraries. The teaching faculty set parameters of student achievement; they are the catalysts of students' inquisitive vigor. If they do not communicate the value of, or demonstrate the need for, being able to discover what is known about their disciplines, one can hardly expect those they teach to invest much interest in such pursuits.[12]

Implicit in Stanger's statement is the need for cooperation between faculty and librarians. Recognition of this need is unfortunately understated in the recommendations of the Think Tank, which chooses instead to emphasize such things as publishing in journals of higher education and attending and presenting papers at discipline association meetings (though these activities do not prepare students to use the library more effectively). Cooperation can enhance the effectiveness of student and faculty use of the library.

While few would question the potential of a bibliographic instruction program with regard to stimulating library use, many could be skeptical of the practical results of the programs. There are too few evaluative studies of the effectiveness of library instruction to allow generalizations of any sort. It may be, though (and this is speculation), that the single most serious failing of most programs is the effort to produce independent library users. In addition to the effects enumerated by McCarthy, frustration could result from a poorly-constructed program. The frustration probably would not be confined to students, but would extend to librarians and faculty as well. Given the goal of the academic institution, the facilitation of learning, mechanical exercises forced on students are probably counterproductive to the learning experience. Peter Fox observes that such measures as library instruction workbooks, used at some large institutions, enable a great many students to go through a certain program each year, but the incentive to complete a workbook is, too often, compulsion and not the prospect of knowledge gained.[13] The same could be true of many "books and berries" courses and library instruction components of freshman English courses as well.

Should library instruction, then, concentrate its efforts on teaching the use of specific tools? From what approach does the student benefit most? It is undeniable that, with an introductory course for students entering the college or university or with a more advanced, subject-related course, the use of basic bibliographic and other reference tools should be part of the instruction. Beyond exposure to basic sources of information, however, library instruction (from the standpoint of teaching the use of specific materials) may quickly reach a point of diminishing returns. Library use is, for many individuals, a pragmatic endeavor, as was stated earlier. An instruction program which spends a great deal of time parading materials before students is likely to meet with resistance, especially if the students see no use for the materials in the near future. This resistance seriously impairs the usefulness of the instruction. Resistance may be heightened if the library instruction course or course component is required of the students. Arthur P. Young states, "Instruction should be relevant, voluntary, and never considered as a substitute for the direct provision of information."[14]

Young's last point is a key one in the relationship between library instruction and reference services. Library users generally seek satisfaction of a need at the time they experience the need. Library instruction attempts, insofar as it is able, to anticipate needs and to supply users with the wherewithal to search for answers to their questions. It must be acknowledged that the reference function is more efficient at meeting this need of the individual user. It remains for library instruction, then, to concentrate on the search rather than the discovery. Since there is no way to anticipate every need of every student, an instruction program should abandon any hopes it has of doing so. The program should attempt to teach students how to formulate questions, how to conduct a search (frequently with the help of a reference librarian). As Ray Lester says, it should promote a kind of lifelong learning that places emphasis on "*process* rather than *produce*—on the pupil acquiring a capability for learning how to learn, rather than on just becoming learned."[15]

An example of a library instruction program putting the above concept into practice would be one that concentrates more on explaining to students the purpose of indexes and the kind of information they can provide, rather than giving examples of many separate indexes. Even more basic than this is the general approach to the problem to be solved. If the student is able to respond, upon completion of a program, to the question of what is sought, then the program has achieved a degree of success. Stanger writes:

> Academic libraries will be productively used, not when students are able to distinguish between article titles and journal names in *Reader's Guide,* but when students demonstrate the desire to gain access to what libraries provide—records of the knowledge and ideas of other human beings—and have the cognitive competence to know what questions to ask of those records so as to realize their utility.[16]

Acceptance of the foundation of library instruction as set forth here demands acceptance of both the limitations and potential of such programs. Library instruction and reference services are not completely discrete functions, but are two means which share a common goal and which, in coexistence, are best able to meet the needs of students and achieve the purpose of the library and the institution.

REFERENCES

1. Frances L. Hopkins, "Bibliographic Instruction: An Emerging Professional Discipline," in *Directions for the Decade: Library Instruction in the 1980s*, ed. Carolyn A. Kirkendall (Ann Arbor, MI: Pierian Press, 1981), pp. 13-24.

2. James Rice, Jr., *Teaching Library Use: A Guide for Library Instruction* (Westport, CT: Greenwood Press, 1981), pp. 6-7.

3. "Think Tank Recommendations for Bibliographic Instruction," *College & Research Libraries News*, 44: 395 (Dec. 1981).

4. Jon Lindgren, "Seeking a Useful Tradition for Library User Instruction in the College Library," in *Progress in Educating the Library User*, ed. John Lubans, Jr. (New York: Bowker, 1978), pp. 71-72.

5. Thomas G. Kirk, "Problems in Library Instruction in Four Year Colleges," in *Educating the Library User*, ed. John Lubans, Jr. (New York: Bowker, 1974), p. 87.

6. Constance McCarthy, "Library Instruction: Observations from the Reference Desk," *RQ*, 22: 36-37 (Fall 1982).

7. Lindgren, "Seeking a Useful Tradition," p. 74.

8. Anita R. Schiller, "Reference Service: Instruction or Information," *Library Quarterly*, 35: 59 (Jan. 1965).

9. William A. Katz, *Introduction to Reference Work: Vol. II: Reference Services and Reference Processes*, 4th ed. (New York: McGraw-Hill, 1982), p. 59.

10. Colin Harris, "User Needs and User Evaluation," in *Library User Education: Are New Approaches Needed?* (London: British Library, Research and Development Department, British Library Research & Development Report No. 5503, 1980), p. 15.

11. Ibid.

12. Keith J. Stanger, "On the Limits of Bibliographic Instruction in Higher Education: An Opinion Piece," *Research Strategies*, 1: 32 (Winter 1983).

13. Peter Fox, "Higher Education in Britain and the United States—Implications for User Education," in *Library User Education: Are New Approaches Needed?* (London: British Library, Research and Development Department, British Library Research & Development Report No. 5503, 1980), p. 6.

14. Arthur P. Young, "And Gladly Teach: Bibliographic Instruction and the Library," *Advances in Librarianship*, 10: 80 (1980).

15. Ray Lester, "Why Educate the Library User?" *Aslib Proceedings*, 31: 369 (Aug. 1979).

16. Stanger, "On the Limits of Bibliographic Instruction," p. 32.

Reference/Technical Services Cooperation in Library Instruction

Lois M. Pausch
Carol B. Penka

Reference librarians and catalogers have been traditionally allied in their efforts in providing instruction to patrons. Both groups are concerned with promoting use of the collection and with encouraging an understanding of the bibliographic mechanisms needed to access that collection. This paper traces the development of cooperation between reference librarians and catalogers and looks at future trends.

Numerous references in library literature have recorded examples of, or suggestions for, closer relations between reference librarians and catalogers. In an article covering what the reference librarian expects of the catalog, Elizabeth G. Henry wrote that the "reference librarian and the catalog should be the best of friends for they are quite necessary to each other and through knowledge and understanding of each other help the patrons in the use of the library."[1] Grace Walker in an article on the relationship of the cataloger to reference service stated that, although the point of view of the services rendered may be different, both the reference librarian and the cataloger have the same goal, that is, the best possible service to the patron.[2] Anna Jacobsen in her article entitled "The Cataloger Looks at the Reference Librarian," made the statement that:

> the best, the main service the cataloger can do the reference librarian is to concentrate her energies . . . on making a "bigger and better" catalog . . . [the] chief service the reference librarian can do the cataloger is to realize that the cata-

Ms. Pausch is Coordinator, Science Section, Original Cataloguing, Library, University of Illinois at Urbana-Champaign, Urbana, IL 61801. Ms. Penka is Assistant Reference Librarian, Library, University of Illinois at Urbana-Champaign.

101

log . . . can do its own work but should not be expected to do several different things it was never intended to do.

In addition, she made suggestions for cooperation such as having the reference librarians refer "certain questions involving bibliographical search to specially qualified members of the cataloging staff" and asking the catalogers to be mindful of the needs for certain materials with some pre-cataloging arrangement by which the reference librarian may have immediate temporary use of the wanted item.[3] Other ideas offered by Helen L. Purdum[4] and Frances Clark[5] included having the cataloger circulate lists of new subject headings and making the reference librarians responsible for noting areas where subject coverage is weak and requesting additional analytics to help.

In the 1950s the articles cited below reflected the continuing concern that the catalog should meet the informational requirements of the patrons and that the catalog itself should instruct these patrons in the effective use of that tool. Indeed both technical services and public service librarians of this and earlier eras conceded the catalog to be the primary reference tool, opening access to the vast collections of the library. In calling for greater dialogue between these two groups, Clara Ann Kuhlman stated that "it is probably safe to say that the bulk of the cataloging rules and routines which have been set up was decided upon by the cataloger alone. This is not a healthy situation."[6] In a companion article "The Reference Librarian Looks at the Catalog," Eugene P. Watson said that:

the modern trained cataloger, knowing that her skills provide the foundation upon which the entire profession of librarianship has been built makes every effort to construct her catalog not so that it will conform to some deified and sacrosanct pattern but so that it will be of maximum service to the reference function of that particular library for which it is constructed.[7]

The role that the cataloger plays in the instructional mission of the institution in which the library is located was aptly articulated by Helen B. Uhrich:

The cataloguer, then, stands between the acquisition of books and the final servicing of these books and it is here that she makes her unique contributions to the instructional program of the school. Between these two actions all the implications of the curriculum, new courses, additions to the teaching staff, size of student body, will have to be understood and interpreted by the cataloger . . . . The use of books is not an incidental or accidental aspect of instruction but central and primary.[8]

In all of the above, the theme was cooperation between reference librarians and catalogers with no mention made directly to library instruction. There are some reports in the early literature on the involvement of catalog librarians in introducing the patron to the use of the library and its resources. In an article published in 1886, Edwin H. Woodruff cited the example of the chief cataloger at Harvard delivering one lecture a year on the use of the catalog.[9] Then in the 1930s, Ella V. Aldrich, in a paper on the experience of a readers' adviser in patrons about the catalog, reported that "much discussion, in a library course, is stimulated by problems prepared by the cooperative effort of the instructors, the readers' advisers, and of the catalog department." She also mentioned that the catalog department in the fall of the next school year planned to cooperate by preparing displays to supplement the instruction.[10] In the 1970s, Anne Roberts in her study on library instruction in ten state university libraries in New York, reported that technical services librarians had been involved as instructors and that there was a high level of agreement among library instruction librarians, library administrators, and technical services librarians that involvement of technical services librarians in library instruction was an idea whose time had come.[11] Still more recently, a statistical study by Lois Pausch and Jean Koch showed that technical services librarians became much more involved in bibliographic instruction during the 1970s and were evaluated as effective instructors.[12]

In addition to these instances of cooperation, patterns of organization of libraries designed to accomplish the same goals have been recorded in the literature. The subject-divisional plan for library organization was an innovative plan which had its beginnings in the early 1940s. Libraries were divided into broad service areas reflecting groups of subjects: social sciences, humanities, physical sciences, life sciences. In libraries utilizing this plan, subject specialist librarians had dual assignments. They spent half their time in cataloging and the other half providing reference or other public service. Thus, the creator of the catalog supplied information about its use to the patrons and was quickly able to produce new cross references, history cards, and analytics that met the needs of the public. While many factors contributed to the abandonment or modification of this type of organization by many libraries which had adopted it, almost all commentators on this plan agreed that cooperation between public services and technical services was an excellent idea resulting in a catalog which met the needs of the public, a classification scheme which indeed put like books on the shelf together at the place where people looked for them, and a system by which books in great demand were automatically rushed through the cataloging process. However, a note of caution was heard in an article by Enid Miller. "Regardless of all intentions, however, this plan would probably not work well if the individuals involved were not above average. They need to be flexible, able to see both sides of the question, and willing to learn."[13]

This type of organization into subject related divisions has resurfaced in the literature of the 1970s and 1980s with several articles suggesting that this plan of organization may be the wave of the future in academic libraries. At Columbia University in the early 1970s, a plan for reorganization of the library was devised in which one group, called the resources group, would provide professional services while more routine library operations were assigned to two other groups. This plan recognized "that the same staff members may have the subject or technical competence to function in. . . performing cataloging, selection, preservation, and in-depth research and reference activities."[14] Later in the decade, both Michael Gorman[15] and David Peele[16] wrote of the benefits to be achieved from the involvement of professional librarians in all professional tasks including both bibliographic instruction and cataloging. In libraries with this form of organization, the need for cooperation between cataloger and reference librarian is eliminated since the two functions are performed by the same individual.

However, for the many libraries with the more traditional public services/technical services arrangement, cooperation in library instruction can produce stronger, more dynamic programs. Just as the subject divisional plan utilizes the subject expertise possessed by the cataloger to benefit the patron, current programs in bibliographic instruction in more traditionally organized libraries can do essentially the same thing. One hour lectures to classes in course-related programs of instruction will be more effective if they are taught by someone who knows the jargon and who, in the course of cataloging the subject-oriented collection, has used the reference sources, knows the subject headings, etc. The cataloger is also the logical person to be responsible for service at any information desk or other service point in the public catalog area. Catalogers who so desire can serve as term paper counselors or as advisers in term paper clinic programs. These direct instruction activities can have a number of beneficial effects for the cataloger, the main ones being the opportunity to discover how the catalog is being used and where problems occur in its use.

Catalogers can also assume responsibility for those parts of any library instruction program that relate to the bibliographic organization of the library, even if they do not serve as the actual front-line instructor. Point-of-use instruction materials and workbooks, both of which are produced behind the scenes, can be worked on extensively by catalogers. As one example, instructional materials including slide-tape presentations, printed materials, etc. on using the *Monthly Catalog* seem logically to be done best by the documents cataloger. Also, catalogers can and should be asked to provide training for all instruction librarians new to the library and to create any informational or directional signs to be used in the public catalog area.

The reference librarian responsible for library instruction programs should take the time and make the effort to articulate the needs of those programs to the library administration and to indicate his/her willingness to share the responsibility for this service with technical services colleagues. Where instruction in catalog use is one of the aims of the bibliographic instruction program, the reference librarian should actively seek the help of the cataloger. In addition, the reference librarian can identify materials needed for library instruction purposes and bring these to the attention of the cataloger for more speedy processing. When problems with the catalog are encountered, the reference librarian can and should ask for help in solving them at the same time recognizing that good cataloging practice limits the options for change. Where the administration allows, the reference librarian can also become involved in cataloging, especially in the application of subject headings and classification and in making recommendations for additional guide cards, cross references, and analytics.

Perhaps the most important task to be undertaken jointly in the near future is instruction in the use of online catalogs and indeed in the construction of the online catalog itself to reflect the information and instructional needs of library patrons. Just as librarians in the past wrote on the purposes and effectiveness of the card catalog, librarians today are having to come to grips with new instruments—either online or COM—all machine produced and capable of being easily changed. Cooperation will not only be desirable, it will be imperative, if these new instruments are to be effective in performing needed functions and in fulfilling patrons' expectations.

Cooperation in library instruction is an ideal that is possible where administrators offer encouragement and both technical services and reference librarians exhibit willingness to share responsibility and recognition. If the trend of the future is truly toward the reorganization of the library with divisions of technical services, such as acquisitions and copy cataloging, becoming the province of non-professionals and with subject cataloging, reference, library instruction, and collection development becoming the province of professional librarians, then discussion of cooperation will become a matter of expediting the delivery of materials to the subject specialists. However, in the near future, the prospects are for the traditional divisions to remain and for the need for cooperation to continue and to become more important. The good will and determination of librarians in both reference and technical services and the recognition by administrators of the need for this cooperation are the surest means to effective collaboration in the provision of instruction in the use of libraries.

REFERENCES

1. Henry, Elizabeth G. "What a Reference Librarian Expects of the Catalog." *Library Journal* 54 (January 1, 1929): 13-15. Quotation is from p. 13.

2. Walker, Grace. "Cataloging from a Reference Viewpoint." *Libraries* 36 (1931): 241-245, 292-294.

3. Jacobsen, Anna. "The Cataloger Looks at the Reference Librarian." *Library Journal* 59 (February 15, 1934): 147-150. First quotation is from p. 147; second and third quotations from p. 148.

4. Purdum, Helen L. "What the Reference Department Expects of the Catalog and Catalog Department." *Library Journal* 59 (February 15, 1934): 150-151.

5. Clark, Frances. "Cataloger's Relation to the Reference Service;" abstract. *ALA Bulletin* (September 15, 1942): p. 53.

6. Kuhlman, Clara Ann. "Catalogers Can Help the Reference Librarian." *Wilson Library Bulletin* 26 (November, 1951): 267-269. Quotation is from p. 268.

7. Watson, Eugene P. "The Reference Librarian Looks at the Catalog." *Wilson Library Bulletin* 26 (November, 1951): 269-270.

8. Uhrich, Helen B. "The Cataloguer and Instruction." Sixth Conference of the

American Theological Association, Louisville, 1952. pp. 20-30. This quotation is from p. 23.

  9. Woodruff, Edwin H. "University Libraries and Seminary Methods of Instruction." *Library Journal* 11 (1886): 219-224.

  10. Aldrich, Ella V. "The Public Catalog for Whom? Experiences of a Readers' Adviser in a University Library." *ALA Bulletin* 33 (October, 1939) *ALA Catalogers' and Classifiers' Yearbook* 8 (1939): 58-61. Quotation is from p. 59.

  11. Roberts, Anne. "A Study of Ten SUNY Campuses Offering an Undergraduate Credit Course in Library Instruction." Washington, D.C.: Council on Library Resources. 1978.

  12. Pausch, Lois M. and Koch, Jean. "Technical Services Librarians in Library Instruction." *Libri* 31, no. 3. (1981): 198-204.

  13. Miller, Enid. "Public Service and Cataloging at the University of Nebraska," *Library Resources and Technical Services* 3 (Summer, 1959): 188-191, Quotation is from p. 191.

  14. Booz, Allen and Hamilton, Inc. "Organization and Staffing of the Libraries of Columbia University." Washington, D.C.: Association of Research Libraries, 1972. Quotation is from p. 12.

  15. Gorman, Michael. "On Doing Away with Technical Services Departments." *American Libraries* 10 (July/August, 1979): 435-437.

  16. Peele, David. "Staffing the Reference Desk." *Library Journal* 105 (September 1, 1980): 1708-1711.

ADDITIONAL READINGS

Bachus, Edward J. "I'll Drink to That: The Integration of Technical and Reader Services." *Journal of Academic Librarianship* 8, no. 4 (September, 1982): 227, 260.

Johnson, Edward R. "Subject-divisional Organization in American University Libraries, 1939-1974." *Library Quarterly* 47, no. 1 (1977): 23-42.

Kohl, David F. "Public Service and the Disappearing Card Catalog." *RQ* 17 (Summer, 1978): 308-311.

Strowd, Elvin E. "Readers' Services – One and All." *Southeastern Librarian* 22 (Winter, 1972): 184-192.

Mental Maps and Metaphors in Academic Libraries

Raymond G. McInnis

In our minds, our ideas about specific things in the everyday world are in large part made up of impressions or perceptions. The sharpness of these perceptions, of course, varies according to the extent of our familiarity with particular things. Along with objects which comprise physical matter or other ''real-world'' materials or concerns, included in this concept are those elements which normally we define as abstract phenomena. That is, the ''thought-products'' of our minds, including the kind of material in the books and scholarly journals on our library shelves.[1]

''Mental map'' and ''cognitive map'' are the labels geographers and psychologists use to identify the images we construct in our minds to help us understand something. And, as we see below, correlations exist between our mental maps and our metaphors. When we speak of perceptions which relate to personal, internalized maps, we may label them either mental maps or cognitive maps, but preference is given mental maps.

In this discussion we argue that geographers' literature on mental maps can provide greater understanding of scientific literature's formats, conventions, processes and formulations. By scientific literature, we mean all published materials which result from our systematic, collective efforts toward producing knowledge.

THE CONCEPT OF MENTAL MAP

Mental maps are not really maps in the ''cartographic'' sense. Instead, they are analogies, or symbolic elaborations, with functions

The author is Head of Reference and Social Sciences Librarian at Western Washington University, Bellingham, WA 98225. He wishes to thank the following colleagues for their suggestions: Cindy Richardson, Jerrold Nelson, Vladimir Milicic, Edmond Mignon, Donna Packer and Kathy Haselbauer.

similar to metaphors, which we construct in our minds to represent specific objects, abstract concepts, or spatial relationships.

Correlations exist between mental maps and metaphors. Metaphors "transform" the meaning we have for one thing into another. By this process, we try to comprehend new, unknown things, by attaching them to older, known things.

Three classes of "perception" analyses developed by geographers who study mental maps provide the background we need to understand how to apply the implications of studies conducted by librarians. In particular, information scientist Blaise Cronin's work suggests that, for instructional purposes in academic libraries, we can utilize examples of the outline structures of scientific articles. A scientific article is, after all, the basic building block, or "brick," with which bodies of knowledge are constructed.

In the view of geographers Roger M. Downs and David Stea, "mapping" is our individual means of "spatializing" information. In this context, our concern is not any specific class of phenomena. Instead, interest is in the idea of "a space acting as a medium of relating pieces of information." And since, in the academic library, when we "relate pieces of information," in large part we deal with abstract phenomena, necessarily we deal with this material metaphorically. The expression, "pieces of information" is itself an example of translating something abstract into something concrete.[2]

Mental maps are convenient sets of shorthand symbols to which we all subscribe, recognize, and employ. While these symbols vary from group to group, and individual to individual, "they are the result of our biases, prejudices and personal experiences." Downs and Stea make clear, however, that mental maps are not necessarily "maps." Instead, to them "mental map" designates "a functional analogue." In this context, while mental maps have all the functions of familiar cartographic maps, the function is an "analogy to be used, not believed."[3]

MENTAL MAPS AND METAPHORS[4]

Independent of one another, Clive Staples Lewis,[5] a literary critic, and Downs[6] suggest that when we think of metaphors, we need to think in terms of two specific kinds: one kind for teaching, and one kind for learning. Metaphors we use for teaching Lewis calls Master metaphors; Downs calls them Decorative metaphors.

Metaphors we use to learn with Lewis calls Pupil metaphors; Downs calls them Generative metaphors. Master metaphors, says Lewis, are "freely chosen." When we want someone to understand something, we relate the new thing with something older, with which the person is familiar. Pupil metaphors are not chosen, however. Instead, Pupil metaphors are our own individual attempts toward understanding something new. We do this by attaching the new object to something old which we understand.

PERCEPTION STUDIES

Geographers are interested in three classes of perception studies.[7] Downs presents these as a set of three "analyses": (1) Structure, (2) Evaluation, and (3) Preference.

In the first, for Gould and White an analytical approach, Structure, inquires into the nature of spatial information stored in our minds which we use everyday. And for this everyday spatial behavior, Downs and Stea argue, people need two complementary types of information: (1) distance and (2) direction. Together distance and direction give "locational information."

In the second approach, Evaluation analysis, in Gould and White's view geographers moved into the wider world of cognition mapping—"a construct or mental map which enables people to acquire, code, store, recall and manipulate information about their spatial environment." With the evaluative approach, we ask "What are the major features of the perceived world which affect decisions?"

To answer this question, rhetorically, Downs and Stea ask, "What do people know?" When we compare a mental map with an actual cartographic map, "we find that mental mapping does not lead to a duplicative photographic process," with three-dimensional color pictures miraculously "tucked away in the mind's eye." Nor, they argue, "does it give us an elaborately filed series of conventional cartographic maps of varying spatial scales." No, instead they claim mental maps "are complex, highly selective, abstract, generalized representations in various forms."

Our understanding of mental maps tells us that they are (1) incomplete, (2) distorted and schematicized, (3) augmented, and have, side-by-side, both (4) group similarities and individual idiosyncratic differences.[8]

First, when we speak of the incomplete nature of our mental maps we distinguish between *denotative* and *connotative* meaning. An object may *denote* something to an individual but have no *connotative* meaning. To Downs and Stea this means that a specific object may have "no significant or valued role in a person's behavior." Further, they continue, an individual's mental maps are frequently "distorted so that the size (scale) of represented phenomena" only "indicates relative connotative significance." And any absence of information about specific phenomena on a mental map reflects what they call "cognitive discontinuity of space" or "symbolic elaboration."

Second, when we speak of distortion in mental maps, we mean "the cognitive transformations of both distance and direction," which, in the end, "deviates from the Euclidian [that is, actual] view of the real world." But, argue Downs and Stea, "far more significant" than distortion, "and as yet little understood, are the results of schematicization."

Next, Downs and Stea claim, evidence suggests that we augment or embellish our mental maps with "nonexistent phenomena."

And finally, there is evidence of significant intergroup and individual differences in how specific populations "construe" particular spatial environments.[9]

The third analytical approach labelled Preference falls into two categories:

First, how are objects evaluated with respect to each other? For geographer C.D. Morley, the images of our environment are best investigated from "the framework of the personal interpretation of space," an approach he claims "emphasizes the uniqueness of the individual's milieux."[10] In this approach, the major theme argues that the level of knowledge available on any environment relates to the level of experience associated with that environment. And when we construct mental maps some maturity appears to be a helpful or necessary, though not absolute, prerequisite. Further maturity, in certain respects, depends upon how successfully we acquire an ability to learn.[11]

Second, for a satisfactory spatial behavior, do "What we need to know" and "What we know" depend upon "How we get our knowledge?" The answer to how we get our knowledge rests in two different sources: (1) sensory and (2) direct and vicarious.[12]

In (1), our sense are influential in determining how we understand or interpret our environment.

In (2), "direct sources" include our "face-to-face contact" with another object. To cope, we must select what we attend to or choose to repeat. But, above all, we "learn by doing." By trial and error we sharpen our skills to achieve the operation level that satisfies our needs. In addition, in (2), "vicarious sources" come, by definition, "secondhand." These sources come to us, "literally and metaphorically," through "someone else's eyes." Such an understanding is true whether it is a verbal description, a cartographic street map, a TV film, a written description, a color photograph, or a painting.[13]

Thus, taken together, all of these factors help explain how we construct our mental maps, the bases upon which our spatial behavior occurs. We behave in our "world" as we see it, regardless of whatever flaws or imperfections exist in our mental maps.[14]

REFERENCING BEHAVIOR IN SCHOLARLY ARTICLES

Cronin describes "a simple experiment designed to demonstrate the extent to which variation occurs in referencing practice." Cronin distributed a scholarly psychological paper, "on the subject of school phobia," to over seventy British psychologists. Stripped of all references, the paper was to be marked with an asterisk at appropriate points where, in the view of the respondents, references were called for.

Not a "content analysis of references," Cronin explains, his study scrutinizes the "context" of references.[15] Cronin's purpose is to examine referencing behavior in terms of the content, structure, and syntactic elements in which the references appear.[16] Cronin asks, "Can we presuppose that, at certain points in a paper, its arguments emit signals about where, for support, references are needed?" To begin, Cronin had to establish the criteria for referencing. Sentences in a research article are "citational foci." Like any scholarly paper, however, only a proportion of the constituent sentences are the focus of citations. And within a single citational focus, the number and locations of citations are variable. To illustrate, Cronin gives an example:

> The mothers of school phobic children are variously described as depressed (Agras, 1959), neurotic (Bery et al., 1974), and as being a dependent personality type (Eisenberg, 1958).

From the citing author's viewpoint, argues Cronin, this is an example of "a multi-reference focus." In each case, the terms "depressed," "neurotic," and "dependent personality type" trigger a reference to an antecedent work. Cronin is not concerned with such matters, however. Instead, Cronin's analysis concentrates on variation in how, for referencing, the focus is chosen.[17] And rather than the validity, quality, or relevance of references, the concern is on occurence or suggested placement "at particular nodes in the text."

Cronin's findings do not show a strong correlation between the perceptions of author and reader for the appropriate locations for references. Indeed, the results lead Cronin to admit that the study fails to increase greatly our knowledge of why authors cite as they do. But, if we look at citation practice through the eyes of the reader, it tempts us to imagine that we can establish a set of "citer" guidelines. If indeed we can establish a set of guidelines, the basic building blocks we would use are those classes of references which, if not universally understood, are at least widely agreed upon.

MENTAL MAPS FOR SCHOLARLY ARTICLES AND OTHER MODES OF SCIENTIFIC COMMUNICATION

From his results, Cronin concludes that areas of agreement between author and reader suggest a shared, though limited, understanding among members of a scholarly community of the function of citations in particular contexts of scholarly articles. From this same evidence, however, we can derive other equally important conclusions. In general, in the minds of experienced researchers, a mental map exists of (1) the outline structure of a scholarly paper (with variations from discipline to discipline) and of (2) the appropriate place for referencing authorities to support arguments in these papers. References, Cronin concludes, give substantive expression to the process of innovation, and if properly marshalled, provide researchers with "a forensic tool of seductive power and versatility."[18]

Fundamental to helping undergraduate students understand that the growth of scientific knowledge is a process of exploration, evaluation, and reevaluation is that they become acquainted with the patterns and processes of scientific inquiry. That is, in the library, we want to help students understand that, in a specific area of research, a knowledge field develops as a consensus is achieved among members of a scholarly community.[19]

Again, the chief communication device in scientific inquiry is the scholarly paper. For a specific knowledge field, its publication marks the first formal presentation of new information. Fundamental to progress in research, scientific papers are the "bricks" with which we construct bodies of knowledge.

For instructional purposes, it is not difficult for us to develop an outline structure of a variety of scientific papers appropriate for various disciplines. In developing models for the outline structures of scientific articles, discipline by discipline, instructors in the particular disciplines which libraries serve can help. The outline structures of these articles, we expect, will go a long way toward helping students construct "mental maps" of the scientific articles in subjects of their "majors." (See Figures 1 and 2.)

But, it is still another matter to teach these same students about such issues as "citational foci." Definitely an individual matter, the accepted (one hesitates to say "proper") way to "reference" must be learned through practice.

What remains speculative about the idea of using outline structures of scientific papers to help students understand scientific communication focuses on whether these articles can become departure points for them to learn how scientific communication occurs.

What is *not* speculative about our discussion of the outline structures of scientific papers, however, is that they fulfill the qualities Downs and Stea specify about the characteristics of mental maps.

FIGURE 1. *Journal of West European History*

OUTLINE OF THE TYPICAL STRUCTURE
OF AN ARTICLE BY A HISTORIAN

HOW AN ARTICLE IS CITED:
Doe, John. "An American Source of Hitler's Ideology,"
  J. West. Eur. Hist., V (1975), 57-85.

TITLE:

An American Source of Hitler's Ideology

AUTHOR:

John Doe
Western Washington University

INTRODUCTION:

In which the author summarizes the problem to be analyzed or the events that will be chronicled (depending on the type of essay). Here, the author may also state his conclusions.

FIGURE 1 (continued)

DISCUSSION OF SOURCES AND PREVIOUS SCHOLARSHIP:

Any matters having to do with 1) historiography and significance of the problem, 2) methodology (if it is significant), 3) any special matters concerning sources (newly discovered, differently employed and the like).

PERSUASIVE ARGUMENT AND DOCUMENTATION OF PROOF:

Development of the argument—each paragraph or section should correspond to some point or points raised initially in the introduction. One might view this as a movement in a piece of music where a theme is first stated and then developed more fully later. Readers (students) should learn to recognize topic sentences in paragraphs and the use of supporting material. In addition, ideas are developed in a logical order in an essay. Paragraph 1 precedes paragraph 2 because the ideas in 2 depend on the ideas in 1, and so on through the essay. In a larger sense, sections should support one another in this way.

Bibliographical references are cited in footnotes throughout the article rather than in a separate bibliography at the end.

CONCLUSION:

Brief recapitualtion and conclusion(s). This is the place to emphasize prominent and/or critical points in the essay once again.

FIGURE 2. *Journal of Abnormal Psychology*

OUTLINE OF THE TYPICAL STRUCTURE
OF AN ARTICLE BY A PSYCHOLOGIST

HOW AN ARTICLE IS CITED:

Kohlenberg, Robert J. "Treatment of a homosexual pedophiliac using in vivo desensitization: a case study." *Journal of Abnormal Psychology*, 1974, 83, 192-195.

TITLE:

Treatment of a Homosexual Pedophiliac Using in Vivo Desensitization: A Case Study.

AUTHOR:

Robert J. Kohlenberg

ABSTRACT:

A concise presentation of the main points of the paper.

INTRODUCTION:

Background information and a presentation of the main purpose of the paper and a listing of the specific questions that are to be answered.

METHOD:

A complete description and presentation of the experimental method that was used.

Subjects: A description of the participants.

FIGURE 2 (continued)

Apparatus: A description of the equipment, tests, measuring devices, other pertinent information.

Procedure: A description of the tasks that were performed and the manner in which the experiment was conducted.

RESULTS:

The data, statistical analyses, and specific answers that they provide to the questions that were asked in the introduction section.

DISCUSSION:

An explanation of the results as they relate to previous research; some suggestions for further research that is indicated by the present results.

REFERENCES:

A list of the articles referred to in the paper.

Mental maps, we note above, are (1) incomplete, (2) distorted and/or schematicized, (3) augmented, and (4) have group similarities and idiosyncratic individual differences. Further, in the sense detailed by both Lewis and Downs, for "Master-Decorative" metaphors, these outline structures of scientific articles are "Master-Decorative" mental maps. That is, they are designed to inform students about how, in fact, scientific articles are structured.

In academic libraries, many of the understandings about mental maps geographers have discovered remain as rich opportunities for further exploration.[20] Among the almost limitless possibilities we can explore, for example, is the mental map of the book. And, after the book, we can look at the mental maps library users construct for the volume (that is, book) of collected literature review articles. Most frequently, publishers call these treatises *Handbook of . . .* Though as a rule little known to people other than reference librarians and experienced scholars, as an aid to the growth of knowledge, their utility is self-evident. But specific measures we can utilize to acquaint these volumes to our students are not well articulated. To date, our efforts are only partially satisfactory.

And, yes, inevitably a discussion of a mental map of the *Handbook*-type volume raises another issue, one that touches on both the "Evaluation" and "Preference" categories of Downs and Stea's analysis of our perceptions of mental maps. If we can teach students about the outline structures of scientific papers, can we help them understand the structure of the literature review article? A variation on the scientific article, which reports the results of new research, the literature review article, we all know, is the primary communication device which, through consensus, helps us change the "information" reported in our scientific articles into "knowledge."[20]

For the moment, hypothetically, let's assume that a given library has two sets of literatures of a body of knowledge. But, to complicate matters, each exists in different formats. In the first set, the format is the *Handbook*-type volume. In the second, the same articles the *Handbook* contains are scattered in various sources on the library's shelves: some are chapters in books, some are articles in journals which normally report new research, and some are articles in "dedicated" literature review publications (for example, the *Review of Research in Education*). Among reference librarians in academic libraries who work with literature reviews, in both types of format, experience suggests that greater value is set upon the usefulness of the first example, the *Handbook*-type of collection. Why is greater value placed on the first—often called "a truly substantive tool," and less upon the second—generally recognized as "fairly broadly useful bibliographic reviews"? Ease of accessibility, perhaps, is one reason. Another is the amount in internal indexing. That is, because the publisher has a substantial investment in the volume, he wants to enhance its usefulness: indexing subjects and names page by page makes the volume's contents more accessible. But, of course, the literature review articles, like ordinary articles, will be indexed in the standard indexes and abstracts, and thus will be accessible in other ways. Taken together, however, these considerations about formats of literature review publications still do not explain the preferential values indicated above. These are issues that we believe fall in the category of mental maps which deserve investigation.

CONCLUSIONS

This paper attempts to demonstrate obvious connections between the theoretical discussions and the empirical finding by geographers of our perceptions on mental maps and enduring problems in academic libraries. Mental maps are shorthand symbols we construct in our minds as functional analogues to represent something. As such, mental maps function like familiar cartographic maps. Features of the three classes of perception studies for mental maps (Structure,

Evaluation, and Preference) reviewed suggest some promising possibilities for applications in academic libraries. Evaluation analysis, in particular, informs us about the characteristic nature of our mental maps. With evaluation analysis, geographers moved into the wider world of cognition mapping—to investigate how we acquire, code, store, recall and manipulate information about our spatial environment. The results of these investigations show that our mental maps are incomplete, distorted and/or schematicized, augmented, and have, side by side, group similarities and individual differences.

Cronin's work on referencing practices in scientific articles provides evidence which indicates that among experienced scholars, there exists a mental map of a scientific article. With this evidence, we suggest that models of scientific articles, in outline format, promise to become aids for students to more rapidly obtain a command of the literatures they are studying. Additional studies of mental maps in academic libraries, particularly which relate to the book, the literature review article, and its larger kin, the *Handbook*-review, are suggested.

REFERENCES AND NOTES

1. According to L.J. Wood, "Perception Studies in Geography," *Transactions of the Institute of British Geographers,* no. 50, pp. 136-8, there is much debate about how to define "perception." Wood cites S.H. Bartley(1958): "Nowhere in the literature can we find in concise and adequate form a well-rounded account of what perception is, what its characteristics are, and/or how it relates to other aspects of behavior." In general, Wood argues, perception studies concern attitudes, opinions or impressions, all of which are aspects of mind extremely difficult to measure.

2. Downs, Roger M. and Stea, David, "Cognitive Maps and Spatial Behavior: Process and Products," in Roger M. Downs and David Stea, eds., *Image and Environment: Cognitive Mapping and Spatial Behavior* (Chicago: Aldine, 1973), pp. 23-4. For a discussion of the metaphorical treatment of library materials, see Raymond G. McInnis, "Do Metaphors Make Good Sense in Teaching Research Strategy?," in Cerise Oberman and Katina Strauch, eds., *Theories of Bibliographic Education: Designs for Teaching.* (New York: Bowker, 1982). Hereafter, this chapter is referred to as "Metaphors in Teaching Research Strategy."

3. Ibid., 1973, p. 11.

4. In "Metaphors in Teaching Research Strategy" is an extensive exploration of the literature and the application of metaphors to the academic library, with particular reference to the problem of teaching research strategies to students.

5. Clive Staples Lewis, *Rehabilitation and Other Essays.* (London: Oxford University Press, 1939), pp. 140-141.

6. Downs, Roger M., "Maps and Mappings for Spatial Representation," in Lynn S. Liben, et al., eds. *Spatial Representation and Behavior Across the Life Span* (New York: Academic Press, 1981): 150.

7. Downs and Stea, "Cognitive Maps and Spatial Behavior," 1973; Roger M. Downs, "The Role of Perception in Modern Geography," *University of Bristol, Department of Geo-*

graphy Seminar Paper Series A, 11(1968); Roger M. Downs, "Geographic Space Perception: Past Approaches and Future Prospects," in C. Broad, et al., *Progress in Geography* 2 (1970); Wood, "Perception Studies in Geography," 1970, p. 131; Peter R. Gould and R. White, *Mental Maps* (Harmondsworth, England: Penguin, 1974).

8. Downs and Stea, "Cognitive Maps and Spatial Behavior; 1973, pp. 1, 18.

9. Ibid., 1973, p. 21. As expressed by Downs and Stea, 1973, their notions have obvious parallels with the conceptual schemes developed by Peter L. Berger and Thomas Luckmann, *The Social Construction of Reality* (New York: Doubleday, 1966) and Thomas S. Kuhn, *The Structure of Scientific Revolutions,* 2nd ed. (Chicago: University of Chicago Press, 1970). Berger and Luckmann develop a framework for explaining how, collectively, society constructs "reality," and Kuhn discusses how "paradigms" structure scientific research.

10. C.D. Morley, as cited by Wood, "Perception Studies in Geography," 1970, p. 131-2.

11. Downs, "Maps and Mapping for Spatial Behavior," 1981, p. 151.

12. Downs and Stea, "Cognitive Maps and Spatial Behavior," 1973, p. 22.

13. Ibid., 1973, p. 23.

14. Ibid., 1973, p. 23.

14. Ibid., 1973, p. 22.

15. Blaise Cronin, "Agreement and Divergence on Referencing Practice," *Journal of Information Science* 3 (1981):28.

16. Cronin, ibid., is not alone when he assumes "pattern" is recognized in referencing behavior. In *New Perspectives* and "Metaphors in Teaching Research Strategy," I discuss attempts by others, primarily G. Nigel Gilbert, "The Transformation of Research Findings into Scientific Knowledge," *Social Studies of Science* 6 (1976):281-306; and "Referencing as Persuasion," *Social Studies of Science* 7 (1977)113-122. Gilbert aruges that, basically, referencing is really a form of "persuasion." Other evidence about referencing behavior is in the Institute for Scientific Information's (1982) *Searcher's Manual.* It argues that the bibliographic citation is really a symbol for a "subject," which makes citation indexing the most precise form of online searching. The manual states: An author does not cite the earlier literature at random. Earlier works are cited by an author to be sure the readers can locate earlier material on the research topic. A paper's bibliography references specific items published earlier, including journal articles, books, material appearing in the report literature, even letters published in journals. References in the introduction a paper are to fundamental papers on which the author's present work is based. If there is a methodology section, it will have references to the earlier papers which describe methods used. The section on the report of the actual work done contains references to earlier papers. And the conclusion and summary sections will also contain references to earlier literature.

17. Ibid., 1981, p. 28.

18. Ibid., 1981. p. 16.

19. See, for example, the study, "Libraries in the Mind: How Can We See Users' Perceptions of Libraries?", *Journal of Librarianship* 15(1983): 19-28. Author Robert James discusses the results of using mental maps drawn by library users as a basis for library planning.

20. As well as a look at the evidence reported in the literature, my speculations on this topic are in chapter 4 of *New Perspectives.*

INSTRUCTION IN PUBLIC LIBRARIES

Library Instruction in Public Libraries: A Dream Deferred, A Goal to Actualize

Patricia F. Beilke

Public librarians are educators too. Although some public librarians may be startled to consider the provision of education as part of their roles, few would challenge that the provision of information to users at the time it is needed and in the form that it is needed is part of their professional aims. Many would concur that provision of programs to stimulate new uses of information is among the activities acknowledged as those provided by public libraries. Ian Malley[1] says few librarians have had any professional preparation for user education. User education, as seen by Malley, involves librarians in education, instruction and learning. Keith G. E. Harris[2] points out that preparation in education is needed by some librarians.

DEFINITIONS

Facilitation of transfer of information is the ultimate goal of reference service. This ultimate goal is stated in the January 1976 Developmental Guidelines,[3] adopted by the Reference and Adult Services Division, American Library Association. The Developmental Guidelines state that substantive interaction with users on direct and indirect levels is the means by which reference librarians ensure optimum uses of information. Examples of these interactions range from the explanation of the use of bibliographical aids—

Patricia F. Beilke is Associate Professor of Library Science, Ball State University, Muncie, IN 47306.

123

catalogs, information data bases and reference works—to interpretative tours and lectures. For the present discussion, these activities concerning ways to locate and pursue information will be referred to as *library instruction.*

Education is defined as "the act or process of imparting knowledge or skill."[4] Library education encompasses library instruction but is not limited to the pursuit of information concerning library resources. *Library adult education* is influenced by the needs and interests of users, societal trends, and the nature of the topic being addressed. The breadth of the term library adult education was explained by Margaret E. Monroe[5] in her article "Adult Services in the Third Millennium." According to Monroe, trends in adult education have implications for public library adult services.

NEED FOR LIBRARY ADULT EDUCATION

Carolyn A. Kirkendall and Carla J. Stoffle[6] acknowledge that library instruction programs have never been widely established in public libraries; however, they avow that the recent explosion in the information-gathering/information-exchange fields as well as the current emphasis on the adult independent learner offer many opportunities for developing continuous working relationships between public librarians and patrons. Kirkendall and Stoffle predict that effective use of the public library will be an important and growing part of total reference service.

Although few librarians may be professionally prepared for their roles in user education, the need for librarians to perform these roles has persisted for many years. Patricia Senn Breivik[7] indicates that some visionary librarians were concerned about library instruction in the 1870s. In 1959 Monroe[8] stated that public libraries had created the field of library adult education in the previous thirty years. She indicated that library adult educational services may be varied as to the means by which they promote or provide continuing cumulative experiences for adults. The services may include: (1) readers' advisory activities with individuals or groups, (2) sequential group programs in the form of presentations or discussions, or (3) programs developed cooperatively with other community groups whereby library materials, skills or insights make appropriate contributions.

TRENDS

Monroe[9] anticipates an increase in the population of adults by 2000 A.D. These adults will be 65 years of age or older and in relatively good health. She says these adults will have leisure, be accustomed to the use of public library services, and be oriented toward learning to satisfy their varieties of interests. Monroe[10] counsels that adult service librarians will need understanding of life tasks of various groups of older adults. Danny Cunningham[11] says shifts in population in the 1980s and 1990s indicate there will be renewed emphasis on library adult education. Cunningham says public library services for persons in the 35–54 year age group should be accelerated. Interests of persons in this age group can be used as bases for the public library adult education programs. Cunningham says basic interests of persons in this age group "include self-education, travel and hobbies, career change, financial investment, planning for retirement, and health care."

Other trends which affect library adult education are those associated with changes within society. Alvin Toffler and John Naisbitt are well-known for their writings about the future. Toffler[12] writes of a Third Wave civilization where information, including imagination, will be very important. According to Toffler the Third Wave civilization will be a world which may be characterized as new in values, technologies, geopolitical relationships, lifestyles and modes of communication. Naisbitt[13] examines several new trends. Two trends which have potential implications for librarians who provide adult education programs are:

> The American society is moving in dual directions of high tech-high touch. The introduction of every new technology is accompanied by a compensatory human response—or the new technology is rejected.
> The most important trend in this century is the continuing shift of the United States from a representative democracy to a participatory democracy.

Toffler and Naisbitt emphasize changes in technologies. These changes will lead to changes in many persons' relationships with: one another, the machines used to accomplish work or pursue leisure activities, and institutions. There will be an accelerated need for sensitivity in human relationships, because traditional responses will no longer be sufficient. More individuals will seek to participate actively in the institutions which affect their lives rather than relying on others to represent them.

IMPLICATIONS OF TRENDS

Rapid changes in technologies and increased participation of citizens in the institutions of society have implications for the continuing education of librarians. Greater sensitivity will be needed for working with other individuals and organizations by librarians as they plan, implement, and evaluate library adult education programs. Changes in technologies will lead to greater need for library users to become updated about new ways of gaining access to information, information related to their interests. As public library adult education programs are provided, library instruction will need to be considered as a necessary component of each program. To meet the needs mandated by accelerated technological changes and increased adult participation in institutions, F. William Summers[14] stresses that greater emphasis should be placed on group and interpersonal communication skills for reference librarians.

Professional readings can provide guidance for reference librarians concerning interpersonal communications. Katz[15] discusses the importance of developing rapport with a patron in volume II of his third edition of *Introduction to Reference Work.* Katz[16] provides suggestions for readings concerning both verbal and nonverbal communications. One can observe that some users can be alienated by a reference librarian who does not approach the patron and conducts the reference interview from a distance of five or six feet. In a like manner, reference librarians who conduct library adult education programs need to gain the confidence of the participants. Librarians who are new to their educational duties may wish to examine their own nonverbal behaviors. Useful information is provided in paperback books about nonverbal behavior, such as Erving Goffman's[17] *The Presentation of Self in Everyday Life* and *How to Read a Person Like a Book* by Gerard I. Nierenberg and Henry H. Calero.[18] Other useful books about working with groups include: Walter M. Lifton's *Groups: Facilitating Individual Growth and Societal Change*[19] and Herbert A. Thelen's *Dynamics of Groups at Work.*[20]

GOALS OF LIBRARY ADULT EDUCATION

Effective library adult education programs provided by public librarians must have subject matter related to the needs and interests of the intended participants. A written statement of the goals of the library adult education program is a useful way to begin. Reference librarians may find it useful to think of the development of goals for library adult education from various points of view. One useful approach may be to state the goals in terms of what ideally a library patron may strive to become. Thelen[21] provides some useful suggestions. He describes the "humane person" as one who is: (1) involved in his culture, (2) aware of his belongingness to the human species and (3) involved in the environment of his society. Thelen elaborates on this involvement in the environment as including: belonging to informal and formal organizations, having a position and status, solving problems, as well as competing for comfort, power, prestige, and the world's goods. Thelen concludes that the humane person is a member of a society, a citizen. In the opinion of this writer, a public librarian can validly develop library adult education programs with aims for contributing to the development of fully functioning citizens. Jesse H. Shera[22] asserts repeatedly that the goals of the library are the goals of society. Library instruction should be incorporated into each library adult education program. Breivik[23] says the needs of library employees for library instruction should be considered also.

Houle[24] contends that it is difficult to know which goals of a public library are educational and which are not. In the opinion of this writer library adult education goals tend to be diffused under various programming efforts. Library instruction is frequently viewed as one component of library adult education. If it were to be viewed as a necessary component of every library adult education program, it would be considered and planned for whenever any type of library adult education is developed. Givens[25] says public librarians provide user instruction in many situations without giving the instruction a name. Givens predicts that this condition is likely to change since the concept of life-long learning and the role of libraries as agents of change in life-long learning are gaining wide acceptance. Givens foresees that user instruction will become a fixture in public libraries as it has become in schools and colleges.

Peter Marshall,[26] reference librarian in Bexley London Borough,

England, reminds librarians not to ignore the needs of citizens who have a problem of literacy or basic understanding. He suggests that it is easy to satisfy needs of those persons who have already acquired basic reference skills. He says it is a more difficult task to work with persons who have not acquired basic reference skills and where a higher level of motivation is needed. Marshall points out that the need to acquire reference skills arises urgently with demands made by either employment or unemployment and by other activities associated with the economic facts of life. His list of practical tools, although oriented toward library practices in England, provides guidance for reference librarians who wish to collect comparable materials in the U.S. These practical materials will help citizens with very basic and urgent information needs develop their competencies in acquiring information for themselves. Marshall[27] advises reference librarians to collect materials which can be used at a very fundamental level to instruct patrons how to locate: (1) materials in libraries, (2) information in general reference sources, e.g., dictionaries and encyclopedias, (3) application forms, and (4) instructions for filling out the application forms. Clearly, opportunities for working with community agencies will occur to imaginative public library reference librarians who are stimulated by Marshall's suggestions. Additional groups to serve may be suggested by examining Thomas Childer's *The Information Poor in America.*[28]

Ron Scrivener,[29] Branch Librarian, Woodbridge, Suffolk, England, says a user education course in a public library can promote good public relations and better understanding between the library staff and the library users. The prototype course which he and his staff developed had three goals:

1. To encourage users to help themselves in the library;
2. To provide an awareness of other library services available through the county library;
3. To develop or improve relationships between staff members and the public.

Scrivener's program[30] deserves study by public librarians. The eight meetings he describes incorporate tours and varieties of practical activities as well as informative presentations. Orientation tours, the mysteries of catalogs and classification, microfiche catalog use, services for children, reference and information services, and computerization were among the topics covered. Half-hour coffee breaks separated the two forty-five minute sessions which comprised each meeting. This approach of Scrivener and his staff illustrates the person-oriented approach to reference service advocated by McFadyen[31] whereby learners are not passive receivers of information but bring their own experiences to the concept of information thus making and remaking their own understandings. Practical steps essential to the establishment of the library adult education course described by Scrivener[32] were:

1. Endorsement of the county library director and the library trustees;
2. Help and participation of a competent and enthusiastic library staff;
3. The willingness of professional colleagues to give up one evening of their time.

IMPORTANCE OF INSTRUCTIONAL OBJECTIVES

After goals are established, learning objectives need to be written in terms of what each library instruction participant will be able to do as a result of having participated in the planned sequence of learning activities. Learning objectives specify in what ways the goals will be actualized and justify why particular teaching-learning events take place.[33] Breivik[34] points out that at the conclusion of an instructional session each participant should be able to do something new and be confident about doing it.

EVALUATION BASED ON OBJECTIVES

A well-written set of objectives is important, because evaluation of the extent to which each participant is achieving the desired objective is much easier if the objective is appropriately written. Robert F. Mager's paperback *Preparing Instructional Objectives*[35] is useful for persons who need guidance about the writing of objectives. Advisory groups composed of library staff members and/or library patrons can be useful for review of both goals and objectives. Each objective must be measurable.

Breivik's[36] instructive comments about evaluation indicate that evaluative plans need to be made concerning learning outcomes, learning experiences, instructional presentations, learners' attitudes, as well as the total program. Particularly helpful are the forms she provides for evaluation of a workshop[37] and of a learner's attitudes.[38]

CONCLUSION

Reference librarians in public libraries can initiate new and improved programs of library instruction. To do so, library adult education programs must address needs of library users or potential users in a rapidly changing communication environment. The library instruction component of each of the library education programs needs to be designed. Goals and objectives for the library adult education programs must be written and, when possible, reviewed by advisory committees. Evaluation should be planned.

Librarians need to be prepared to function as educators. Much of the information which users wish to obtain must be transferred in face-to-face encounters, in small groups and, in some cases, in large groups. Professional preparation in the areas of adult education and interpersonal communications can help. Professional readings can help. Insights gained from these readings can facilitate the friendly, approachable image librarians wish to project. Participation in professional associations and inservice meetings can contribute to professional growth. Librarians need practice in planning, implementing and evaluating educational programs from a behavioral approach while using verbal and nonverbal communication skills.

Effective library instruction occurs in a personal context. Effective library instruction involves the human dimension as well as the imparting of knowledge and skills about the most recent means of locating and accessing information. The teachable-moment for a child occurs when interest in a curricular project is supported by expert guidance provided in a warm supportive environment. An adult, likewise, responds favorably to learning environments which meet current interests and needs. New competencies gained from socially-supportive learning sessions can fulfill the library user's aspirations as a life-long learner. Library instruction offered in the context of library adult education programs will no longer be a dream deferred. Now is the time to plan for the competencies to be gained.

REFERENCES

1. Ian Malley, "National Clearinghouses for User Education," *Libri* 32 (March 1982):55.

2. Keith G. E. Harris, "User Education," *Libri* 32 (December 1982):331.

3. Reference and Adult Services Division, American Library Association, "A Commitment to Information Services: Developmental Guidelines," *RQ* 18 (Spring 1979):275-76.

4. *The American Heritage Dictionary of the English Language,* (1970), s.v. "Education."

5. Margaret E. Monroe, "Adult Services in the Third Millennium," *RQ* 18 (Spring 1979):272.

6. Carolyn A. Kirkendall and Carla J. Stoffle, "Instruction," in *The Service Imperative for Libraries: Essays in Honor of Margaret E. Monroe,* ed. Gail A. Schlacter (Littleton, Colorado: Libraries Unlimited, 1982), pp. 56-57.

7. Patricia Senn Breivik, *Planning the Library Instruction Program* (Chicago: American Library Association, 1982), p. 124.

8. Margaret E. Monroe, "Educating Librarians for the Work of Library Adult Education," *Library Trends* 8 (July 1959):91.

9. Idem, "Adult Services in the Third Millennium," p. 272.

10. Ibid., p. 273.

11. Danny Cunningham, "Population Shifts Demand Library Response," *American Libraries* 13 (September 1982):505.

12. Alvin Toffler, *The Third Wave* (New York: William Morrow and Company, 1980), pp. 368, 18.

13. John Naisbitt, "The Major National and International Societal Problems and Issues Whose Resolutions Require Information Service in the Year 2000," in *Strategies for Meeting the Information Needs of Society in the Year 2000,* ed. Martha Boaz (Littleton, Colorado: Libraries Unlimited, 1981), pp. 30-31.

14. F. William Summers, "Education for Reference Service," in *The Service Imperative for Libraries: Essays in Honor of Margaret E. Monroe,* ed. by Gail A. Schlacter (Littleton, Colorado: Libraries Unlimited, 1982), pp. 166-67.

15. William A. Katz, *Introduction to Reference Work,* 3rd ed., 2 vols. (New York: McGraw-Hill Book Company, 1978), vol. 2: *Reference Services and Reference Processes,* pp. 62-78.

16. Ibid., pp. 79-80.

17. Erving Goffman, *The Presentation of Self in Everyday Life* (Garden City, New York: Doubleday and Company, 1959).

18. Gerard I. Nierenberg and Henry H. Calero, *How to Read a Person Like a Book* (New York: Hawthorn Books, 1971; Pocket Books, A Division of Simon and Schuster, 1973).

19. Walter M. Lifton, *Groups: Facilitating Individual Growth and Societal Change* (New York: John Wiley and Sons, 1972).

20. Herbert A. Thelen, *Dynamics of Groups at Work* (Chicago: The University of Chicago Press, 1954).

21. Idem, "Comments on 'What It Means to Become Humane,' " in *To Nurture Humaneness: Commitment for the '70's,* eds. Mary-Margaret Scobey and Grace Graham (Washington, D.C.: Association for Supervision and Curriculum Development, NEA, 1970), pp. 29-30.

22. Jesse H. Shera, "Response," in *Changing Times: Changing Libraries,* eds. George S. Bonn and Sylvia Fabisoff (Urbana-Champaign, Illinois: Graduate School of Library Science, University of Illinois, 1978), p. 15.

23. Breivik, p. 48.

24. Cyril O. Houle, "Adult Education," in *Encyclopedia of Educational Research,* 4th ed., ed. Robert L. Ebel (New York: The Macmillan Company, 1969), p. 52.

25. Johnnie E. Givens, "User Instruction: Assessing Needs for the Future," in *Reference Services and Library Education: Essays in Honor of Frances Neel Cheney,* eds. Edwin S. Gleaves and John Mark Tucker (Lexington, Massachusetts: D.C. Heath and Company, 1983), p. 99.

26. Peter Marshall, "Our Role as Rescue-Educators in an Age of Basic Needs Information," *Library Association Record* 84 (February 1982):57.

27. Ibid., pp. 57-58.

28. Thomas Childers, *The Information Poor in America* (Metuchen, New Jersey: Scarecrow Press, 1975).

29. Ron Scrivener, "User Education in Public Libraries—A Practical Exercise," in *Second International Conference on Library User Education Proceedings, Keble College Oxford, 7-10 July 1981* (Loughborough, Leicestershire, England: Loughborough University of Technology, INFUSE Publications, 1982), pp. 64, 61.

30. Ibid., pp. 65-66.

31. Don McFadyen, "The Psychology of Inquiry: Reference Service and the Concept of Information/Experience," in *The Professional Development of the Librarian and Information Worker,* Aslib Reader Series, vol. 3, ed. Patricia Layzell Ward (London: Aslib, 1980), p. 133.

32. Scrivener, p. 61.

33. *Measuring and Attaining the Goals of Education,* by Wilbur B. Brookover, Chairman (Alexandria, Virginia: Association for Supervision and Curriculum Development, 1980), pp. 6-7.

34. Breivik. p. 59.

35. Robert F. Mager, *Preparing Instructional Objectives,* 2nd ed. (Belmont, California: Fearon Publishers, 1975).

36. Breivik, p. 97.

37. Ibid., p. 101.

38. Ibid., p. 106.

SELECTED BIBLIOGRAPHY

The American Heritage Dictionary of the English Language, 1970. S.v. "Education."

Breivik, Patricia Senn. *Planning the Library Instruction Program.* Chicago: American Library Association, 1982.

Childers, Thomas. *The Information Poor in America.* Metuchen, New Jersey: Scarecrow Press, 1975.

Cunningham, Danny. "Population Shifts Demand Library Response." American Libraries 13 (September 1982):505.

Givens, Johnnie E. "User Instruction: Assessing Needs for the Future." In *Reference Services and Library Education: Essays in Honor of Frances Neel Cheney,* pp. 95-108. Edited by Edwin S. Gleaves and John Mark Tucker. Lexington, Massachusetts: D.C. Heath and Company, 1983.

Goffman, Erving. *The Presentation of Self in Everday Life.* Garden City, New York: Doubleday and Company, 1959.

Harris, Keith G. E. "User Education." *Libri* 32 (December 1982):327-36.

Houle, Cyril O." Adult Education." In *Encyclopedia of Educational Research,* 4th ed., pp. 51-57. Edited by Robert L. Ebel. New York: The Macmillan Company, 1969.

Katz, William A. *Introduction to Reference Work.* 3rd ed. Vol. 2: *Reference Services and Reference Processes.* New York: McGraw-Hill Book Company, 1978.

Kirkendall, Carolyn A., and Stoffle, Carla J. "Instruction." In *The Service Imperative for Libraries: Essays in Honor of Margaret E. Monroe,* pp. 42-93. Edited by Gail A. Schlacter. Littleton, Colorado: Libraries Unlimited, 1982.

Lifton, Walter M. *Groups: Facilitating Individual Growth and Societal Change.* New York: John Wiley and Sons, 1972.

McFadyen, Don. "The Psychology of Inquiry: Reference Service and the Concept of Information/Experience." In *The Professional Development of the Librarian and Information Worker*, Aslib Reader Series, Vol. 3, pp. 125-34. Edited by Patricia Layzell Ward. London: Aslib, 1980.

Mager, Robert F. *Preparing Instructional Objectives*, 2nd ed. Belmont California: Fearon Publishers, 1975.

Malley, Ian. "National Clearinghouses for User Education." *Libri* 32 (March 1982): 54-67.

Marshall, Peter. "Our Role as Rescue-Educators in an Age of Basic Needs Information." *Library Association Record* 84 (February 1982): 57-58.

Measuring and Attaining the Goals of Education. By Wilbur B. Brookover, Chairman. Alexandria, Virginia: Association for Supervision and Curriculum Development, 1980.

Monroe, Margaret E. "Adult Services in the Third Millennium." *RQ* 18 (Spring 1979):267-73.

_____. "Educating Librarians for the Work of Library Adult Education." *Library Trends* 8 (July 1959):91-107.

Naisbitt, John. "The Major National and International Societal Problems and Issues Whose Resolutions Require Information Service in the Year 2000." In *Strategies for Meeting the Information Needs of Society in the Year 2000*, pp. 30-42. Edited by Martha Boaz. Littleton, Colorado: Libraries Unlimited, 1981.

Nierenberg, Gerard I., and Calero, Henry H. *How to Read a Person Like a Book.* New York: Hawthorn Books, 1971; Pocket Books, A Division of Simon and Schuster, 1973.

Reference and Adult Services Division, American Library Association. "A Commitment to Information Services: Developmental Guidelines." *RQ* 18 (Spring 1979):275-78.

Scrivener, Ron. "User Education in Public Libraries—A Practical Exercise." In *Second International Conference on Library User Education Proceedings, Keble College Oxford, 7-10 July 1981*, pp. 60-66. Loughborough, Leicestershire, England: Loughborough University of Technology, INFUSE Publications, 1982.

Shera, Jesse H. "Response." In *Changing Times: Changing Libraries*, pp. 14-22. Edited by George S. Bonn and Sylvia Fabisoff. Urbana-Champaign, Illinois: Graduate School of Library Science, University of Illinois, 1978.

Summers, F. William. "Education for Reference Service." In *The Service Imperative for Libraries: Essays in Honor of Margaret E. Monroe*, pp. 157-168. Edited by Gail A. Schlacter. Littleton, Colorado: Libraries Unlimited, 1982.

Thelen, Herbert A. "Comments on 'What It Means to Become Humane.' " In *To Nurture Humaneness: Commitment for the '70's*, pp. 27-32. Edited by Mary-Margaret Scobey and Grace Graham. Washington, D.C.: Association for Supervision and Curriculum Development, NEA, 1970.

_____. *Dynamics of Groups at Work*. Chicago: The University of Chicago Press, 1954.

Toffler, Alvin. *The Third Wave*. New York: William Morrow and Company, 1980.

Library Instruction
Through the Reference Query

Jane A. Reilly

Note: This topic is being considered from the point of view of a public librarian, although the techniques of instructing through response to the reference query have application in all types of libraries. The article does not cover training aspects of techniques of the reference interview nor interpersonal relationships, assuming that the adult services librarian has acquired these skills and is motivated to use them. Given this assumption, much of the literature favors the person to person eclectic approach because of elements of motivation and immediacy. Stressed is the helping relationship of a trained professional to the learner.

This consideration is posited upon the premise that librarians are educators as well as information specialists. Without entering into controversy, it may be well to recall that academic librarians regularly speak out for faculty status, calling attention to their academic backgrounds and subject specialties. Media personnel in elementary and high schools, too, owe the viability of their positions to their success in complementing and enriching the curriculum. Such specialists further the learning goals of their institutions by providing a variety of learning modes.

Library science is usually a double specialization in addition to a broad humanistic foundation with intensification in one or two subject areas. It is the science of selecting, acquiring, organizing, classifying, accessing and arranging of materials. It also involves managerial skills in directing staff in various aspects of these tasks and business skills for budgeting and programming the use of materials

Dr. Jane A. Reilly is with the Hild Regional Library of the Chicago Public Library System, and assigned to reference duties with special responsibility for selection and collection development in the social sciences. She is also Chairperson of the Organization and By-Laws Committee of PLA's Alternative Education Programs Section and also holds membership in the Continuing and Independent Learning Services Committee of the same section.

and resources. The multiplication of media forms and the complexity of the classification systems sometimes make aspects of librarianship concerned with collection building seem more important to the public and to the practitioner than is logical or feasible in an institution founded for public service to independent readers and learners.

Some librarians are concerned merely with the provision and location of materials. Their stance is that it is none of their business what the browser wants with the materials. In cases where there is an imbalance of professional and clerical staff, perhaps this is the only stance possible. It does not justify the title of educator for the librarian, and in a larger context of concern, it will do nothing to strengthen the profession by insuring numbers of practitioners who can be of assistance to learners in the role of advisors. It will only insure that the elitist concept of libraries for the already educated will endure. Certainly it will strengthen the growing conviction of business managers and federal job revisers that there is really no need for persons trained to the master's level to run libraries. The function of efficient book or materials location does not, indeed, require that level of expertise. At worst it may hasten the demise of libraries as too expensive to maintain for so few users. Having laid down a premise and expressed some related concerns, it will be well to describe the educator's function of the librarian as learner's advisor at the level of instruction in the use of the library.

The person coming to the library in search of a specific book or topic is need-motivated. The need may be personal, such as the desire to know how to handle a specific health problem, or it may be necessary in order to fulfill an assignment or to learn more about a work-related skill. If the person is coming in for the first time, no matter what the level of education, it will be necessary to supply some orientation about how the collection is organized. A study of traffic flow and graphic signage may be helpful, but the human voice is a great comfort at this stage. Some libraries offer tours on audio cassettes for the new registrant. Some have video cassettes at carrels. Slide-tape presentations and sound filmstrips are also used. Self-directed tours in print format have found favor in many places. An excellent overview of the methods which may be used is found in a chapter by Mary Jo Lynch in *Educating the Library User,* annotated in the bibliography for this article. The group tour has been found ineffective in many instances and wasteful of staff time and energy, though if it is employed merely to acquaint the newcomer with the physical arrangement of the building and collection without trying to communicate too much detail, it can be a positive experience. Some self-learning method seems preferable if this can be introduced in a friendly and personable way. Perhaps the best time to do this is after the initial request for help has been fulfilled, as an invitation to make further use of the library's resources. This could be the time to invite registration and application for a library card, and the directional helps could be introduced while the application is being processed. The aim is to insure a positive first impression and an invitation to return. This type of overture goes beyond the mere satisfaction of the request for information, though since this has been the motivating force for the patron's visit, it should be handled first.

The question of motivation is crucial. It is simply not productive to put the user through a complete course of library instruction which is unrelated to the need of the moment. Even to provide many useful examples or hypothetical search problems is not sufficient to spark interest if need is not present. This indeed is a hazard of the curriculum of library science as a graduate discipline, though at least here the knowledge of resources is recognized as a tool to bring to professional practice. Librarians who have been through the crucible know that they have used what they have learned, but the journey to competence often palled. This is not to say that the independent learner or library patron may not find manuals of library practice helpful, especially if these are tailored for the library which is being used. With rapidly changing technology the card catalog may have given way to the systemwide union catalog in book format or on film, fiche, and increasingly, interactive computer terminals. Bibliographies with abstracts are computer-produced. Printouts of magazine and journal articles can be obtained on call. Classification systems are in process of expansion and change, networking may mean that the physical resource is not on the premises but can be obtained by drawing from other collections.

STRUCTURING THE PROGRAM OF LIBRARY INSTRUCTION

How, then, is a program of library instruction, whether in the school library, the academic library or the public and special library structured? A practitioner's answer, bolstered by the opinions of other librarians here and abroad is simply that the best structure is dictated by responsiveness to the needs of the user. Here is a credo:

- A library should be generously staffed by professional librarians.
- These librarians should be available, accessible and "on the floor" when patrons are using the library.
- The needs of local users will affect the character and selection of the collection on a continuous basis.
- Every library should provide a good working reference collection so that overview information on a wide variety of subjects is available.
- Every library should seek to develop its collection with maximum responsiveness to user requests and with close attention to requests which cannot be filled with existing resources so that this condition can be swiftly remedied.
- Systems should provide for this type of swift responsiveness by expediting special purchases.
- If patrons or customers are expertly attended to, the use of libraries will increase and libraries can be educational institutions according to their mission.
- Librarians should be person-centered communicators as well as managers, administrators, bibliographers and technical processors. Areas of library education recruitment and hiring should focus on individuals capable of outreach and human service.

Idealistic and unrealistic as such a credo may appear, it will restore credibility to the profession and help to insure needed funding for services which will become increasingly indispensable.

Having approached this subject the long way round, it is time to address the question of illustrating how the librarian can approach library instruction through the use of the reference query by furnishing examples of how the process works.

Teaching Skills Related to the Use of the Encyclopedia

Imagine the shelves housing the library's general encyclopedia collection. For a good-sized library branch, the sets in the adult reading room might include *Americana, Britannica Colliers* and two sets of the *World Book.* When the after school influx of high schoolers has gone home to supper, it will be noted that the *World*

Book shelves will show the most missing volumes and disarray. The simple, straightforward alphabet on the cover attracts the user, and the richness of graphics and illustrations yield a good report on most topics generally assigned. Other sets with more detailed treatment are used less frequently; inclusive key word lettering on the cover makes uniform sized volumes possible, but deters the less sophisticated user who finds it difficult to pinpoint a subject.

The reference librarian with an attentive ear knows what the students are looking for and is on site to see that all available resources are well-used. Two skills that can be taught are approaching the subject through the index volume and targeting the desired word from the information on the cover. Often this can be done for a group at the reference desk, or simply by talking the process through to an individual as the librarian helps to locate the desired material. In the course of the day many adult learners also can benefit from this kind of help.

Talking aloud to users about the qualities of various encyclopedias is instructional. The *Britannica Micropedia* for ready reference with guidance to related articles in the Macropedia or full set will give the searcher a good overview of the topic. The *World Book* is superior for number and clarity of graphics. *Colliers* dates back to the editorship of the late Louis Shores in its concern for the independent student. *Americana* is highlighting readability and is valuable for coverage of literature and history in the United States. This is not to suggest that the librarian should be chattering constantly to users, but valuable and interesting information can be tactfully and judiciously conveyed. There is no substitute for a well-selected and extensive reference collection which insures that the staff can give some help on most topics. Handing materials to users is far better than merely pointing them out.

Library Instruction on Special Subjects: Health

A survivor need is information on health topics. Several sets of family health encyclopedias with suggestions for home treatment of minor ills should be available as well as standard dictionaries for the definition of medical terms. The *Merck* handbooks give descriptions for patrons able to handle the specialized vocabulary and they include side-effects of various drugs. Some of the consumer-oriented manuals in this area are good additions to the collection. The *Physician's Desk Reference* with latest supplements is essential. Inquirers often need assistance in the kinds of help available, and it is very rewarding to supply a patron with a collection of self-help materials as an aid to further understanding of a health problem.

Two recent examples come to mind. One involved a young man just released from the hospital for treatment of a spontaneous lung collapse, an emergency he had been told might recur. He spent several hours reading and sought out the librarian before leaving to thank her for the special help in knowing how to manage his health situation.

A young woman came in quite distraught. She had just been told at the Air Force recruiting station that blood tests showed an irregularity, a hereditary condition, which would need lifelong medication and disqualify her from consideration by any of the United States military services. This represented an end to a dream of escape from the ghetto which was especially hard to accept, since she had passed entry tests with high marks. She was additionally concerned with the hereditary factor transmitted through the female line. Some time after she was supplied with information on her subject of concern, she returned to say that she felt better able to cope with her problem, since she understood it better and had reflected that her mother and grandmother had lived normal and productive lives in spite of this condition. Even though she could not undertake the severe physical stress of required military training, she felt that there would be other avenues open to her in view of her grades and ability.

Both of these library patrons had learned to use encyclopedias, dictionaries and handbooks in the health field because of their personal motivation and outreach met by the response of a librarian who could answer their needs. These individuals required more than a direction to use the catalog or to search the subject shelves.

ASSISTING THE PATRON TO GATHER MATERIALS ON-SITE AND INTRODUCING NETWORK AND SUPPLEMENTARY SERVICES

In the event that a search for information via the reference collection is not sufficient, the user needs help in gathering relevant subject materials available at the library. Here a collection of call numbers listed from the catalog or various finding lists such as directional posters are helpful. Browsing subject areas will yield what is on hand. Often the subject approach is more fruitful than a specific title, and this can be pointed out and illustrated by bringing materials to the inquirer: clippings, pamphlets and collections of current periodicals. The union catalog for the system will yield the location of indispensable titles and other agencies can be called to locate the desired title. Interagency delivery of books can then be effected, and the use of interlibrary loan forms can be explained to tap network sources. When the librarian is active in such a search with the help of shelvers or pages, it is usually possible to come up with much helpful material that the user might overlook. A reference query that would yield results might begin with a question as broad as ''What is a bibliography?'' Skills taught as the librarian interacts might be:

- What a short printed bibliography looks like.
- What items are included in a citation.
- How to compile items on individual slips using the materials which have been gathered.

While it is true that Turabian or a Harbrace handbook would accomplish the above, much time could be saved if the techniques are indicated by the librarian. Here again, the central premise of this article is that there are client-centered librarians with a human services outlook on the reference floor. Admittedly the procedure described goes beyond traditional expectations. What better service might mean for the future of the profession and the increased use of libraries is an intriguing question, and the time for an answer may be here. Certainly, slashed budgets for staff, materials, hours, services, and maintenance are not heartening at this time.

Arriving at State-of-the-Art: Teaching the Use of Current and Local News Resources

In a neighborhood agency, even of full-service size, the provision of really current information can be a problem. The subscription budget must include a news encyclopedia such as *Facts on File* to provide for this necessity. It is very rewarding to see how users respond to this particular tool when they are instructed in its use. This is an instance when individual recourse to the card catalog would hardly yield the desired information. Some of the librarian's time to point out the looseleaf accumulations for recent years and to show how the index is used to locate a brief factual story is indicated here.

Dates for the insertion of these stories are leads to back issues of news magazines such as *Time, Newsweek,* and *U.S. News and World Report.*

For a wealth of annually updated materials on various regions and countries of the world, *Statesman's Yearbook* is desirable in a collection of any size. It includes names of governmental leaders, figures on the current budget and state of the national economy, as well as an overview of the state of agriculture, health, and education.

Bibliographical helps should be plentiful. The *Afro-American Almanac* has very good coverage of well-known Black Americans in every field, current and historical. *Who's Who in the United States* and *Current Biography* with a library of its back issues are essential. Questions such as: Who is the alderman here? and What are the issues in the current elections? can be answered by getting the whole staff interested in spotting and clipping helpful items from the local press. Let's explode the mystique of the vertical file. What we want are some brown envelopes, a felt-tipped pen to print on subject headings and some file drawers. If we can keep our subject headings consistent with all others, fine, but what is really important is a living, moving, circulating bank of current information. What does this person need? is the only relevant question.

Paperback non-fiction subject packages on current topics supplement the reference section. Special neighborhood interests such as the need for Black Heritage materials or Spanish language collections can be inexpensively enriched in this way, and the materials can be given out for use in the reading room. Logan Square Branch of the Chicago Public Library system has extended the circulation of materials to both patrons and other branches of the system by organizing and keeping updated a tremendous collection of materials. Duplicate copies of magazines are kept and circulated. A file of pertinent resources on topics for term paper research is maintained, and a borrower can call for a packet of materials or can pick it up at the neighborhood branch which requests the materials through system delivery. With the availability of photocopy and bibliographies with abstracts through computer-assisted research as well as the possibility of maintaining complete serials files on film or fiche, the physical copies of the serial or magazine can be used for circulation purposes, rather than keeping them for binding. This may represent a plus both as regards cost and user satisfaction.

One last eclectic example of library instruction through response to a reference query will lead to a re-emphasis of the argument of this article: that the librarian's role is increasingly to be responsive in a way which indeed is a new interpretation of how a qualified professional functions in a public library when that person is assigned to the reference area.

The question: "Do you have any information on how to make a course outline?"

What level do you need to prepare for, elementary, high school or college?" "Junior college."

"Are you familiar with Robert Mager's book on preparing educational objectives? We don't have a copy in, but I could get one for you to pick up here in a couple of days, or you could go to the education department at Central which has a more extensive collection."

"I'm really in a bind. I need something for class tonight for a starter."

"Here is what we have on the shelves. You may find some help in browsing through this collection. In the meantime I'll try to locate something for you."

The librarian returned to the user with a brief outline of a typical college syllabus which she had jotted down and with the citation for Mager which could be used as a bibliographic reference in submitting the assignment.

> Here is an outline which would be a help in your class discussion until you can investigate further, and I have provided the call number for Mager so that you can read more on goals and objectives when you can get downtown. I see that you did find some material on this.

In this instance a patron in a hurry was introduced to the library's subject collection and to the availability of further resources at the central library through interlibrary loan. The librarian herself was an additional resource in this particular case. Was it completely beyond the call of duty to provide the outline? Was it, indeed, unwarranted interference, effrontery and obnoxious didacticism? The user within the context of the situation seemed happy to have the help, and the librarian had that pleasant glow that comes from being able to help. It would not be possible always and in every subject to take the extra step, but why not when one can? Or why not call on a more qualified colleague? Let's hope that there will be more qualified colleagues in libraries to the great benefit of citizen learners, of library schools, of our profession.

The model, then, is:

> The motivated need of the user gives rise to the query which is met by the response of the librarian:
>
> a good overview
> an introduction to the subject collection
> to the use of network services
> and to community resources.

In the process the patron receives needed library instruction and becomes increasingly more independent in the use of the library for pursuing personal learning goals.

SHARING A DREAM

As the phenomenon of independent study and therefore the need for instruction in the use of libraries grows, public libraries could evolve into study centers for a national university or a consortium of universities offering the option of courses taken in the home, viewed from public service TV or pursued within the library. England's Open University is one model utilizing BBC broadcasts, videotape, kits, and compiled sourcebooks mailed to students. In the U.S. there could be a liaison with the private sector utilizing modern technology such as the videodisc, and interactive computer systems for instruction and reference.

Public librarian specialists could serve as adjunct faculty of this university, assisting the learner by selecting, organizing, locating, dispensing, interpreting, supplementing media chosen for instruction. Interaction for reference purposes would be the order of the day in libraries as thousands would pursue higher education in spite of constraints of work and family obligations. College professors could be active in formulating curricula, designing courses, media presentations, and evaluation and grading for credit. Problems of financing could be worked out cooperatively among learners, manufacturers of media, employers, local, state, and federal government.

It is interesting to speculate what this could mean for faltering institutions such as libraries and universities, for full utilization of high tech as applied to education, and for the upward mobility of those individuals who are intellectually capable and motivated to seize upon such alternative opportunity.

ANNOTATED BIBLIOGRAPHY

Fjallbrant, Nancy and Malcolm Stevenson, *User Education in Libraries*. Hamden, Conn., Linnet Books, 1977.

The book is oriented to the academic library, surveying the present state-of-the-art of user education in the United Kingdom, Scandinavia and the U.S.A. It emphasizes the need to define goals and objectives for programs of user education and describes the efficacy of varying teaching methods: the lecture-seminar and tour for group instruction; the audiotape for groups and individual instruction; film, videotape, tape/slide, illustrated audiotape for use in carrels as well as small and large groups; books, printed guides, practical exercises, programmed instruction, self-instruction, tours and signage supplemented by librarian help to the individual. Concludes that methods and media for the library user should involve the student at a point where he/she feels motivation to use the library.

Miller, Roz, "Library Service to Adults," *ALA Yearbook,* 1982. Chicago: American Library Association, 1983, pp. 26-34.

Cited as a trend: certain librarians moving from a passive role to a more active one in the seventies because of the Adult Independent Learners' Movement inaugurated by Orlando Toro. These sought an active interchange in which needs assessments were developed, study programs planned and appropriate referrals made. New technologies are being introduced: videocassettes, microcomputers, COM-Cats, on-line databases, motorized indices, in-house video, cable TV. Budget cuts are widely experienced on federal, state and local levels affecting materials purchase and severe reduction in services. The arrival of diverse groups poses new challenges for libraries. Other trends are fees for non-residents, decrease in binding, use of paperbacks for replacements, reduced backlists, cuts in programming and emphasis on practical programming for those with special needs, promotion of networking and the return of censorship.

Lubans, John Jr., *Educating the Library User.* N.Y., Bowker, 1974.

An edited volume containing a series of practical well-selected articles on the topic, several of which are annotated here:

Edwards, Margaret A., "The Public Library and Young Adults: a Viewpoint," pp. 56-58.

Edwards says that teens see the catalog as the librarian's tool, not theirs. She decries teaching the use of the catalog and other formal library skills and says the time should be spent in introducing the joys of reading, in good book talks and the introduction of good books. Public librarians should help young adults with their assignments with kindness and grace, inspiring them with the love of libraries and books.

Jeffrey, Penelope S., "Library Instruction for Young Adults in Public Libraries," pp. 53-55.

Points out that the usual practice in public libraries is to give individual assistance. Teachers are often unrealistic in their assignments and in their demands on the ordinary library collection. The New York Public Library gives the student a form which states that the student has not been helped, giving the reason. The library makes every effort to educate young people in the help that is available from the people who work in libraries.

Lynch, Mary Jo, "Library Tours: the First Step," pp. 254-268.

The author considers and evaluates the conducted tour, tours in print, tours on cassette, armchair tours utilizing films, TV and slide/tape. She considers the slide/tape format successful and easiest to revise. Lynch researches thoroughly and presents conclusions without preconceptions or hackneyed assumptions.

Murphy, Marcy and Nancy Mildred Nilon, "The Reference Advisory Interview: Its Contribution to Library-User Education," pp. 287-306.

Treats climate, question-negotiation, follow-up. Gives the qualifications of a good interviewer. Reports on survey of library schools showing that only a few require training in interpersonal communication.

Newman, Ruth T., "Instructing the Out-of-School Adult in Public Library Use," pp. 59-68.

Traces shift from individual reader-guidance toward group services. Outlines several effective group instruction approaches.

Stevens, Charles H., and Jeffrey J. Gardner, "Point-of-Use in Library Instruction," pp. 269-278.

Describes A/V devices or instructions at point-of-use for more difficult reference tools. These may be located at the table where the tool is housed and require pushing a button or lifting a phone.

Penland, Patrick R., *The Library as a Learning Service Center.* New York: Marcel Dekker, 1978.

Emphasizes a theme that Penland has pioneered: "the role of the librarian as a learning consultant has to be developed as more than a simple service reaction to expressed demand." (p. IV). From the viewpoint of a professor in a graduate library school, Penland describes the library as a learning environment, the role of the librarian in such an environment and techniques for developing the needed skills to function as an adult educator in a library setting, facilitating "shopping center access to the community helping system."

The Reference Librarian, Spring, 1982, #3.

Several relevant articles from this issue are annotated here:

Cuyler, Alison E., "The Management of Library Reference Services: an Overview of the Literature," pp. 127-147.

There are expanding perceptions of library obligations. On-line data base search services are being incorporated. There is a shift of role perception of the librarian from archivist in residence to information specialist. Reference librarians have a stronger voice in decision making. On the other hand, finance cuts pose a dilemma. Nonprofessional staff are being trained for reference service. Statistics are being gathered and interpreted as a key to the library market. Articles on the subject are most numerous on topics of management, administration, training of non-professionals, incorporating on-line services, and evaluation of reference services.

King, Geraldine B., "Try It, You'll Like It: A Comprehensive Management Information System for Reference Service," pp. 71-78.

Describes a reference transaction slip for gathering output data. 4×6 inch slip gives date, time, name of librarian, category of questioner, the question and its disposition. If it is a telephone request, this is indicated. Provides workload information, differentiates document and subject requests, provides numbers of telephone vs in-person requests, individual performance record, available resources, data for networking and collection building.

Voight, Kathleen, "Selective Guidelines for a Beginning Manager of an Academic Library Reference Department." pp. 39-45.

Guidelines suggested: 1) Read a text on management theory and practice 2) Fit the reference department into the organization chart of the university library 3) Develop a job description for each member of the department 4) consult or develop a reference philosophy, mission statement, goals and objectives for the department 5) Consult or develop a policies manual, staff manuals, standards or philosophies for your department 6) Read a text on human development and interpersonal communications 7) Market your services 8) Develop an evaluation form for your staff.

Wade, Gordon S. "Managing Reference Services in the Smaller Public Library," pp. 107-112.

Focuses on training non-professional staff to answer questions through role-playing, question review, group solution.

Reilly, Jane A., *The Public Librarian as Adult Learners' Advisor, An Innovation in Human Services.* Westport, Conn.: Greenwood Press, 1981.

Describes the role of the librarian as a learners' advisor; factors promoting the development of this role; opportunities to practice it; services performed; necessary background and skills; choices to be made in the process of graduate library education to prepare for this function and needed support from administration in public library systems. Developments in learning technology such as the computer and the videodisc are emphasized and the desirability of national standardization of opportunity for the independent learner in public library study centers is suggested.

Library Use Instruction
in the Small and Medium Public Library:
A Review of the Literature

Jerry Carbone

INTRODUCTION

To begin: the title to this article is somewhat of a misnomer—the literature regarding library instruction in the small and medium public library is apparently non-existent. These libraries, because of their size, limited staff, and, sometimes, geographical remoteness, do not write about experiences in library instruction programs.

According to the latest survey of the habits and attitudes of forty-nine small libraries in rural Pennsylvania, over seventy percent have a commitment to instruction in library use; over ninety percent give instruction to school classes; and ninety percent conduct library tours.[1]

Being cut-off from that literature which might aid small public libraries to improve their library instruction programs is a serious problem in our profession.

In this "literature review" an attempt will be made to identify the nature of the problems affecting library instruction in the smaller public library, and report on the writings—in the opinion of the author—which may be most helpful to those libraries that have no formal library instruction programs.

TRENDS

The recent Pennsylvania survey of small public libraries showed a definite commitment to library use instruction. For comparison sake, a survey of Indiana public libraries in 1970, the Olsen study, provides a startling contrast in statistics: the Olson study showed only ten percent of the small public libraries in Indiana promoting ex-

---

Jerry Carbone is Reference Librarian, Brooks Memorial Library, Brattleboro, VT.

149

tensive instructional service; about fifty percent of small public libraries not providing any general instruction; and a large amount (nearly seventy-five percent) of the libraries surveyed not providing any instruction.[2]

Allowing for differences in the survey questions and the size of the sample between the two surveys, the surprising statistic is that between 1970 and 1980 small public libraries have discovered that some form of library instruction is an important component of library service.

DEFINITION OF THE PROBLEM

The dearth of writings on library instruction in the small and medium public library has forced many librarians to adapt the experiences of large public or academic libraries to their much different situations.

Some statistics to consider: the *Digest of Educational Statistics* reports that eighty-two percent of the public libraries in the United States serve populations under 25,000. Populations of 10,000 or below are served by sixty-six percent of all public libraries.[3]

Now consider the growth of library use literature relating to all libraries and public libraries in particular. Using Hannelore Rader's annual review of this literature from 1973 to 1981 as an index, a total increase of 989.6 percent of entries was reported on all types of libraries.[4] The only significant numbers for public libraries began in 1979 with five citations of the total: 1980 and 1981 saw the percentage increase dramatically—eighty and sixty-seven percent respectively.

Another numerical gauge of the literature is the recent book by Deborah Lockwood, *Library Instruction; A Bibliography.* Of the 934 items annotated only nineteen entries are included in "Public Library and Adult Education" category. (The scope included only published works, or those available through ERIC, in English, since 1970. The list is very selective for those works published before 1970.)[6]

THE LITERATURE

The main tools for bibliographical control of the information were the Lockwood, *Library Instruction; A Bibliography,* and the Rader, "Library Orientation and Instruction [date]; An Annotated

Review of the Literature''—an annual bibliography in *Reference Services Review* since 1973.[8]

The literature reviewed for this essay was limited to the published articles and books on library use instruction programs in public libraries. Because of the lack of published writings for small and medium public libraries, special consideration was given to those articles that have adaptability to the smaller public library situation. Reports on methods, technique, audio-visual applications, self-paced manuals, etc were omitted from this review. The reader is referred to the exhaustive Lockwood bibliography and the Rader annual review for these citations.

PHILOSOPHY OF LIBRARY INSTRUCTION

The *raison d'état* of library instruction may be best quoted by a British librarian, Anne Irving, who states:

It is the recognition, development and dissemination (or teaching!) of these abilities [strategies for reading, library skills] that is our strongest contribution for life-long learning and an educative society.[9]

In 1968 Kathleen Molz reported her findings of a survey sent to over 700 libraries regarding the out-of-school adult and library instruction. She concluded that public library use instruction should go beyond mere orientation to assessing the patron's need for information and establishing a relationship between librarian and patron to reduce the frustration and intimidation people feel when they enter the library.[10]

In an essay written in 1980 entitled, ''Reference Service as Teaching Function,'' Hannelore Rader elucidates the breaking down of barriers to library use as stated by Molz twelve years earlier.[11]

Discussing the approach to reference service along the ''conservative/minimum to liberal/maximum'' lines, Ms. Rader examines the dilemma of ''reference librarian as teacher'' versus ''reference librarian as information provider'' schools and their implications for library use instruction.[12]

Breaking down the barriers and frustrations to library use is a main component of library instruction, but other justifications are just as valid for implementing library instruction programs in public libraries.

Hannelore Rader's article, "Bibliographic Instruction," gives several goals which reference staff should follow in approaching library instruction programs.[13] Although these goals are written in the context of academic libraries, they are, nonetheless, appropriate for public library settings. These goals for reference staff are as follows:

1. Instruct users in the effective identification of information resources;
2. Help users to be life-long learners;
3. Teach community groups the appropriate use of library resources;
4. Cooperate with community social agencies to facilitate the fullest use of library resources.[14]

The end result, according to Ms. Rader, is for people to be functional and productive in a democrative society by nurturing life-long information gathering skills.

The life-long learner's concept no longer the province of formal academic degree programs is now firmly in place in most communities to keep pace with this increasingly complex world. In 1980 the American Library Association adopted a policy statement in support of user education. Entitled, *Policy Statement: Instruction in the Use of Libraries,*[15] the organization recognized that individuals in society, "have an inadequate understanding of how to determine the information needed, locate the appropriate information, and use it to their best advantage."[16] The statement concludes, "It is essential that libraries of all types accept responsibility of providing people with opportunities to understand the organization of information."[17] The A.L.A. supports the idea of life-long learning; the means by which it may be encouraged throughout society is to include instruction in the use of public libraries—large and small—as a main goal of service.[18]

LIBRARY INSTRUCTION: THE PROGRAMS

Library instruction programs over the past ten years have been aimed at out-of-school adults; independent learners—such as, ABE students; and groups in the community with special information needs—secretaries, business people and students.

As early pioneer of the literature in public library use instruction, the Denver Public Library, incorporated both orientation and in-depth instruction in a very successful program. According to Ruth Newman in an essay, "Instructing the Out-Of-School Adult in Public Library Use," the Denver program began in 1968 with a four part, two hour workshop combining public relations and user instruction. The Library Director, Technical Services Director, and a representative from the reference staff, planned the sessions and published a twenty-five page booklet on the library. The first session began with a lecture on books, printing, book-buying policies, and information on general library services. The second session was devoted to an explanation of the basics of the card catalog. The third session was represented by the reference staff, who covered various helpful reference sources. The fourth and last session involved participants in a guided tour of the library, concentrating on areas normally removed from public exposure.[19]

A wonderful and elaborate program for a large public library, but somewhat, at least in financial and personnel resources, out of reach for the smaller public library. Yet, the ideas employed are worthy of examination; they include: use of personnel other than the reference staff in library education functions; the combination of public relations and library use instruction; and the publication of an in-house user guide to explain library functions and services.

Expanding on the theme of instruction to the out-of-school adult, Christopher Compton—a former college reference librarian—adapted an academic program of instruction in library use for freshman to an informal "free university" course for out-of-school adults. The program entitled, "How to Find Out about Anything; A Library Skills Course," attracted individuals from all walks of life and background.[20]

Mr. Compton's different approach was to expose the class to the various ways information is organized and accessed in the many special libraries in the Denver area. The tours were conducted by staff members of the libraries, and, after the tour, participants had the opportunity to work through prepared lessons on the reference sources found in the collections.[21]

Cooperation with libraries outside the public library boundary and in-depth instruction in various information sources insured the success of this altered academic library use instruction program. As a model, Mr. Compton's experience might prove successful in small public libraries by expanding the scope of their reference collection and the knowledge for their users.

The value of cooperation between academic and public libraries in presenting library use instruction is reported effectively by Margaret Hendley of the Kitchener Public Library. Ms. Hendley organized "Research Skills Workshops" in her library to meet the need for library skills training by patrons enrolled in college classes offered at the library.[22]

Although the program was geared toward the continuing education student, the "Research Skills Workshops" drew a majority of people not involved in any structured education program.

The workshop sessions ran for two hours, twice a year. Each began with an explanation of the card catalog, followed by a detailed discussion of reference indexes. Ms. Hendley reported that user guides were prepared on basic Dewey schedules, periodical indexes, and book reviews. These guides were subsequently given to the reference staff for daily use in the library.[23]

Continuing education courses and public library use instruction apparently go hand-in-hand as was seen in the Kitchener Public Library experience. Another example of this marriage is at West Hartford (Connecticut) Public Library, where a library use instruction program was sponsored by and publicized through the West Hartford Continuing Education Program.[24]

Designed to meet the needs of out-of-school adults, the course began with a series of six workshops conducted twice a day (morning and evening), oriented around discussion and demonstration of various types of reference works.

An instructional workbook was developed that contained annotated bibliographies and question/answer worksheets. Core sessions revolved around the use of the card catalog and periodical indexes.

Due to several changes made in the schedule—elimination of the morning session—and focus—emphasis on popular reference titles rather than academic titles—satisfaction with the workshop was very high.[25]

The West Hartford experience—although not in a small public library—is important to all libraries in its concentration on *planning* and *reevaluating* library use programs.

THE ATTIC DOOR OPENED . . .

Port Washington Public Library serves a population of over 30,000 with approximately 120,000 volumes: a smaller, medium public library by today's standards. An article appeared in the Fall

1979 *Bookmark,* entitled, "Opening the Attic Door: Bibliographic (and Other) Instruction at the Port Washington Public Library." Written by Sheldon Tarakan, Head of Information Services at Port Washington, the article pointed to several successful and well-developed bibliographic instruction programs that, in their variety and scope, are befitting of a much larger public or academic library.

As reported by Mr. Tarakan, library instruction and orientation is a significant part of the library's program of service. Professional staff are available on a daily basis for individual orientation tours and one-to-one instruction. In addition to the normal reference service, a one-to-one and one-half hour "mini-course" is conducted twice per month. Requiring no advance registration and emphasizing informality, the overall goals of the mini-course is to break down barriers to library use by presenting the library in understandable, layman terms. The major ingredients at each of the sessions are *orientation, instruction,* and *application*—the three elements which guarantee the course's success. Participants are asked for their own topic of interest, and each is given ways of finding the information of his or her choice.[26]

Instruction in the use of the library goes beyond the mini-course; a model program which in itself may be sufficient for library users interested in the operation of video are trained on the library's own equipment. As a result of this training, the library owns a collection of locally produced tapes on community programs.[27]

Another instruction service includes library orientation and skills training for parents to better help them take part in their children's education. Of course, library instruction occurs continuously throughout the year for children with class visits and story hours.[28]

A major component of Port Washington's library instruction program is an ambitious series of workshops on research paper writing. Similar in concept to the Kitchener experience, this program consists of research skills training and term paper writing over the span of three sessions, lasting three hours apiece. Each session is divided into 1½ hours of research training—in depth reference work—and 1½ hours of writing skills.[29]

An important part of this program is the necessary cooperation which must take place between a library staff member, who is responsible for the research skills segment of the workshop, and the neighboring university staff member, who teaches writing skills in the session.

The variety and scope of the Port Washington program is staggering. Its valuable and successful programs in library use instruction go quite substantially beyond the "mere orientation" of such programs warned by Kathleen Molz over ten years earlier.

More tales like these must be written; for certainly they do exist.

CONCLUSION

Although the author was unable to find any published literature on the small public library and library use programs, and only several articles relating to medium public libraries, the trend toward more articles on library use instruction in large public libraries should continue.

The chances that reporting by small and medium public libraries on their experiences will grow also. We have seen the indications already in place: (1) the number of library use programs in public libraries are rising each year, as reflected in the annual bibliography by Rader; (2) and the Pennsylvania survey of small public libraries definitely shows a commitment to library instruction programs.

Small and medium public libraries serve the greater share of this nation's public library users. Those libraries that do not have library instruction programs in place can learn from the literature written on the larger public library.

As it has been reported to date and summarized here, the writings on library use instruction must have good publicity and planning; if necessary, a willingness to adapt an attractive program to specific local needs; and a realization—especially in the smaller public library—that cooperation with other libraries and social agencies can insure the success of a program.

The literature expresses the justification for library use instruction in public libraries: to encourage the life-long learning concept by preparing users to find the information for themselves and be intelligent consumers of it.

Smaller public libraries can add their own voice to the writings of successful library use instruction programs, and—in the end—all libraries will benefit.

REFERENCES

1. Bernard Vavrak, "A Struggle for Survival: Reference Services in the Small Public Library," *Library Journal* 108 (May 15, 1983): 969.

2. Edwin A. Olson, "Survey of User Policies in indiana Libraries and Information

Centers," Indiana Studies Report No. 10, Peter Hiatt, gen. ed. (Bloomington: The Center, 1970), quoted in Penelope S. Jeffrey, "Library Instruction for Young Adults in Public Libraries," p. 60, in *Educating the Library User,* ed. John Lubans, Jr. (New York, London: R.R. Bowker, 1974).

3. W. Vance Grant and C. George Lind, *Digest of Education Statistics,* 1979, quoted in Vavrak, "A Struggle," p. 966.

4. Hannelore Rader, "Library Orientation and Instruction—(date); An Annotated Review of the Literature," *Reference Services Review,* 2 (Jan.—Mar 1974): 91-93; *Reference Services Review,* 3 (Jan.-Mar. 1975): 29-30; *Reference Services Review,* 4 (Oct.-Dec. 1976): 91-93; *Reference Services Review* 5 (Jan.-Mar. 1977):41-44; *Reference Services Review* 6(Jan.-Mar. 1978):45-51 *Reference Services Review* 7 (Jan.-Mar. 1979): 45-56; *Reference Services Review* 8 (Jan.-Mar. 1980): 31-46; *Reference Services Review* 9 (Apr.-Jun 1981):79-89; *Reference Services Review* 10 (Summer 1982): 33-44.

5. Deborah L. Lockwood, comp., *Library Instruction; A Bibliography* (Westport, CT.: Greenwood Pr, 1979), pp1-166.

6. Ibid.

7. Ian Malley, "National Clearinghouse for User Education," *Libri* 32(Mar 1982): 55-56.

8. Lockwood, *Library Instruction;* and Rader, "Library Orientation and Instruction—(date)," *Reference Services Review.*

9. Anne Irving, "New Directions for Libraries," *Library Association Record* 81(Apr. 1979): 179.

10. Kathleen Molz, "The State of the Art of Public Library Orientation," *Maryland Libraries* 34 (Winter 1968): 15.

11. Hannelore B. Rader, "Reference Service as a Teaching Function," *Library Trends* 29(Summer 1980):95-103.

12. Ibid.

13. Hannelore B. Rader, "Bibliographic Instruction," *Reference Services Review* 10 (Spring 1982): 65-66.

14. Ibid, p66.

15. American Library Association, "Policy Statement: Instruction in the Use of Libraries," Council Document No. 45, American Library Association Annual Meeting, New York, 1980, quoted in, Ibid., p65.

16. Rader, "Bibliographic," p. 66.

17. Ibid.

18. Ibid.

19. Ruth Newman, "Instructing the Out-of-School Adult in Public Library Use," in Lubans, *Educating,* p63-67.

20. Christopher Compton, "Innovation in Library Instruction Applied to an Adult Education Course," in *Progress in Educating the Library User,* ed. John J. Lubans, Jr., (New York, London: R R Bowker, 1978), pp 135-7.

21. Ibid.

22. Margaret Hendley, "The Librarian as Teacher," *Ontario Library Review* 63(Mar 1979): 45-8.

23. Ibid.

24. Amy S. Frey and Saul Spigel, "Educating Adult Users in the Public Library, *Library Journal* 104 (April 15, 1979): 894-6.

25. Ibid.

26. Sheldon L. Tarakan, "Opening the Attic Door: Bibliographic (and Other) Instruction at Port Washington Public Library," *Bookmark* 38 (Fall 1979):249-52.

27. Ibid., p250.

28. Ibid., p251.

29. Ibid., p252.

INSTRUCTION IN
ACADEMIC LIBRARIES

The Administrative Climate for Bibliographic Instruction in Large Academic Libraries

Ron Blazek

"The time is when a library is a school and the librarian is in the highest sense a teacher, and the visitor is a reader among the books as a workman among his tools." *Melville Dewey, 1876*[1]

INTRODUCTION

Through the years, the issue of library instruction in academic libraries has sustained interest for both readers and writers of the library art as witnessed by the steady flow of articles and letters printed in library journals. Recently it has become a matter of compelling interest if we are to use references from *Library Literature* as a gauge. Although Farber and Kirk may have exaggerated somewhat the total number of such publications, they quite correctly describe a "resurgence of interest" in the topic during the 1960s.[2] Rader has consistently documented an increased quantity of publications with each succeeding year since 1974 with the exception of 1980,[3] while Cravey describes the development of what she considers to be a "hot topic."[4]

The investigator found an average of seven titles per year reported by *Library Literature* during the mid-1930s, four per year during the decade of the 1940s, nine per year during the 1950s, to over 16 per year during the 1960s, and 32 per year during the 1970s. The 1980–82 period has produced an increased interest with

Professor Blazek is with the School of Library and Information Studies, Florida State University, Tallahassee, FL 32306.

161

an average of over 42 per year. Contributing to this spiral has been the addition of columns and departments in various periodicals such as "Library Literacy" appearing in *R. Q.* and "Library Instruction: A Column of Opinion" in *Journal of Academic Librarianship.* Finally, the year 1983 saw the birth of a journal, *Research Strategies,* which provides a strong focus for the activity.

The resurgence in the form of increased writing has been evident at the doctoral research level as well. Whereas, Schlachter and Thomison were able to report only five dissertations under the category of "Library Orientation Programs" (only three of which dealt with academic libraries) for the entire period of 1925–1972; they cited 16 works on academic library instruction for the period of 1973–1982, and another one which treated the topic in a peripheral manner.[5]

This heightened interest in the form of research and publication of course reflects its place in the profession as an issue of importance and not a little controversy. The concept of the instructional role and responsibility of reference librarians has been argued and debated for many years. As numerous as the proponents have been in the past, they have had most worthy opposition such as that offered by Schiller who, in convincing terms, denounced the instructional role as being in conflict with information provision responsibilities of reference people.[6] More recently, Sayles spoke for many librarians of all generations in reporting his discomfort with the practice of bibliographic instruction due to its natural dichotomy with his role to provide information service in line with patrons' needs.[7]

The profession, itself, appears to have moved ahead in both directions promulgating the ascendency of information provision on the one hand, yet laying firmer and broader foundations for its role in library education on the other. Tucker has provided a good history of the movement in academic library user education and traces its development from the 19th century as part of the academic revolution along with the elective system, through the period of the surveys of the 1920s in which a sizable number of libraries reported instruction to some extent, to the broad-based involvement of the present.[8]

It has been the impetus of the almost frenetic activity of the past decade, however, which has further spurred and paralleled the increased publication rate. Creation of the ACRL Bibliographic Instruction Task Force was a giant step forward in 1971, followed by the development of the national clearinghouse (LOEX) in 1972. The year 1977 was of signal importance with the Task Force's publication of the "Guidelines for Bibliographic Instruction in Academic Libraries" and the emergence of both the ALA Library Instruction Roundtable and the ACRL Bibliographic Instruction Section. This activity at the national level has been equalled by similar progress at the state and regional levels.[9]

Throughout all this publishing and organizing, one of the major concerns is that which relates to the management and support of bibliographic instruction. Murphy, in her 1979 dissertation, identified library instruction programs along with interlibrary loan and special collections as the three areas least understood by academic faculty and students.[10] Meyer embraced "Marketing and Management" as the last of three phases of bibliographic instruction, one which involved "selling programs to library administrators and college administrators."[11] Gwinn, in describing the increased interest of the Council of Library Resources in the integration of the library into the teaching and learning process, viewed lack of support or indifference on the part of both library and university administrators as a major problem.[12]

It is obvious that like any other organizational policy, bibliographic instruction will depend on the support of those in authority. To reinforce this point, one may consider the report of the ACRL Bibliographic Instruction Section Research Committee which published its agenda for research in 1980. The three areas identified as needing research were needs assessment, design and implementation of programs, and management aspects.[13] A study of perceptions of various managerial groups associated with the activity is meaningful in ascertaining the type of existing supportive structure and predicting future progress.

Statement of the Problem

It was the purpose of this study to examine the administrative climate or disposition toward the provision of bibliographic instruction in large academic libraries by comparing the attitudes of top level library managers with those of middle managers. Each of these categories differ, of course, in the proximity or degree of direct contact, responsibility, and authority for the activity. It is obvious that much of the debate over the value of bibliographic instruction is rooted in philosophical concerns for impact on other parts of the library program, and decisions are made generally by those holding a more global view. Thus, it is of utmost importance to determine the feelings of top level library administrators who are knowledgeable of the numerous demands and constraints placed upon them in reaching organizational goals. If Library Directors and Assistant Directors have positive attitudes, there is a potential for active support in future allocations of money and personnel, and a good possibility that a strong case be made with university administrators for increased funding.

Similarly, it is important to determine the attitudes of those more closely associated with the day-to-day practice. If Reference Heads and Instruction Coordinators are not enthusiastic about what they manage, then the chances of initiative being shown from top level administrators is lessened considerably. A further point of inquiry lies with these middle managers' perceptions of the attitudes of top-level administrators since they may well influence their own expectations. In short, attitudes were selected for their importance not only as proxies or indicators of present administrative encouragement, but as predictors of future support as well.

Hypotheses and Research Question

Because we were examining the conduct of a professional task, support, encouragement, and depth of feeling on the part of managers was seen to be linked to the degree of direct involvement with that task. It is logical to expect that those most closely associated with its management on a day-to-day basis would have the most supportive attitude in judging its value. Thus Instruction Coordinators were seen to be the group closest to the action and Library Directors the group most removed. Making use of this concept of vested interest thus provides us with the basic general hypothesis: *Supportive attitude toward bibliographic instruction is a function of its direct proximity to managerial responsibility.*

From this were derived three specific research hypotheses:

1. Bibliographic instruction managers are more supportive of the activity than are top-level library administrators.
2. Of the two types of bibliographic instruction managers in this study, Instruction Coordinators are more supportive of the activity than are Reference Heads.
3. Of the three types of top-level library administrators in this study, Directors of Public Services are more supportive of the

activity than are Library Directors and Associate Library Directors.

The final phase of the study dealt with the perceptions of middle managers regarding attitudes held by both their superiors and colleagues. Since there was no justification for predicting a direction for this phenomenon, nor any real reason to conjecture, a research question rather than a hypothesis was posed: *What are the perceptions of middle managers with respect to the attitudes held by both superiors and peers toward bibliographic instruction?*

Definitions

- *B.I. Managers.* For purposes of this study, the grouping of middle managers most closely and directly associated with the conduct of bibliographic instruction. These were, in order of proximity, Instruction Coordinators and Reference Heads. Subject specialists with instructional responsibility were considered part of the former group.
- *Top-level Administrators.* The grouping of managers less closely involved with the direct conduct of bibliographic instruction but more heavily involved with the overall management of the library organization. These were Library Public Services Directors, Associate/Assistant Library Directors, and Library Directors in order of proximity to the instructional program.
- *Support for Bibliographic Instruction.* For purposes of this study, the score obtained on the measurement scale indicates an existing attitude identifying a degree of support and encouragement. Highly supportive attitudes are represented by a mean score of 4.5 and above, moderately supportive attitudes, 4.0–4.4, while an attitude of low or nominal support is registered by mean scores of 3.9 or less on a five point scale.

Assumption

The basic assumption for the study is that attitudes are meaningful indicators of likely future activity and are treated here as "dispositions toward overt action."[13] Supportive attitudes on the part of decision makers, therefore, establish a favorable climate for future progress in bibliographic instruction.

Limitation

The study is limited to the examination of attitudes of certain management groups in only the very large academic libraries. Findings cannot be generalized to other types of libraries nor to smaller academic libraries. Library Technical Services Directors (who, of course, also wield influence in decision making) are excluded here, therefore, the phenomenon of administrative attitude with respect to decision-making which affects support levels may not be complete. It is felt, however, that knowledge of the attitudes of those embraced in this study will provide a greater understanding of the administrative climate as it relates to bibliographic instruction.

REVIEW OF THE LITERATURE

Doctoral Dissertations

Doctoral research in this area has been increasing of late as pointed out previously. The majority of these studies, however, have examined the effects of different instructors or teaching modes or techniques on the learning of skills. Results have been mixed at best and not indicative of any potential panaceas, although the various modes and techniques of instruction appear to have some merit. Of the studies which explore such instructional facets, Brevik (1974) provided the conceptual framework of greatest magnitude by attempting to show library-based instruction as a possible factor in the academic success of disadvantaged college freshmen. She found that the group instructed on a weekly basis did, indeed, show more improvement in homework than did either a control group which received no instruction, or another group which received the traditional tour and lectures on the card catalog and indexes.[15]

Two dissertations examined existing practices in the field, although these were separated by a time lag of 17 years. Breen (1954) surveyed over 200 colleges of teacher education and found that library instruction programs in most instances are lodged within either an orientation course or freshman English class. The library was responsible for instruction in 136 of 242 cases responding.[16] Wilkinson chose the case study approach in 1971, to identify and evaluate reference services for the undergraduate in four institutions: Michigan, Cornell, Swarthmore and Earlham. He found that of the four, Earlham had developed an extensive program of library instruction.[17]

Three recent studies were judged to be most relevant to this investigation since they dealt more closely with administrative aspects. Yee (1979) examined the status of instructional programs in Michigan community colleges through a survey of 34 institutions. Some type of instruction was offered by 70% of the respondents, although administrative support was not being given in a majority of the colleges responding. Lack of adequate time, staff, and budget were still perceived to be the hindrances to more formal library programs.[18]

Also in 1979 Benson investigated successful course-related library instructional programs in academic libraries to determine how they functioned with respect to certain administrative and organizational factors. The successful programs reached a substantial portion of the undergraduate student body and normally began at the freshman level. Smith (1981) examined the training, education, and experience levels of librarians engaged in bibliographic instruction. She found that most acquired their skills through education beyond their professional degree with the majority having specialized in reference during their MS program. They appeared to be interested and active in the profession.[20]

Journal Articles, Reports, Guidelines

The landmark 1977 Guidelines from the ACRL Bibliographic Instruction Task Force provided a strong focus on administrative aspects. Planning and evaluation were seen as integral to the success of the program and the recommendations covered needs assessments, community profiles, statement of objectives, financial support, facility, involvement of the academic community, and evaluation.[21] O'Donnell (1981) urged that all professional staff should participate in policy development in order to strike the necessary balance between bibliographic instruction and adequate reference service;[22] while Kirk saw closer cooperation and communication between library administrators and instructional librarians as the means to improve user education.[23]

A number of surveys have been reported in the past 15 years which attempted to report on and clarify the administrative condition. Phipps (1968) in a survey of 157 small colleges found among other things that there was little cooperation between the library and the college administration or between librarians and faculty in the question of library instruction.[24] Dyson (1975) examined the organization of library instruction in 10 American and 12 British libraries and concluded that the "overriding factor" determining success of an instructional program was the degree to which the library administration was committed to it.[25]

Miller (1978) examined instruction in 13 colleges and reported that bibliographic instruction required an allocation of more personnel, and the necessity of cultivating the support of faculty to retain financial support.[26] In a 1979 survey of New England academic libraries it was found that more than 1/3 of the professional staff participated in the activity.[27]

Obviously, the selections above represent only the tip of an iceberg in which both opinions and facts are freely given and generally are granted audience by the profession. To be sure, the administrative and managerial component has been recognized as an indispensible ingredient in the composition of an effective program. Thus, it is necessary to determine with some precision the attitudes represented in this all-important segment.

METHODOLOGY

Design

The survey method was chosen to elicit data from a randomly selected nation-wide sample. The purpose of this study was to compare attitudes toward bibliographic instruction as represented in the responses of both middle managers and top-level administrators to a measurement scale of 10 value statements. It was hypothesized that those managers serving in capacities which required more direct contact with the activity would tend to be more favorable and possess a more supportive attitude than those further removed from it.

The hypotheses are restated in the null form for purposes of testing:

1. There is no difference between bibliographic instruction managers and top-level administrators in their attitude toward the activity.
2. There is no difference between the two types of bibliographic instruction managers (Instruction Coordinators and Reference Heads) in their attitude toward the activity.

3. There is no difference between the three types of top-level library administrators (Directors, Associate Directors, and Public Services Directors) in their attitude toward the activity.

Another factor, that of attitudes perceived by bibliographic instruction managers to be held by fellow department heads and superiors, was also examined through the posing of a research question since there was no reason to hypothesize the condition.

Population and Sample

The population for the study represented managerial groups in large academic libraries of the U.S. and Canada since a systematic random sample of 51 of the 101 academic members of the Association of Research Libraries was drawn.

Using American Library Directory,[28] one top-level administrator was identified for each library with respect to the following priorities:

1. Assistant or Associate Library Director
2. Library Public Services Director, if there was no Associate Director
3. Library Director, if neither an Associate Director nor Public Services Director was present in the organizational structure.

It was felt that the Associate Director represented an ideal study participant, an influential voice in policy making with a global view, who was not called upon to participate in such investigations as often as was the Library Director. The Public Services Director was seen as a suitable respondent if there were no listings for a second-in-command. Although part of top-level administration and highly influential, the position was viewed, however, as one which is less global and more disposed to favor a public service activity. Finally, the Director, who of course has ultimate authority as well as the greatest breadth of responsibility was, in truth, the best representative of top-level administration. To assure a good return, however, it was considered prudent to include this individual only when necessary.

The response rate from top-level administrators was surprising in that it was exceedingly high; 20 of 23 Assistant/Associate Directors (87% return); 19 of 21 Public Service Directors (90% return), and 6 of 7 Directors (86% return). The total return of 45 of 51 represented a rate of 88% from a group for which the investigator was at first apprehensive. This is an indication either of real interest on their part or (at worst) an acknowledgement of the ease of filling out the brief measurement scale.

From each of the libraries a middle manager was also selected in the following order:

1. Bibliographic Instruction Coordinator
2. Head of Reference, if no Instruction Coordinator was present
3. "blind" letters sent in cases where neither title was listed.

The original mailing was sent to 29 Coordinators, 14 Reference Heads, and 8 blind "To-Whom-It-May-Concern" type addresses. Returns from these groups to a lengthier instrument were respectable but not so high as those from the top-level administrators: 22 of 29 Instruction Coordinators (76%); 9 of 14 Reference Heads (64%); 3 of 8 blind letters (38%). One of the latter group was added to the Instruction Coordinator segment and two became part of the Reference Head category. Two subject specialists with instructional responsibilities were considered part of the Coordinator group. Responding to the measurement scale then were 23 Coordinators and 11 Reference Heads for a 67% usable return. In addition there was a partially answered questionnaire and two polite refusals to participate.

Data Collection and Instrumentation

Based on a literature review, a questionnaire was prepared for bibliographic instruction managers which revealed much factual information on the practice as conducted in their libraries; also included was a Likert scale of five points ranging from Strongly Agree to Strongly Disagree to value judgments presented in 10 statements. This scale was also sent to top-level administration and was precoded to represent an attitude supportive of the activity. Bibliographic instruction managers were asked, in addition, to predict the attitudes of both peers (department heads) and superiors by responding to three more statements not found on the scale sent to top-level administrators.

The questionnaire and scale were pretested on reference librarians at the Florida State University and Florida Agricultural and

Mechanical University in March 1981, further refined, then mailed to the sample group along with a cover letter.

Treatment of the Data

The basis for comparison and analysis between groups were the mean scores on the 10-statement form. These were computed both individually for each statement and in a summated fashion for all 10 responses; the higher the score on the scale, the more positive and supportive the attitude. Chi square analysis was utilized as the statistical technique to determine the differences which existed between groups, and the .10 level of significance was employed.

ANALYSIS OF DATA

Table 1 provides an overview of mean scores received by individual members of each of the managerial groups, and it is clear that the anticipated differences do not appear to exist. Although

TABLE 1

Mean Scores of Individuals Within Different Managerial Groups on 5-point Scale of Supportive Attitude.

Instruction Coordinators		Reference Heads		Public Service Directors		Assoc. Library Directors		Library Directors	
$\overline{X}$	Freq.	$\overline{X}$	Freq.	$\overline{X}$	Freq.	$\overline{X}$	Freq.	$\overline{X}$	Freq.
4.9	2	4.7	3	4.6	2	5.0	2	4.8	1
4.8	1	4.6	1	4.5	1	4.8	2	4.5	1
4.7	2	4.3	3	4.4	2	4.6	1	4.4	1
4.6	2	4.1	1	4.3	2	4.5	3	4.2	1
4.5	2	4.0	2	4.2	4	4.3	1	4.1	1
4.4	2	3.2	1	4.1	1	4.2	1	4.0	1
4.3	3			4.0	2	4.1	2		
4.2	2			3.9	2	4.0	3		
4.1	2			3.8	1	3.9	3		
4.0	2			3.6	1	3.6	1		
3.9	1			3.5	1	3.0	1		
3.8	1								
3.7	1								

Totals

$\overline{X}$ = 4.34 (23)   4.26 (11)   4.14 (19)   4.24 (20)   4.33 (6)

Grand Totals

$\overline{X}$ = 4.26 (79)

ranges for the groups vary considerably (both the lowest and highest individual scores for the study were found in the Associate Director segment) the mean scores for each group were remarkably similar as well as remarkably high. The highest group score of 4.34 belongs to the Instruction Coordinator segment as predicted, but this is only .08 above the total mean and only .20 above the lowest group score (Public Service Directors). Surprisingly, the Library Directors score next highest, only .01 below the Instruction Coordinators. In short, there appears to be little support for the general hypothesis predicting differences based on proximity to the activity. Instead, all groups were judged to be supportive.

Table 2 displays the responses to individual statements on the measurement scale. Greatest support was evident with respect to Statement 1 which enumerated the beneficial effects on rapport and public relations with other parts of the university. This was especially true of the Director's responses for which they all strongly agreed, but each of the other top-level administrator groups scored higher on this point than did either of the middle-managers. Even in the latter groups, however, it was this statement which earned the highest rating.

Least total support was garnered for statement 8 which established bibliographic instruction as a top priority regardless of the impact on other activities, although it should be noted that Directors were less reluctant in this regard than were any other managers. Most surprising was the fact that only Public Services Directors showed some agreement with statement 10 which indicated the need for some caution in weighing the emphasis given to bibliographic instruction as opposed to information provision. The dichotomy does not appear to exist in the minds of Directors and their Associates. Again, it shall be noted that all differences herein described are slight since the totals for each group averaged near the 4-point mark on the 5-point scale.

Table 3 focuses on the responses to individual statements as registered by the combined categories of bibliographic instruction managers with a mean total of 4.32 on the 5 point scale as opposed to that of the top-level administrators with a total mean of 4.21. The difference of .11 between these categories does not appear to be of practical significance since both groups are judged to have supportive attitudes of similar dimension.

Table 4 presents a test of hypothesis one, however, to determine if statistical significance does exist. With the failure to achieve the

TABLE 2

Supportive Attitude of Managerial Groups as Determined
by Mean Response to Each Statement on Scale

	Instruction Coord.(22)	Ref. Head(11)	Pub. Service Director(19)	Assoc. Lib. Director(19)	Library Director(6)	Totals
*Statements 1	4.61	4.45	4.63	4.65	5.00	4.63
2	4.57	4.09	4.42	4.10	4.67	4.35
3	4.43	4.73	4.26	4.10	4.17	4.32
4	4.30	4.09	3.84	4.20	4.17	4.12
5	3.83	4.18	4.16	4.20	3.83	4.05
6	4.52	4.36	4.37	4.25	4.50	4.40
7	4.13	4.00	4.05	4.45	4.33	4.18
8	4.13	4.18	3.84	3.90	4.33	4.03
9	4.57	4.36	4.11	4.50	4.33	4.40
10	4.35	4.18	3.74	4.00	4.00	4.05
$\bar{X}$ =	4.34	4.26	4.14	4.24	4.33	4.25

* 1. Rapport with faculty and good public relations with other parts of this university are enhanced by bibliographic instruction activity.

2. Skills in bibliographic instruction should be expected of recent library school graduates.

3. Bibliographic instruction creates an increased awareness of and ultimately increased demand on other library services (circulation, interlibrary loan, reference, etc.)

4. The costs to this library in terms of staff time, training, equipment, materials, photo duplication, etc., are excessive when compared to gains or benefits of bibliographic instruction.

5. Bibliographic instruction improves the skills and adequacy of its consumers only slightly, if at all.

6. The mission of bibliographic instruction is necessary to the accomplishment of the goals of this library and of this university.

7. Librarians in this library should not be encouraged to publicize bibliographic instruction activities in view of current budget constraints.

8. Planning and implementation of bibliographic instruction should be a top priority in this library even if they impact on some other library activities.

9. Bibliographic instruction enhances and improves the skills of those librarians who participate in it here.

10. There is a danger of too much emphasis on bibliographic instruction at the expense of reference and information provision.

.10 level in a one-tailed test of predicted direction, we were unable to reject the null hypothesis in favor of the research hypothesis. Instead, we must report no difference between the attitudes of middle managers and those of top-level administrators in their support for bibliographic instruction.

There was no need to test hypothesis 2 since it is clear that the difference between means for each group of middle managers was of

TABLE 3

Supportive Attitude of B.I. Managers as Compared
to Library Administrators by Mean Responses to Scale Statements

	B.I. Managers (34) (Reference Heads and Instruc. Coordinators)	Library Administrators (45) (Directors, Associate Directors, Public Service Directors)
Statements 1	4.56	4.69
2	4.41	4.31
3	4.53	4.18
4	4.24	4.04
5	3.94	4.13
6	4.47	4.33
7	4.09	4.27
8	4.15	3.93
9	4.50	4.31
10	4.29	3.89
$\overline{X}$ =	4.32	4.21

TABLE 4

Supportive Attitude: B.I. Managers vs Library

Administrators - Chi Square Test

	Supportive Attitude		
Position	High (4.5-5.0)	Moderate (4.0-4.4)	Low (3.0-3.9)
B.I. Manager	13 (11.19)	17 (16.78)	4 (6.03) 34
Lib. Administrator	13 (14.81)	22 (22.22)	10 (7.97) 45
	26	39	14 79

x^2 = 1.71, 2 df

$p > .10$

slight consequence (.08). Therefore, we are again unable to reject the null hypothesis and must agree with its premise that there is no difference between Instruction Coordinators and Reference Heads in their attitude toward the activity. Both groups must be considered to be supportive in general.

Table 5 provides a test of hypothesis three. In this test, Directors and Associate Directors were combined for purposes of comparison with Public Service Directors. The direction originally hypothesized was reversed since it was not the Public Services Director but the others which had shown a more supportive stance. Rather than employ the one-tailed test, then we utilized a two-tailed test to determine if the differences were significant. Having failed to reach a .10 level, however, we again were unable to reject the null hypothesis. Therefore, we must report no differences between the three types of top-level library administrators in their attitude toward bibliographic instruction. All were considered to be supportive.

Lack of Support for General Hypothesis

Tests of the specific hypotheses failed to confirm the general hypothesis of the study. Although there were differences among groups those differences were slight and in each case insignificant.

TABLE 5

Supportive Attitude: Directors and Associate Directors

vs Public Service Directors - Chi Square Test

Position	Supportive Attitude			
	High (4.5-5.0)	Moderate (4.0-4.4)	Low (3.0-3.9)	
Directors/Assoc. Directors	10 (7.51)	11 (12.71)	5 (5.78)	26
Public Service Directors	3 (5.49)	11 (9.29)	5 (4.22)	19
	13	22	10	45

$$x^2 = 2.76, \text{ 2 df}$$

$$p > .10$$

Based on the data in this study we must report that *Supportive attitude toward bibliographic instruction is not necessarily a function of its direct proximity to managerial responsibility.*

Perceptions of Bibliographic Instruction Managers

With respect to the research question, Table 6 indicates that middle managers' perceptions are somewhat faulty with respect to the responses of their superiors (statement 12). Both groups failed to achieve a 4.0 (perceived agreement with their own responses). Instead, their perceptions of the academic climate are mixed and unsure with more than a bit of indecision. This is important for it shows a perception of conflict when none exists between the values and judgments of administrators and their own beliefs. Colleagues or fellow department heads were seen to be supportive of bibliographic instruction. Least faith was placed in the attitudes of university administrators who were seen to be less knowledgable and less concerned, judging by a number of comments made.

FINDINGS, CONCLUSIONS AND IMPLICATIONS

Findings

1. The general hypothesis was not supported by the data in this study: Supportive attitude toward bibliographic instruction *is not necessarily* a function of its direct proximity to managerial responsibility.
2. All managerial groups were supportive of bibliographic instruction with no real differences between them.
3. Middle managers underestimate the value placed on bibliographic instruction by their library administrators.
4. University administrators are seen by middle managers to be less knowledgeable and less enthusiastic in their support for bibliographic instruction than are library administrators.
5. Fellow department heads are perceived to be supportive of bibliographic instruction.
6. Good public relations and rapport with faculty are major points of agreement and support regarding bibliographic instruction for all groups in the study.

TABLE 6

Perceptions of Supportive Attitude on the Part of Other
Administrators - Mean Responses of B.I. Managers

	Statements	Instruction Coords. (21)	Reference Heads (9)	Total
11	Top-level university officials here would provide approximately the same responses to #1-10 above.	3.05	2.89	3.03
12	Top-level library officials here would provide approximately the same responses to #1-10 above.	3.71	3.78	3.72
13	Colleagues (fellow department or division heads) in this library would provide approximately the same responses to #1-10 above.	4.00	4.22	4.07
	$\overline{X} =$	3.59	3.63	3.61

Conclusions and Implications

The results of this study are encouraging to those who promulgate the importance of bibliographic instruction, for the administrative climate is receptive with supportive attitudes of those in authority. Evidently, with all the attention and publicity given to the activity in professional circles over the past decade and a half, administrators of large academic libraries have become convinced of its value whether or not they personally participate in its management and supervision. It appears that middle managers, if they are, indeed the true believers, may well consider the present as an ideal time to become more vocal in expressing their needs and more energetic in designing additional programs and applications with the expectation that administrative support will be forthcoming.

Judging by many of the comments of the middle managers in the study, at this time they feel frenzied and overworked with little anticipation of relief. Responses from the administration, however, would lead us to speculate that possibly the case for additional personnel, if made convincingly by middle managers, might provide unexpectedly successful results. The administrators might be well-advised to enlist the aid of these dedicated individuals in adopting a strategy to approach university officials in order to render the needed "education." The fact that public relations interests are well-served may suggest the possibility of seeking additional assistance from faculty and deans whose academic departments utilize and benefit from the service.

This study does not go far enough, of course. What needs to be done is to survey university faculty and administrators to determine their awareness and attitudes. If these are not what they should be, subsequent needs assessments should be undertaken with the idea of "marketing" the service. Similar studies such as this should be undertaken at small colleges and universities and junior colleges as well to determine just how thoroughly the concept of bibliographic instruction has been ingrained on the minds of managers. In this way we will become aware of the "total administrative climate" in higher education regarding this activity.

NOTES

1. Melville Dewey, "The Profession," *Library Journal* 1 (September 30, 1876): 5-6.

2. Evan I. Farber and Thomas G. Kirk, Jr., "Academic Libraries – Instruction in Library Use," in *The ALA Yearbook 1976:* Chicago: American Library Association, 1976. p. 59.

3. Hannelore B. Rader, "Library Orientation and Instruction – 1980," *Reference Services Review* 9 (April 1981): 79-89; 10 (Summer 1982): 33-41.

4. Pamela J. Cravey, "The User and Bibliographic Instruction in the Academic Library," *Georgia Librarian* 16 (February 1979): 2.

5. Gail Schlacter and Dennis Thomison, *Library Science Dissertations 1925-1972,* Littleton, Colo: Libraries Unlimited, 1974, 293 pp.; *Library Science Dissertations, 1973-1982,* Libraries Unlimited, 1983, 414 pp.

6. Anita R. Schiller, "Reference Service: Instruction or Information." *Library Quarterly* 35 (January 1965): 52-60.

7. Jeremy W. Sayles, "Opinion About Library Instruction," *Southeastern Librarian* 30 (Winter 1980): 198-200.

8. John M. Tucker, "User Education in Academic Libraries: A Century in Retrospect," *Library Trends* 29 (Summer 1980): 9-27.

9. Fred Hamilton and Susanna J. Turner, "Bibliographic Instruction: Just Formalizing a Trend?" *Mississippi Libraries* 43 (Summer 1979): 97-98.

10. Marcie Murphy, "Criteria and Methodology for Evaluating the Effectiveness of Reference and Information Functions in Academic Libraries: A Regional Case Study." (Ph.D. dissertation, University of Pittsburgh, 1978) 242 pp.

11. Wayne Meyer, "Three Phases of Bibliographic Instruction," *Wisconsin Library Bulletin* 75 (March 1979): 63-65.

12. Nancy E. Gwinn, "Academic Libraries and Undergraduate Education: The CLR Experience," *College and Research Libraries* 41(January 1980): 5-16.

13. ACRL Bibliographic Instruction Research Committee, "Research Agenda for Bibliographic Instruction, *College and Research Libraries News* 41 (April 1980): 94-95.

14. Rensis Likert, "A Technique for the Measurement of Attitudes," *Archives of Psychology* 22 #140 (1932): 9.

15. Patricia S. Brevik, "Effects of Library-Based Instruction in the Academic Success of Disadvantaged College Freshmen" (D.L.S. Dissertation, Columbia University, 1974) 176 pp.

16. Mary F. Breen, "Library Instruction in Colleges for Teacher Education in the United States," (Ed.D. Dissertation, University of Buffalo, 1954) 184 pp.

17. Billy R. Wilkinson, "Reference Services for Undergraduate Students: Four Case Studies" (D.L.S. Dissertation, Columbia University, 1971) 520 pp.

18. Sandra G.B. Yee, "Administration of Library Instruction Programs in Michigan Community Colleges" (Ed.D. Dissertation, University of Michigan, 1979) 190 pp.

19. Stanley H. Benson, "Administering Course-Related Library Instruction Programs in Selected Academic Libraries," (Ph.D. Dissertation, University of Oklahoma, 1979) 215 pp.

20. Barbara J. Smith, "Education and Training Characteristics of Librarians Engaged in Bibliographic Instruction in Eighteen Colleges and Universities in Pennsylvania," (D. Ed. Dissertation, Pennsylvania State University, 1981) 91 p.

21. ALA/ACRL Bibliographic Instruction Task Force, "Guidelines for Bibliographic Instruction in Academic Libraries," *College and Research Libraries News* 38 (April 1977): 92.

22. Michael O'Donnell, "Library Instruction During a Period of Retrenchment" *Bookmark* 38 (Fall 1979): 231-236.

23. Thomas G. Kirk, "Library Administrators and Instructional Librarians: Improving Relations," *Journal of Academic Librarianship* 6 (January 1981): 345.

24. Barbara Phipps, "Library Instruction for the Undergraduate" *College and Research Libraries* 29 (September 1968): 411-423.

25. Allan J. Dyson, "Organizing Undergraduate Library Instruction: The English and American Experience" *Journal of Academic Librarianship* 1 (March 1975): 9-13.

26. Stuart W. Miller, *Library Use Instruction in Selected American Colleges,* Occasional Paper, No. 134, Urbana: University of Illinois. Graduate School of Library Science, 1978, 47 pp.

27. "Bibliographic Instruction in New England Academic Libraries," *College and Research Libraries News* 41 (May 1980): 152.

28. American Library Directory, 35th edition, New York: R.R. Bowker Co., 1982, 1917 pp.

Library Instruction
and Reference Service:
Administration of a Bibliographic
Instruction Program
in the Academic Library

Maureen Pastine

INTRODUCTION

Bibliographic instruction is an important facet of academic librarianship. Its primary purpose, at present, is the teaching of research methodologies in the various disciplines. "The college and university library performs a unique and indispensable function in the educational process. It bears the central responsibility for developing the college and university library collections; for extending bibliographic control over these collections; for instructing students formally and informally; and for advising faculty and scholars in the use of these collections."[1] Bibliographic instruction and reference desk assistance are closely related. Both aim to attain "the democratic goal of fostering independent learning."[2] Because of this similar goal, reference librarians have frequently been the impetus for establishment and development of bibliographic instruction programs in academe. The focus of this paper will be on the advantages and disadvantages of centralizing the administration of a bibliographic instruction program in the reference department and what to expect in the future.

Ms. Pastine is University Librarian, Clark Library, San Jose State University, One Washington Square, San Jose, CA 95192.

181

ADMINISTRATION OF BIBLIOGRAPHIC INSTRUCTION

Prior to a discussion of responsibility for the administration of a bibliographic instruction program, it is necessary to define what is involved in the administration of such a program. A number of objectives seem clear:

1. A needs assessment of the academic community must be undertaken.
2. Results of the needs assessment should then be compiled profiling the needs of each group to be served.
3. Written goals and objectives will be necessary to identify methods and levels of instruction needed.
4. A budget plan for implementation of the bibliographic instruction program and for continued financial support for personnel, equipment, facilities, and materials will be needed.
5. Determination of how the bibliographic instruction program will fit into the library's organizational chart must be completed.
6. A job description for the administrator of the program must be written. Similar job descriptions must be written for all staff involved in planning, implementing, and evaluating the program.
7. Appropriate space within the library must be designated for storage, classroom facilities, and offices.
8. Essential equipment must be purchased to accommodate the requirements of the bibliographic instruction program.
9. Resource people on campus should be identified to assist with integration of the program into the curriculum. This may include, but is not limited to, faculty, audiovisual technicians, testing and evaluation authorities, and others who have expertise not available within the library.
10. Evaluation methodologies for testing the effectiveness of the various methods of instruction must be determined.

Once the stated objectives are completed, personnel can be hired or internal shifts of staff can be made to ensure that the program becomes an active integral part of library services. The bibliographic instruction administrator may want to review Anne Roberts' pamhlet on "Organizing and Managing a Library Instruction Program-Checklists."[3]

RESPONSIBILITY FOR A BIBLIOGRAPHIC INSTRUCTION PROGRAM

The responsibility for administration of an academic bibliographic instruction program has not been adequately covered in library literature, even though there is a plethora of current literature on bibliographic instruction. "The position of library orientation in the library, in all probability, will be influenced by the stimulus for its initiation. A Reference Department-based program may have started as the result of certain problems at the reference desk." Or administration of the program may be the responsibility of the Circulation Department. It may have originated with the director of the library, or it may have started as a separate department within the library. But the "majority of plans reported" are "conducted as part of the Public Services Area, the most frequently being an auxiliary unit of the Reference Department or occasionally the Circulation Department."[4] A study conducted by Barbara J. Smith of academic instruction librarians in Pennsylvania demonstrated that the majority of bibliographic instruction librarians "have major assignments in reference work, an area of activity that is closely associated with instruction by the profession."[5] Regardless of the organizational method decided upon, responsibility must be clear. There seems to be general agreement that this responsibility must be centered with one individual. There also seems to be a feeling by many bibliographic instruction librarians, or reference librarians with bibliographic instruction responsibility, that there is frequently a lack of administrative support for bibliographic instruction programs. I suspect this is because programs were often initiated and implemented without adequate planning. I also suspect that there is more administrative support than bibliographic instruction librarians admit, but it is not readily apparent because of the lack of planning by, and budget reports to, those most closely involved. For example, the amount of staff time involved does translate into significant institutional dollars. If a large portion of that staff time is beyond the traditional forty hour work week, the administrator either needs to request additional staff or attempt to target a smaller portion of the user population. Often it is not the number of users reached that is of significance, but whether the instruction given is aimed at students in the appropriate courses and at an appropriate time—i.e., when the user most needs it. I have seen programs that attempt to reach all incoming freshmen, but the bibliographic instruction is offered before the students are given a library assignment. Orientation has become a "bad word." However, orientation tours may be more useful to an entry-level student than an in-depth bibliographic instruction session on research methodologies and subject-oriented tools before the student has a use for them. More emphasis needs to be placed on librarians targeting bibliographic instruction sessions for research methodologies and writing courses and less on the entry level courses where library use may be extremely limited. A bibliographic instruction administrator should consider contacting and working with faculty on designing effective library assignments prior to offering bibliographic instruction sessions, particularly in those entry level courses where bibliographic instruction is needed.

One of the major problems is that librarians with bibliographic instruction responsibilities have little preparation in administering these courses. Only eleven graduate schools of library and information science offer separate bibliographic instruction courses.[6] In an examination of the syllabi of the eleven courses, there is little discussion time alloted to administration of a bibliographic instruction program, and even less about when and why the program fits within the organization.

Prior to a decision on who, within the organizational structure, administers the bibliographic instruction program, several concerns must be addressed:

1. Is the library large enough to support a separate bibliographic instruction department or program? Will all librarians assist?
2. What is the difference between a coordinator and an administrator and which would be most effective in the library's organization?
3. What priority is bibliographic instruction in the list of library-wide priorities?
4. How much staff time can be allocated to the bibliographic instruction program?
5. How much funding can be made available for the bibliographic instruction program?

6. What staff should be involved in the bibliographic instruction program?
7. Will bibliographic instruction be offered only within existing library facilities, only in teaching department classrooms, or will it be offered within and outside of the confines of library space?
8. What user populations will be offered bibliographic instruction and through what methods?
9. Will the bibliographic instruction program be integrated into general education requirements?
10. Will bibliographic instruction librarians team teach research methodology courses with teaching faculty? Will bibliographic instruction librarians offer separate bibliographic instruction courses?

Resolution of these ten issues can assist in the final determination of administration of the bibliographic instruction program. If the program is one of the highest library-wide priorities, it may be more effective as a separate department so that it will not be viewed as a reference or circulation department function. If all librarians are to assist, it may be more effective if it reports to the Library Director rather than to a reference department head or an associate university librarian for public services. If the number of librarians in the organization and the size of the institution are limited, the program may be more effective if it is housed in the reference department where staff can be used for other duties as needed. If funding and staff time are limited, the program may require greater use of media and less personal staff time in the classroom. In such cases, the program might be more effective if administered by the media department where appropriate equipment and technicians are available.

ADMINISTRATION OF BIBLIOGRAPHIC INSTRUCTION THROUGH REFERENCE DEPARTMENTS

Because the purpose of reference service and bibliographic instruction are so closely linked (i.e., both offer information and instruction), many libraries have opted to establish the administration of the bibliographic instruction program within the reference department. Mary Mancuso Biggs states "that to maximize the effectiveness of both services, all reference librarians should do some instruction, and vice versa.''[7] Reference librarians are often more familiar with user research needs and problems than are other staff. Thus the reference department head, or a member of the department, is assigned administrative responsibility for bibliographic instruction. Advantages of this are obvious. Reference librarians are experts in the bibliographical content and control of various disciplines, as well as in research strategies and techniques. They do teach on a one-to-one basis every day. Thus it does seem that they are the logical staff to administer the program. Because of their daily contact with users in answering questions and providing guidance and direction to users, they are familiar with the curricular, research, and recreational needs of users. Reference librarians are available practically all, if not all, hours the library is open, and thus are often expected to provide instruction to evening and weekend classes when other staff are not on duty. In addition, users frequently know reference librarians by name because of frequent interaction with them at the reference desk. Most students are more willing to approach a reference librarian who gave their class a bibliographic instruction presentation than someone they have never met. Reference librarians are, it seems, better equipped initially to participate in bibliographic instruction than are other staff (this may be reason enough to involve all librarians in both reference services and bibliographic instruction programs). However, the reasons used to involve reference librarians in bibliographic instruction presentations are not necessarily the best reasons to locate administration of the bibliographic instruction program in the reference department. Few reference department heads have time to administer three, four, or more major library priorities, e.g., reference desk assistance, online search services, reference collection development, and bibliographic instruction. And, if the reference department heads administer bibliographic instruction programs, they may find that it is difficult to rely on assistance from outside their departments for the bibliographic instruction programs. Most reference department heads with this responsibility are well aware of the friction between departments if they ask for assistance from other departments without providing equal staff time from the Reference Department. Yet, they often react with resistance when the administration of the bibliographic instruction program is outside of their purview but requires reference librarian and support staff time. Conflicts may arise in assignment of priorities between other reference functions and activities and the bibliographic instruction program.

What then is the best solution? There are several alternatives:

1. The bibliographic instruction program could be limited to one aspect of reference departmental priorities and administered and offered by reference department staff with no outside assistance.
2. The bibliographic instruction program could be divided with several departments responsible for different aspects of the program. For example, the circulation department could be responsible for instruction in the use of online public access circulation terminals; the catalog department for instruction in the use of online public access terminals; the media department for preparation and maintenance of audiovisual point-of-use instructional aids; etc. This might require a coordinator to ensure consistency and lack of duplication.
3. The bibliographic instruction program could be a separate department with its own staff (may not be as feasible as other alternatives due to costs associated with a new separate department).
4. The bibliographic instruction program could have a program head who was responsible for the administration of the program with a percentage of librarian time from other departments to carry out the instructional and evaluative activities.
5. The heads of public and technical services could split the assignment and involve librarians, support staff, and student assistants in their divisions as appropriate.

Larger research libraries, with branch and/or departmental libraries, and an undergraduate library, and main library have greater problems in resolving the conflict of coordination and administration of a bibliographic instruction program. But initial planning may help in resolving problems that arise if there was inadequate preplanning. Advance planning is a necessity to avoid conflicts, resistance, resentment, and problems related to increasing demands of successful bibliographic instruction programs (without increased staff to handle the workload).

SUMMARY

There is no simple solution to how a bibliographic instruction program should be administered. However, advance planning prior to implementation of the program allows for anticipation of problem areas before they become insurmountable. Even though reference department activities are now more closely linked to bibliographic instruction than any other library operations or services, changing technology and increased use of automated or computerized services requires bibliographic instruction expertise beyond the traditional classroom lecture or orientation tour. This shift in bibliographic instruction responsibilities and activities calls for a re-examination of how bibliographic instruction programs should be administered, and, in my view strengthens the position of bibliographic instruction as a separate service, equivalent to other library-wide priorities. I anticipate that in the future there will be no question that a bibliographic instruction program should be administered outside of the confines of the reference department, or public services division, as a bonafide library-wide priority incorporating staff talents, expertise, and time of each department and division of the library. The administration of the program of the future will face difficult problems in provision of adequate support (professional, clerical, and student assistant) because of tight fiscal constraints and declining federal and state funding. In the meantime, each library should reassess its present program and begin planning for the future.

The most successful bibliographic instruction programs contain the following precepts:

1. An administrator who is knowledgeable about teaching methodologies, has personnel management skills, has budgeting and long range planning experience, is able to set priorities, goals and objectives, is knowledgeable about measurement and evaluation techniques of library services and programs, is able to recognize and target its user population and meet their needs.

2. Adequate funding based on: a. Personnel needed (librarians, support staff and student assistants). b. Equipment needed (including overhead projectors, video cameras, and closed circuit television monitors, large viewing screens, slide-tape and microfilm tape projectors, access to typewriters or word processor, signage equipment, and even 35 mm cameras and flood lights for preparation of slides). c. Adequate photocopy/duplicating/printing resources. d. portable terminals for dial-up access demonstrations. e. Travel funds for attendance at appropriate workshops and seminars.

3. Adequate physical facilities for training purposes, as well as

for provision of bibliographic instruction to large and small groups, preferably within the library.

4. Job descriptions for administrator and staff with reporting and cooperative relationships clearly delineated.
5. Release time for professional development in maintaining and expanding skills.
6. Results from a needs assessment of user population for use in management decisions.
7. Clear guidelines for advance scheduling and preparation time, and written limitations of the program.
8. A highly motivated, enthusiastic staff.
9. Effective faculty liaison.
10. An ability to adapt to change.

As long as the library and university administration, faculty and students, as well as library staff see the need for, and provide the appropriate resources for, the bibliographic instruction program, location of the administration within the organizational structure becomes less important. What is of paramount importance is the commitment to bibliographic instruction and follow-through on its effectiveness in preparing users for life-long learning.

NOTES

1. "Guidelines for Bibliographic Instruction in Academic Libraries," Chicago, Illinois: Association of College and Research Libraries, January 31, 1977.

2. Frances L. Hopkins, "A Century of Bibliographic Instruction: the Historical Claim to Professional and Academic Legitimacy," *College and Research Libraries,* 43 (May 1982), 196.

3. Anne Roberts, "Organizing and Managing a Library Instruction Program–Checklists," Chicago, Illinois: Association of College and Research Libraries, June, 1979.

4. James E. Ward, "The Position of the Orientation Program Within The Library," in *Planning and Developing a Library Orientation Program,* ed. Mary Bolner, Ann Arbor, Michigan, Pierian Press, 1975, pp. 24-27.

5. Barbara J. Smith, "Background Characteristics and Education Needs of a Group of Instruction Librarians in Pennsylvania," *College and Research Libraries,* 43 (May 1982), 206.

6. Maureen Pastine and Karen Seibert, "Update on the Status of Bibliographic Instruction in Library School Programs," *Journal of Education for Librarianship,* 21 (Fall 1981), 169.

7. Mary Mancuso Biggs, "On My Mind . . . The Perils of Library Instruction," *The Journal of Academic Librarianship,* 5 (July 1979), 159.

Bibliographic Education and Reference Desk Service—A Continuum

Mary Reichel

In academic libraries, bibliographic education, reference desk service, online searching, and interlibrary loan services are all aspects of reference service and form a continuum, that is, the four services have a "fundamental common character."[1] The "fundamental common character" among these four services is that they are part of an overall process geared to helping researchers—whether they are students, staff, or faculty—to understand the process of literature searching and to execute a literature search successfully. The common character of these services is strengthened by having the same librarians participate in all services. The librarians can then form an ongoing relationship with researchers as well as providing continuity for reference service. Establishing the relationship among these services means that librarians take a more active view of their responsibilities.

Literature searching is a complex process. To conduct a successful literature search, a researcher must know where to start for his or her level of expertise in the topic. The researcher must be able to proceed logically from one type of library resource to another; for instance, it is often more effective to go from the library's catalog for general book material to the periodical indexes for more specific periodical material. A researcher should also have an idea of where to stop a literature search when a comprehensive search is not needed. A researcher must know types of resources generally, including those outside the scholarly mainstream, such as government documents, statistical sources, and technical reports. A researcher must

Mary Reichel is Head, Reference Department, Pullen Library, Georgia State University, Atlanta, GA 30303.

191

know how to evaluate sources, and this involves both judgment of relevance from bibliographic citations and in depth analysis from serious reading of the item.

How do researchers learn all of this in an academic environment? They learn from faculty, peers, reading, practice, and from *librarians.* They learn from librarians in the classroom, at the reference desk, and with the computer terminal. The different aspects of reference service are appropriate for different stages of the literature searching process. Bibliographic education is appropriate at the beginning of a literature search when general information is needed. Reference desk service is the appropriate mode for answering more specific questions which come later in a literature search. Online searching and interlibrary loan are for even more specific needs.

Bibliographic education comes at the beginning of a search when a researcher needs to know the kinds of library sources available, what their purposes are, how they relate to each other, and how they are used. Bibliographic instruction presentations are well suited to helping a researcher understand the general principles of literature searching. A presentation or lecture is a good way to stimulate interest and enthusiasm.[2] In giving presentations, librarians need to limit the material to an overview of the subject. For instance, when talking to doctoral students in education, a librarian could discuss the publication sequence of material in the field from conference papers to journal articles and research reports, etc. and the various access tools which lead to these kinds of resources. Another method of keeping presentations general is to use an example of a literature search as the organizing structure.[3] With the assurance that follow up can be provided at the reference desk and through individual appointments, librarians can comfortably keep presentations on a conceptual level. In bibliographic instruction presentations, specifics are very hard to present in an interesting manner. Further, there is much that students at the beginning of a literature search simply do not need to know. For example, they do not need to be told the beginning dates of sources nor the alphabetization patterns of various sources. They will learn these specifics as they use the sources and with the help of librarians at the reference desk.

The idea that bibliographic instruction presentations must present general information with more specific help given at the reference desk has implications for the view that learning to use libraries is like laboratory work in the sciences. McCarthy, in her thought provoking article on bibliographic instruction as observed from the reference desk, makes this statement: "Learning to use libraries is analogous in some ways to laboratory training, and laboratory sessions in the reference room seem to work."[4] A better analogy for bibliographic instruction is to scientific training as a whole. A body of knowledge, including a methodology, is needed that can be tested and put to use in the laboratory. Literature searching is dependent on previous knowledge that can be tested and used in the library. In scientific education, laboratory work reenforces and expands on what is learned in the classroom. Theory and experimentation are used to complement each other. The same should be true in bibliographic education. Near the end of her article, McCarthy states that "successful library instruction entails practical experience illuminated by principles and concepts."[5] Experience must be combined with principles, but the order in which they are taught and learned is important. I would reverse McCarthy's idea and suggest that principles and concepts of bibliographic information should be learned first and reenforced with practical experience.

To proceed with the continuum, at the reference desk specifics can be handled effectively on an individual basis. The reference desk is the appropriate place for suggesting such tools as bibliographies and indexes to use for a particular topic. The reference desk transaction is excellent for explaining the use of a tool. However, since interactions at the reference desk are relatively short, it is very difficult to give an overview. More lengthy individual assistance serves to complement service at the reference desk; many librarians encourage and routinely schedule appointments with researchers for extensive individual assistance.

Time is an interesting factor in different aspects of reference service. Reference desk transactions are usually brief. This is partly because reference desks are busy, and there are not enough librarians to spend long periods of time with questioners. In addition, patrons approach the reference desk expecting a short answer. They are usually beginning or in the midst of a literature search and eager to get on with it. Most patrons will not have the patience for even a twenty minute overview at the reference desk. In the classroom, of course, students expect a much longer discussion.

Online searching and interlibrary loan services are parts of reference service which provide even more specific assistance for researchers. Online searching seems to be most useful and practical when the researcher has done some preliminary work and has a fairly well defined topic. Bibliographic instruction presentations are very important for setting the stage for online searching because researchers should gain a general understanding of what can be expected from online data bases. Of course, online searching is an important tool for various types of questions received at the reference desk, such as bibliographic verification. Interlibrary loan services provide information on locating the physical item when it is not available in the home library. Interlibrary loan and other location services are for the most specific kinds of questions. The researcher has identified the item bibliographically and needs physical location. Most often, researchers will have progressed quite far in their literature searches before they need interlibrary loan services.

To synthesize, bibliographic education and reference desk service together with online searching and interlibrary loan services form a continuum. These activities share a fundamental purpose of helping researchers with various parts of the literature searching process. Bibliographic education provides the most general information and interlibrary loan service provides the most specific information while the level of information provided by reference desk service and online searching falls between these two extremes.

To strengthen the relationship among bibliographic education, reference desk service, online searching, and interlibrary loan, librarians should be involved in all of these services. This involvement allows librarians to form ongoing relationships with researchers; it makes the librarians better at what they do; it gives continuity to the services; and it helps librarians to take an active view of their responsibilities.

Viewing all aspects of reference service as a continuum assumes that students and other researchers will not just see a librarian once, but will have continuing contacts with librarians. Librarians should interact many times with students on individual projects and also throughout their academic careers. On individual papers or projects, students should deal with a librarian for the overview of literature searching, for specific help, for help with constructing the bibliography, and, ideally, with feedback on how the paper was received. These different points of interaction between researchers and librarians allow the librarian to reenforce what has been said previously and to place into context much more specific information. Many librarians participating in both bibliographic instruction and reference desk service establish this kind of ongoing relationship with students. It is very common for students to ask for the librarian who taught their class; it is also relatively common for students to return to librarians with information on the grades they received on papers, especially if the grades were good!

It is also important for students to have an ongoing relationship with librarians on a programmatic level. Students need one level of bibliographic information when they are freshmen and more sophisticated information when they are juniors and seniors. The highly successful bibliographic instruction program at Earlham College[6] certainly has this fundamental idea built into it. Students at Earlham get various levels of bibliographic instruction throughout their four years.

By being involved in all aspects of reference service, librarians become better at what they do. Librarians are more aware of the whole literature searching process when they deal with it in the various aspects. When librarians prepare for bibliographic instruction presentations, they learn about new resources and even whole new subject areas. For a presentation on library materials related to taxation, for example, a librarian would need to learn about specialized tools such as Prentice-Hall's *Federal Taxes*[7] as well as how that source and similar ones relate to standard legal sources. One of the real pleasures of involvement in bibliographic instruction is learning new material well enough to teach it.

Working at the reference desk provides insights into what researchers need to know, and these insights can in turn be used for effective bibliographic education. Similarly, librarians are constantly learning about new sources and approaches as they help people at the reference desk. Participation in online searching helps librarians understand what topics are realistic and suitable research projects. Also, in online searching, librarians can actually judge how relevant citations are to the search terms and strategies used. Participation in interlibrary loan helps to give awareness of the kinds of material which can and cannot be located. All of this makes the librarians more knowledgeable about library resources and their strengths and weaknesses.

Involvement by librarians in bibliographic education, reference desk service, online searching, and interlibrary loan gives continuity to these services. A specific example of the benefit of having the same librarians participate in bibliographic education and reference desk service is the common occurrence when students have library related assignments which are unrealistic. The assignments may be unrealistic because the students are not prepared or because library resources are unavailable. In either case, reference librarians often contact the professors who give such assignments and suggest a bibliographic instruction presentation and perhaps a modification of the assignment. In fact, it is often ideal when librarians at the reference desk are helping to answer assignment questions which they helped to design. A very common example of this phenomenon is library skills workbooks. Continuity is also seen in the ability of the librarians to explain each type of service.

Finally, librarians' involvement in all these services has advanced the idea of active reference service. Dougherty states that:

> Public service librarians must recombine their skills and interests. They must take a broader view of public services to include bibliographic instruction, traditional reference, and data base services, all as important parts of an *integrated information services* program. Librarians must abandon the reference desk and heighten their profile within the academic community. Changing the image of the public service librarian will be about as easy as scaling Mount McKinley—difficult, but achievable.[8]

Librarians need not abandon the reference desk in order to become more visible. But they must be aware of how reference desk service and other services relate to each other. Reference desk service as a sole means of delivery is primarily a passive service. Librarians wait for questioners to come to them and then react. Adding bibliographic education to the reference process has increased the active nature of reference service.

Bibliographic instruction has given more control to reference librarians. Budd makes this statement:

> The educational experience is ideally geared to enquiry. That the library is vital to enquiry cannot be denied. The librarian as teacher, is able to initiate and facilitate enquiry from a position unique in the academic structure.[9]

Control and initiative are vital parts of good reference service, although it would be foolish to hope to control everything. Librarians need to be in the habit of seeing where library information fits into what is happening on campus. There is a need to view library resources and procedures from the user's perspective and to emphasize what is important to the user.

Reference librarians need to assume explicit responsibility, shared with the other faculty, for the bibliographic knowledge of researchers on their campus. Once this responsibility is acknowledged, it follows that reference service should be active. Active reference service includes letting faculty, staff, and students know about new information sources and processes. For example, reference librarians must inform patrons about the possibilities and limitations of online searching. Reference librarians must be alert to the curriculum, and how, when, and why students need to gather information. In fact, librarians should be helping to decide the curriculum on campus and on a broader level.[10] Further, for faculty, staff, and students, reference librarians must anticipate needs, help to build appropriate collections, and keep the academic community informed of new developments. One of the most important ways for librarians to know what is needed in the academic community is by the questions asked at the reference desk. Librarians must use all other available avenues to keep informed from the college newspapers to attendance at departmental meetings.

From the librarian's perspective, acknowledgement of bibliographic education, reference desk service, online searching, and interlibrary loan as aspects of reference service which form a continuum has many advantages. By having librarians involved in all these activities, they increase their expertise and add variety to their responsibilities. From the researcher's perspective, it is important to have reference service that will help with the total literature search. As the researcher progresses from general to specific, appropriate types of reference service will be available.

REFERENCES

1. *Webster's Third New International Dictionary of the English Language Unabridged* (Springfield, Massachusetts, G. & C. Merriam Company, 1976.)

2. Nancy Fjallbrant, "Teaching Methods for the Education of the Library User," *Libri* 26 (December, 1976), p. 257.

3. Beverly A. Pierce, "Librarians and Teachers: Where is the Common Ground," *Catholic Library World* 53 (November, 1981), p. 166.

4. Constance McCarthy, "Library Instructor: Observations from the Reference Desk," *RQ* 22 (Fall, 1982), p. 39.

5. McCarthy, p. 40.

6. A description of the program is found in Evan Ira Farber, "Library Instruction Throughout the Curriculum: Earlham College Program" in John Lubans Jr., ed., *Educating the Library User* (New York: R. R. Bowker Company, 1974), pp. 148-155.

7. *Prentice-Hall Federal Taxes* (Englewood Cliffs, New Jersey: Prentice-Hall).

8. Richard Dougherty, "Avoiding Burnout," *Journal of Academic Librarianship* 7 (January, 1982), p. 333.

9. John Budd, "Librarians are Teachers" *Library Journal* 107 (October 75, 1982), p. 1944.

10. John Lubans, Jr., "Curriculum Reform: A Quick Fix or Revolution" in his column on "Library Literacy", *RQ* 22 (Spring, 1983), pp. 235-237.

Library Instruction for Faculty Members

Eric W. Johnson

The necessity of library instruction for college students is almost universally accepted. Few college or university libraries do not offer some sort of orientation, whether a single session introduction to the library or a formal course taken for credit. The number of libraries offering the same service for instructors, however, is minimal, yet the need for "library re-education" (or, in some cases, primary orientation) is certainly just as vital. How can librarians expect faculty members to promote library use among their students if they themselves are ignorant of what is available to them? At an orientation class I once presented to first-year English students, their instructor was astounded to learn of the *MLA International Bibliography* and, despite having a master's degree in English, had obviously never been exposed to it. This may be an extreme example, but it is certainly not an isolated one.

At the Fifth Conference on the Library Orientation for Academic Libraries held in 1975, A.P. Marshall, Dean of Academic Services at Eastern Michigan University, stated that:

> faculties are notoriously ignorant of library resources, particularly of items outside of their normal classification. Many of them are only familiar with the simplest of library procedures, but hesitate to seek help because they think this would reveal their ignorance. . . . Actually, few faculty have developed the expertise necessary to ferret out all related materials in a research library.[1]

The need for faculty library orientation exists.

There are several possible approaches to the orientation process,

Eric W. Johnson is Associate Librarian, Public Services, University of New Haven Library, New Haven, CT 06516.

from casual assimilation to structured classes, depending on the particular needs of the faculty involved and the availability of library staff for the programs.

THE STUDENT ORIENTATION CLASS

Faculty members who are not regular users of the library can be painlessly introduced to its resources during the course of the basic bibliographic instruction class, especially if it is not handled as a separate course. Most students will pay better attention to the librarian instructor if their regular instructor is present. Thus, requiring his or her presence will serve double duty, since the instructor will reap the benefits of the class along with his students.

There naturally should exist a rapport between the faculty instructor and the librarian. The librarian should meet with the instructor beforehand to determine the specific needs of the class. In an English class, for example, students may be required to research literary topics, and emphasis might be placed on literature reference sources, while a speech class might be more interested in current event sources. By discussing the scope of the orientation, the librarian will not only have a good idea of the class's needs, but also an indication of the instructor's familiarity with the material to be covered.

At almost every specialized orientation session I have conducted, the instructor has been exposed to at least one new reference source in his field. If he finds it worthwhile, he may include it on a class syllabus, emphasize its use by his students, or tell his colleagues about it.

The orientation class should be reviewed periodically by both the library staff and the pertinent faculty members. In this manner both students and faculty are assured of keeping up with the constant flow of new reference tools and library services.

FACULTY MEETINGS

There is often a lack of awareness on the part of a faculty as to what the library can offer them. While some faculty members are habitual library users and take an active part in library affairs, others seldom if ever use the library, are not familiar with its holdings, and may even pass on their disinterest to their students. Just as the patron who is hesitant to ask for help at the information desk must be approached, so must the non-library user be made aware of what the library can offer. Librarians cannot always sit back and wait for people to come to them; we must take an active part in advertising the library.

An excellent way to do this is to take part in departmental meetings, if not on a regular basis then at least once or twice a year. A quick presentation of a new reference service or a brief survey of the most essential subject tools will keep the regular users up to date and hopefully generate interest among the recalcitrants. A handout of some sort, possibly a photocopy of one of the pages of the reference tool or a brief annotated bibliography, will reinforce the presentation in the faculty's minds.

In addition to the obvious result of acquainting faculty members with new items, the librarian is also instilling an awareness of the library in the minds of users and non-users alike, many of whom may encourage its use among their students while at the same time neglecting it for their own use. The interest developed in the library will extend to other areas, as faculty are able to provide assistance in collection development, promotion of use, and—a very important consideration indeed—support at budget allocation time.

THE FACULTY ORIENTATION CLASS

A logical off-shoot of the orientation class for students, the faculty orientation class performs the same function for a different audience. Like its counterpart, the class may take a number of forms, from a short session in the library on perhaps an annual basis to a longer, more formalized presentation with hands-on practice and bibliographies for the participants.

The concept of faculty library orientation is not a new one. In a paper presented at the American Library Association Conference in October, 1933, E.M. Feagley mentioned that the Teachers College at Columbia University had inaugurated a system of group meetings with teachers to explain reference materials for their subjects.[2] At the same time the Library School of the George Peabody College for Teachers in Nashville, Tennessee offered a course instructing school administrators and teachers in library methods.[3] Most of these early courses were designed for elementary and secondary school teachers enrolled in advance degree programs rather than for college and university faculty members.

Despite these programs, however, the American Association of School Librarians in 1960 felt the need to send a letter to professional associations and agencies charging teacher-training institutions with inadequate training of teachers in the use of libraries.[4] College libraries had meanwhile begun to prepare library handbooks for faculty members, explaining rules and regulations as well as basic reference tools.

By the early 1970s actual orientation classes and workshops for faculty were being provided at such diverse schools as the Bergen Community College in New Jersey[5] and the Universite de Clermont-Ferrand in France.[6] Other schools, such as the Miami-Dade Community College South Campus, soon followed suit.[7] The need had reached a critical level, and librarians were attacking the problem in a logical and professional manner.

One such program has worked extremely well. Since June 1976, faculty seminars on social sciences and humanities research have been offered on an annual basis at the University of California, Berkeley. The program has been a success from its inception, with some faculty members returning to several sessions. From the sessions, the librarians discovered that many faculty did indeed need a refresher course, some being in need of even more basic orientation; that faculty were eager to learn about the library; and that, in addition to becoming familiar with the library, faculty were also instructed in the role of librarians in the information-retrieval process.[8]

In setting up an instruction program for faculty members, librarians will probably find the most difficult task is determining the level of instruction, i.e., deciding what items will be included. Although some faculty may be extremely proficient, it is better to assume that they possess only a rudimentary knowledge of the library. Even items which are familiar to them may not have been consulted for some time, and a quick explanation will refresh their memories. At the same time, it would be unwise to attempt to cover too much ground, especially if the orientation consists of a single session. Instead, the librarian should narrow the subject and concentrate on fewer, key sources, emphasizing the most useful ones, than overwhelm with a wide range of items.

Handouts and bibliographies are essential. A brief explanation of how to find periodical articles, for example, might accompany an annotated list of indexes and bibliographic materials. A map of the library is always useful. By taking the mystery out of the library's sytem of arrangement the librarian makes the task of getting faculty into the library that much easier.

Librarians may find that a single session is not adequate to cover the needs of the faculty. The faculty themselves may not be satisfied with one lesson. Conversely, the faculty may be more sophisticated in library usage than anticipated, and one or two sessions will be sufficient. It makes more sense to start small and then expand the program, to a regular course if warranted.

Critical input from the faculty is important. Since any faculty orientation program would be attended on a voluntary basis, it is essential that the faculty be satisfied with such a program. By assessing the program with its students, the librarian will be able to determine the necessary level of sophistication as well as the correct amount of material to cover. Some instructors may prefer hands-on practice with the tools being discussed via chosen or assigned topics, while others may be satisfied with being made aware of their existence. The success of the venture depends on the cooperation between teacher/librarian and student/faculty.

In the program's initial stages, librarians will probably feel odd preparing to teach faculty members, some of whom may be experts in their field. There is no need to feel this way, since those faculty who are taking part will be doing so because they are interested in learning more about the library. Indeed, most faculty will welcome the opportunity to expand their knowledge of their special subject, and some may care to familiarize themselves with areas outside of their chosen field.

Once designed and implemented, the orientation program should continually be examined and discussed by both librarian and faculty in order to upgrade it. The latest worthwhile reference tools should be introduced as necessary, and the format or materials covered changed if needed. A single session may divide into basic sources and advanced sources; a broad topic may subdivide into its component parts. The program should not be viewed as immutable; on the contrary, all parties involved should cooperate to insure the best possible format and coverage for the intended audience.

Both faculty members and librarians will be impressed with the wide range of results of the faculty orientation program. First, and most basic, faculty will be afforded the opportunity to expand their knowledge, not only of their subject area but of the library in gen-

LIBRARY INSTRUCTION AND REFERENCE SERVICES

eral. Secondly, a heightened interest in the library by the faculty will be passed on to their students. Once they have become familiar with reference tools, they will recommend them in class, resulting in an increased use of these tools and of the library.

Finally, the library orientation will help to dispel the mysteries of the library by acquainting the faculty with what services it can offer them. At the same time, they will see librarians in a new light—not as mere guardians of books, but as co-educators and peers—and hopefully seek a new cooperation with them for the better good of both the college community and the entire library profession.

REFERENCES

1. A. P. Marshall, "Library Orientation—What's That?" *Faculty Involvement in Library Instruction,* ed. Hannelore B. Rader (Ann Arbor: Pierian Press, 1976), pp. 97-100.

2. E. M. Feagley, "The Teacher and the Library: Possibilities and Responsibilities," *ALA Bulletin,* 28 (March 1934), 116-23.

3. L. Shores, "Library Instruction for Teachers," *Peabody Journal of Education,* 14 (November 1936), 128-33.

4. "Teacher Training Inadequate AASL Charges," *Library Journal,* 86 (January 15, 1961), 345.

5. Margery Read and Sara Katharine Thomson, "Instructing College Faculty in the Bibliographic Resources of Their Subject Field: A Case Study," *Educating the Library User,* ed. John Lubans, Jr. (New York: Bowker, 1974), pp. 191-201.

6. J. Archimbaud, "L'enseignement de la bibliographie à la Faculté mixte de médecine et de pharmacie de Clermont-Ferrand," *Association des Bibliothecaires Francais Bulletin d'Informations,* No. 68 (1970), 167-75.

7. Lucinda A. Hofmann, "Educate the Educator: A Possible Solution to an Academic Librarian's Dilemma," *The Journal of Academic Librarianship,* 7 (July 1981), pp. 161-63.

8. Anne Grodzins Lipow, "Teaching the Faculty to Use the Library: A Successful Program of In-Depth Seminars for University of California, Berkeley, Faculty," *New Horizons for Academic Libraries,* ed. Robert D. Stueart and Richard D. Johnson (New York: K.G. Saur, 1979), pp. 262-67.

Bibliographic Instruction in the Academic Library: Looking at the Adult Student

Mary Ellen Kennedy

In the academic library, users comprise an increasingly varied group of adults of all ages, from those just out of high school onward, who may be in the library for quite diverse reasons. Bibliographic instruction in the academic library is part of adult education, and should in fact be based on the recognition that learning patterns of adults are different from those of children or adolescents. It has been considered necessary because students were supposed to be coming into a rather strange and forbidding environment from high school libraries that varied from nothing to facilities and resources that were quite extensive. However, bibliographic instruction is not only for incoming freshmen, but for any group of academic library users who need it.

Furthermore, it is increasingly evident that incoming freshmen are not as homogeneous a group as was previously thought. Therefore, it is necessary to examine what bibliographic instruction is or can be in terms of the users.

Bibliographic instruction has become a discipline of its own in library science, particularly in academic librarianship. It is sometimes thought of as synonymous with library orientation, library instruction or user instruction, or as embracing a combination of the library tour and instruction in use of significant reference sources. It is a function of academic library practice that has been around for a long time, but not until recently has become a more recognized and distinct area. This discussion of bibliographic instruction concerns only that service offered by academic libraries. The population served

Dr. Kennedy is Reference Librarian at Purdue University Libraries, West Lafayette, IN 47907.

by the library of an academic institution is chiefly post high school and inclusive of students who are matriculating in full time programs, taking occasional courses or short term programs like ELDERHOSTEL (A short term, low cost residential program for older adults), or simply using the college/university library for personal information needs.

Between the years 1974 and 1979, the increase in total enrollment of college students aged 35 years or older increased by 36.8 percent, while the group 18-24 years of age increased by only 10.7 percent.[1] "Students 35 years of age and over represented 10.4 percent of the total enrollment in 1974 compared with 12.3 percent in 1979."[2] The increase in percentages for that age group does not seem large for a five year period, but it does reflect the changing demographics of college populations. A further statement in this regard is the profile of age ranges for students entering institutions of higher learning initially, during the fall term of 1980. These were defined a "full time freshmen enrolled in college for the first time."[3] In 1980, while the greater bulk, 72.6 percent were of age 18, six percent were of age 20 or older.[4] Another source indicates that "from 1957 to 1975, the number of adults involved in continuing education rose from 8.2 million to 17.1 million."[5] This would include those enrolled in colleges and universities. Many of those adult students are attending college to complete a degree that they had left unfinished years ago, to prepare for a new career, or to simply learn something new.[6]

The age of the population of students and other users of the library spans a wide range of years. Life experience of persons who come into the college programs nowadays would therefore be expected to be much broader than it would be if students all came directly from high school to college. College students beginning and matriculating through college are not a homogeneous group. Rather they consist of persons just out of high school and beginning their freshman year with little or no life experience to those adults much older with several years of life experience.

How is bibliographic instruction actually defined? Beverly Renford and Linnea Hendrickson define bibliographic instruction as work that "encompasses all activities designed to teach the user about library resources and research techniques."[7] Beaubien notes that bibliographic instruction involves activities through which "users are made aware of the whole complex system of information organization and retrieval."[8] Thomas Kirk distinguishes library instruction from orientation. He defines orientation as comprising "activities which orient a person to a particular library facility . . .," while instruction "means some type of teaching activity in which methods of library use are covered. This teaching usually covers reference tools, both published and library produced, and strategies for using these tools . . ."[9] Anita Schiller discusses the two aspects of reference service, information and instruction. Instruction is defined as that type of reference service in which the patron was provided with direction and guidance in the search for information.[10]

Bibliographic instruction is more than teaching people how to access books and periodicals; it is also teaching them how to use online equipment, in-house library files custom made for access to specialized information, and human resources throughout the community, all of which function as information sources. If bibliographic instruction can also enable the user to recognize his own power to get information, it can give the user a greater incentive to continue learning begun in the classroom or elsewhere, or to initiate learning projects of his own, independent of classroom experience. Therein lies its relationship to adult education, or what is known as life-long learning or independent learning.

Why should librarians be concerned with adult education as distinct from any other in a discussion of bibliographic instruction? Educational methodology has dealt with the learning habits of children and young people. Higher education has continually focused on the type of student whose whole learning career was fairly uninterrupted by adult responsibilities and whose schedule permitted learning in large blocks of dedicated time. Now, however, it is apparent that more enrollees in college and university courses and programs are people whose lifestyles are devoted to work, leisure activities, homemaking, child raising and other prior commitments. These persons also want to obtain degrees or to enter into learning experiences. Methodology appropriate to children and young people will not work for them; adults learn differently.

As Malcolm Knowles notes, the term "andragogy" or the art of teaching adults is based on four assumptions about adults and their learning patterns:

> As a person matures, (1) his self-concept moves from one of being a dependent personality toward one of being a self-directed human being; (2) he accumulates a growing reservoir of experience that becomes an increasing resource for learning;

(3) his readiness to learn becomes oriented increasingly to the developmental tasks of his social roles; and (4) his time perspective changes from one of postponed application of knowledge to immediacy of application, and accordingly, his orientation toward learning shifts from one of subject-centeredness to one of problem-centeredness.[11]

The above assumptions form the basis for some principles of adult education that librarians can use for approach to adult users in the academic library. As to first assumption, the self-directed motivation of the adult user will suggest an approach that allows maximum freedom to use the library's tools and resources independently. The librarian can suggest many sources from which an adult user can choose to begin or to continue a search for information. Regarding second assumption, the adult's life experience will provide him with multiple approaches to the subject material. An example could be of an English teacher who comes back to take a summer graduate class in research. He may know some of the tools (if not all of them) but he will also have his teaching experience to draw upon in writing a paper for the graduate class. This second assumption is closely related to the third and fourth assumptions. The English teacher will relate use of library tools and the paper he will write to his own work. He will not be operating from a theoretical or hypothetical base as would an inexperienced graduate student just out of college, but look at problems inherent in his work. The research will be geared toward solutions to those problems.

Patricia Cross further delineates the differences between how adults learn and how children learn. In summary, she points out that child learning methods are premised on dependency of the learner, lack of immediacy of need for the knowledge acquired, subject focus of the knowledge, and the predominant leadership of the teacher. Whereas adult learning behaviors imply independency of the learner, self-directed acquisition of knowledge, and a mutual sharing of knowledge and ideas.[12]

Given these qualities of the adult learner and the differences from the child learner, as well as the fact that colleges and universities are dealing with this type of individual, it stands to reason that library service in those institutions should be geared to this type of user. More recognition of adult learning patterns must be shown in the way that librarians teach adults use of the library so that these adults may begin or continue learning on their own with effective use of the library's resources. Librarians are addressing a group of learners who are interested in carrying away from the experience some practical knowledge that they can use immediately. Most bibliographic instruction sessions tend to be of the single lecture format. Beaubien defines the single lecture as a ''unique encounter between the teacher and a group of any size where there is no guarantee of personal followup or evaluation of what has been taught or learned.''[13] Therefore the users must go away from this session with some ability to attempt to access the subject,[14] in this case, to begin to obtain with a measure of independence the information they want from the library.

Certain qualities inherent in social services relationships of clients and counselors are applicable to adult education, and thus to the continuing education of adults in the library setting. In fact, these ideas have already permeated thinking in the public service area of librarianship, as well as in adult education. These ideas concern attitudes of behavior of librarians toward client/patrons that they serve.

Specifically, these attitudes of librarians toward persons who reflect many backgrounds as previously discussed, must move from an orientation toward a group of college students and faculty perceived as fairly homogeneous to the larger community perceived as diverse. No studies of academic librarians' attitudes toward patrons had been done prior to this author's doctoral work. That study covered discussion of a survey of academic librarians' attitudes toward service to older adults in the ELDERHOSTEL programs. ELDERHOSTEL was used as an example group of adult patrons. Most librarians surveyed felt that service for older adults would essentially be no different than for patrons of any other age group who customarily use the library.[15] More work needs to be done in this area, especially to see exactly how librarians do perceive their patrons as to background, age, orientation to the library and other factors.

Because attitudes have a great impact on the type of service and services offered, as well as how programs are planned and carried out, it would be well to note specific skills that are applicable to bibliographic instruction and reference services for adult patrons in the academic library. Ralph Brockett points out several helping skills that can be used in general adult education situations and therefore would have library applications. Such basic helping skills that he mentions are those of attending, responding and understanding.[16] These skills are exercised in a ''helper/client'' relationship. Often conceived in a one to one context, they could be applied to groups as well.

In the library, "attending" can refer to the bibliographic instruction situation in that the librarian gives full attention to the hearers, and they know that the librarian is interested only in them at that time. The librarian understands the group that he is dealing with, and notes reactions of the group. These reactions will vary among individual members. The librarian can be flexible, allowing members of the group who feel confident with the library material to work independently. No bibliographic lecture should consume the entire meeting period, especially if there will be only one meeting. Part of that time should be geared so that even the least library-oriented persons come from the meeting having successfully used the reference tools presented. Adults coming back to college often feel threatened by the school milieu, and look for immediate success.

Another skill cited by Brockett is that of "responding," which includes skills of empathy, respect, genuineness, and concreteness.[17] The skill of responding is most applicable to the reference interview itself, wherein the librarian tries to understand what a patron is asking. However, it is also pertinent in teaching a group of adults use of the library. Responding to patrons means that the librarian can sense whether or not adult users are assimilating material given in a bibliographic lecture. He can see the way they look, or he can note the question they ask, and tell that he has perhaps given too much material at once, or has not been clear. Adult users are attentive to detail; they do not want to bother with extraneous matter that is not relevant to use.

Among the subskills noted above, empathy is one of the most important. It means the understanding of the position of the patron. Many adults are unfamiliar with the academic library and may not even be users of the public library. Recognizing where the adult is in his learning progress at the time of the bibliographic lecture and instruction in use of materials can make the one to one contact that follows more effective. It is not possible to really know these persons as individuals at the time of a lecture; however, following certain principles can open the way to giving more effective attention to individual needs. For example, it is not wise to assume that everyone knows *Readers' Guide* simply because it is routinely introduced in school and college library reference situations.

It is necessary for the librarian to respect the patron as an individual with specific needs, and to attempt to meet those needs as much as possible. Recognizing how adults learn and that more adult learners are present on college campuses in classes and programs can help librarians work toward meeting their needs more effectively. It is necessary that the library and especially the public service sector be informed about any special adult programs that the university or college is offering. Of 171 librarians responding to the question concerning general publicity of ELDERHOSTEL on campus, 73.1 percent believed it was well publicized; almost 70 percent of 165 responses indicated that librarians felt that the library had received sufficient information about course offerings in this program.[18] This is especially necessary if such programs run for a different time length than regular term courses, or if they fall in between terms. Such programs, if successful, as ELDERHOSTEL has been, will often be repeated in the future. Librarians may often have to seek out that information through visits to college/university administrative offices, and to department heads and deans. Liaison work between librarians and faculty should be encouraged by directors of libraries. Breivik notes the importance of liaison work with subject divisions of the campus community, where most students and faculty are involved. She emphasizes the need for careful planning of the liaison role of the librarian.[19] Without planning it becomes haphazard and formless. Liaison work involves planning the bibliographic lectures for classes, and using appropriate followup for individual students.

Alluded to previously in this paper are some of the fears that adults often bring to the learning arena. It will be necessary for librarians to work to break down such inhibition and fear through individual understanding and assistance. Adults are sometimes afraid to try something new, even investigating new library tools, and finally writing a paper for a course, because of fear of failure. These inhibitions are among the greatest barriers to undertaking a learning project in a formal setting, and continuing it once it is begun. Other barriers to comfortable learning for adults include such factors as limited time allotments for learning due to other commitments mentioned previously. Adults do not have large blocks of time to devote to homework, preparation for tests, or research for term papers. However, these events in courses are inevitable in most cases. Therefore, the time adults spend in the library must be used to get the most precise data they will need for such work, or for their own questions.

Another barrier to learning for adults is often age, more a product of attitudes than a factor in itself. Stereotypes about age as a deterrent to learning still prevail. However, age does not in itself inhibit learning. It was found that librarians dealing with older adults perceive them as not having any problems with learning that are associated with age. Strongest disagreement among 171 librarians who responded to a range of "Strongly agree/strongly disagree" was to the statement "Older adults cannot learn new things." Ninety-seven percent of the responding librarians disagreed with the statement.[20] Other physical factors may of course enter into this on an individual basis. Related to age are attitudes of friends and relatives which may discourage adult participation. However, older adults have proven themselves to be eager and enthusiastic learners. They have been and are attending school and undertaking learning enterprises on their own.

Martha Boaz notes another set of barriers that can have a major influence on adult learning plans—institutional regulations and procedures. She emphasized that institutions should make it easier for adults of all ages to register and be admitted; part-time students with limited time and energy should be considered; women, older adults and minorities should be strongly encouraged to come to the campus.[21]

In summary, bibliographic instruction and accompanying reference service for adults who use academic libraries should be premised on principles of adult learning behaviors. It behooves librarians to review attitudes toward all patrons, and to recognize that more post-college age persons are involved in learning programs at the college/university level. To best do this librarians must be well informed about developing curricula and programs within their institutions.

REFERENCES

1. U.S., Department of Education, Educational Research and Improvement National Center for Statistics, *Digest of Educational Statistics* (Washington, D.C.: Superintendent of Documents, 1982), p. 93.

2. Ibid.

3. Ibid., p. 98.

4. Ibid.

5. Ralph B. Rauch, "Education for the Growing Majority: Adults," *Lifelong Learning: The Adult Years,* 5 (September 1981): 11.

6. Ibid., p. 12.

7. Beverly Renford and Linnea Hendrickson, *Bibliographic Instruction: A Handbook,* (New York: Neal-Schuman, 1980), p. 84.

8. Anne K. Beaubien, Sharon A. Hogan, and Mary W. George, *Learning the Library: Concepts and Methods for Effective Bibliographic Instruction* (New York: R.R. Bowker, 1982), p. 3.

9. Thomas Kirk, "Past, Present and Future of Library Instruction," *Southeastern Librarian* 27 (Spring 1977): 15.

10. Anita R. Schiller, "Reference Service: Instruction or Information?" *Library Trends* 35 (January 1965): 53.

11. Malcolm Knowles, *The Modern Practice of Adult Education: Andragogy Versus Pedagogy* (New York: Association Press, 1970), p. 39.

12. K. Patricia Cross, *Adults As Learners* (San Francisco: Jossey-Bass, 1981), p. 224.

13. Beaubien, *Learning The Library,* p. 155.

14. Rauch, "Education for the Growing Majority," p. 12.

15. Mary Ellen Kennedy, *Service to Older Adult Users of Academic Libraries: A Study of Librarian Attitudes* (Ann Arbor, Michigan: University of Microfilms, 1980), p. 168.

16. Ralph Brockett, "Facilitator Roles and Skills," *Lifelong Learning: The Adult Years,* 6 (January 1983): 8.

17. Ibid.

18. Kennedy, *Service to Older Adult Users of Academic Libraries,* p. 125.

19. Patricia Breivik, *Planning the Library Instruction Program* (Chicago: American Library Association, 1982) pp. 11-12.

20. Kennedy, *Service to Older Adult Users of Academic Libraries,* p. 118.

21. Martha Boaz, "The Leadership Role of Library Education: Crisis in Confidence," in *Reference Services and Library Educational Essays in Honor of Frances Neel Cheney,* eds. Edwin S. Gleaves and John Mark Tucker (Lexington, Massachusetts: Lexington Books, 1983), pp. 239-240.

Library Instruction and Foreign Students: A Survey of Opinions and Practices Among Selected Libraries

Frank Wm. Goudy
Eugene Moushey

The importance of the foreign student to the enrollment of many colleges and universities appears to be increasing. In 1970-71 the number of foreign students reported was only 144,708, a decade later this figure had increased to 311,882 students.[1] One forecast reported in the *Chronicle of Higher Education* indicated that by the early 1990's there could be more than one million foreign students on the nation's campuses.[2] The 1980-81 student enrollments in American universities from specific countries included: Iran, 47,550; Taiwan, 19,460; Nigeria, 17,350; Japan, 13,500; and Saudi Arabia, 10,440.[3] With the projected tripling of the number of students coming to study in this country, reference and other public service librarians must play a key role in developing plans to resolve the problem of library instruction for foreign students. This is essential as the reference librarian is often the first to encounter students who have complex information demands but who do not have the skills essential in accessing the library's resources.

Relatively little has been written in the library literature about academic libraries and their attempts to provide such services to these students.[4] Indeed, if this paucity of published literature is indicative of the attempts to provide such instruction, then academic libraries have apparently been negligent in recognizing this responsibility. In addition to the scant attention paid to these students and their special needs for library use skills, many foreign students ap-

Dr. Frank Wm. Goudy is Associate Professor and Reference Librarian, Western Illinois University Libraries, Macomb, IL 61455. His co-author, Eugene Moushey, is Assistant Professor and Reference Librarian, Western Illinois University Libraries, Macomb, IL 61455.

pear to have fundamental communication problems. Or simply stated, they often cannot either understand or speak English sufficiently well to communicate in an English speaking ambience. That many foreign students have had this problem for years is rather clear from the literature.[5-9] This research also reveals that this problem is not limited to students from any one area or country. Although the references emphasize that many academic problems can arise from a lack of English proficiency by foreign students, these difficulties could seemingly be compounded when the students are faced with research that requires the use of library resources.

English proficiency in some countries thought to be bilingual is low. In Bangladesh and Pakistan, for example, many teachers are natives and the emphasis is now on regional languages with a change in Bangladesh from English to Bengali as the official language.[10] Sharma thinks that "the most severe academic problems concern giving oral reports, participation in class discussion, and understanding lectures. The problems require a long period of time for their resolution."[11] A 1969 article by Lewis on library orientation for Asian students states that "most Asians come to the American college campus with at least minor, often serious deficiencies in English."[12] Of course, Asians have no monopoly on English language troubles. One student caps her problem when she says "I think in Thai, I am fluent in Japanese, I read French, I cry in English."[13]

Foreign students' problems are compounded when the language deficiency is either not considered important or is willfully overlooked in the screening process. In a strongly worded statement, the American Council Education's Committee on Foreign Students and International Policy warned that "growing economic pressures may tempt some institutions into compromising on standards and in indulging in unprofessional behavior" in the recruitment of foreign students.[14] In addition, one of the A.C.E.'s six considerations is that "All segments of the academic community, especially the faculty, should be involved in the development of policy."[15]

Whether librarians are formally faculty or not, they should be involved in the development and implementation of such policies. Library research composes a significant part of the total learning process and thus librarians should be consulted in whatever planning is effected for foreign students. Librarians can not be expected to teach English to foreign students. However, they can and must provide some kind of instruction in the use of the library if the students are to be effective in their class assignments. One can imagine the problem when the foreign student is working in a foreign language (English) and in a new environment. The problems to be overcome in using library resources can lead to discouragement and frustration from the beginning.

A parallel can be drawn between foreign students and disadvantaged students from this country. Briefly, at least three of the similarities include: a lack of experience with libraries in general; little or no experience in using indexes, abstracts, reference works, etc.; and little or no practical experience in the use of the card catalog. Although most libraries have apparently done little in library instruction specifically designed for disadvantaged students, Shaughnessy presents a viable program which might be adapted for use with foreign students.[16]

The inability of students to effectively use the library has been the subject of much discussion for many years. And these workshops, articles, and books focused almost exclusively upon students who were presumed to have a command of the English language and at least a passing acquaintance with libraries.

A questionnaire was designed to ask selected libraries if they have special problems in assisting foreign students (from non-English language or cultural backgrounds) in their library needs, what these problems consist of, and if they have developed specific programs of library instruction to aid such students.

METHODOLOGY

A questionnaire was mailed to the directors of forty-four academic libraries. These libraries were selected from the forty universities with the most foreign students as well as those which had at least ten percent of their student body from other nations. The data identifying the selected schools were obtained from the publication *Open Doors, 1980/81.* Each questionnaire was accompanied by a self-addressed, postage paid return envelope to facilitate replies and to help ensure a favorable return. Of the forty four academic libraries contacted, thirty-one (70.5 percent of the sample) completed the survey. The institutions they represented accounted for a total of 58,925 foreign students during 1980-81.[17]

The survey had several objectives including: the perceived adequacy of library skills possessed by foreign students as compared to native born students; whether library instruction would be helpful to foreign students, and if so, how it could best be accomplished; what existing library instruction programs are already being implemented by the library or another part of the university; and finally, what coordination, if any, exists between the library and other components of the university responsible for the academic needs of foreign students.

Not all of the respondents answered all questions while two libraries provided a total of five separate responses as the library directors forwarded a copy of the questionnaire to branches or areas with responsibilities for library instruction and/or public services. Thus, the total number of responses for each question varies. One library did not fill out the questionnaire but did provide several insightful comments.

FINDINGS

Level of Library Skills and Need for Instruction

The first question attempted to determine the level of difficulty that foreign students have, as compared to native born students, in using the resources of the library. The choices selected by the libraries were as follows: "extreme difficulty" (1), "significant difficulty" (11), "some difficulty" (18), and "little difficulty" (1). Not a single library reported "no difficulty" although some remarked that it varied significantly depending upon the individual. Thus, there seems to be rather solid agreement that foreign students, as a group, do have more problems adapting to and using the library than does the average student from this country.

In the use of various library tools such as the card catalog, indexes and abstracts, reference works, etc., there was a clear indication that foreign students have below average ability in effectively utilizing necessary resources for library research. Problem areas specifically mentioned were: difficulty in understanding the arrangement of periodicals, subject entries in the card catalog, the classification scheme, unfamiliarity with indexes, and the purpose and organization of the vertical file. Naturally, such difficulties often occur with all students; however, foreign students were perceived as having even more problems than would normally be expected. In effect, the foreign students would appear to be confronted by obstacles of major proportions in using the library.

Another opinion question that was asked was whether foreign students who had "extreme," "significant," or "some" difficulty in using the library would benefit by a specific program of library instruction. Of the thirty-one libraries which responded in this manner, twenty-nine indicated that such a program would be valuable while only two responses were negative. And of the twenty-eight libraries answering positively to having a specific program of library instruction, nineteen indicated that such instruction should be a separate program exclusively for foreign students and ten libraries thought library instruction should be integrated regardless of the student's background or nationality. One respondent stated that "I feel very strongly" about foreign students being integrated but did not offer any further explanation. Another respondent observed that a separate program exclusively for foreign students was necessary. "at least the first time they have library instruction."

As to why there should be a separate program of library instruction for foreign students, the following answers were selected: poor pronunciation and difficulty in oral communication (14 responses), lack of adequate vocabulary (14 responses), and the inability to conceptualize and apply the English alphabet (10 responses). Other representative answers included: "need for repeated personal assistance"; "difficulties are language and culture bound"; "need for very basic instruction and the speed of presentation"; "most students are from developing countries and have had no exposure to libraries"; and "total unfamiliarity with North American libraries—their arrangement, open stacks etc." One library noted that the dilemmas of foreign students varied dramatically depending upon from what part of the world they came from and therefore it was necessary to take this into consideration when generalizing about foreign students. A statement provided on one of the questionnaires perhaps best summarized the overall impression given by others when commenting "while both foreign and native born experience lack of familiarity with available resources, it is more severe with foreign, because of communication (lack of vocabulary and grasp of concepts)."

Library Instruction: What Is Offered and Who Offers It?

The next set of questions in the survey became less of subjective opinion about the ability, problems, and needs of foreign students. Instead, there was an inquiry about specific programs of library instruction being offered on campus and the degree, if any, of coordination that exists between the library and other areas of the university who teach or have responsibilities for the academic needs of foreign students.

The first question in this sequence was whether the library at their institution was responsible for offering specific programs of library instruction for foreign students. Twenty-four libraries marked that some type of program was available while ten libraries gave a negative response. If they answered that some form of program was in existence, they were then requested to indicate whether there was a separate program exclusively for foreign students or whether it was integrated with native born students. This was further divided into a series of responses to indicate exactly what form of instruction was available.

Of those who acknowledged that there was a program exclusively for foreign students, eighteen checked that it consisted of bibliographic instruction on an ''as requested basis'' by a member of the teaching faculty and that library orientation (a physical tour of the library) was presented. Seven libraries each provided various forms of self-instructional materials and were willing to extend a formalized program of ''one-on-one'' instruction as requested by students. One library offered a non-credit course in library use that was designed for foreign students. Other responses indicated that a library skills workbook had been developed and that ''foreign students and their families have a university-wide orientation in which the library participates.''

For those libraries which integrate foreign students with native born students, there was a more varied response as to the types of library instruction provided. Although again, bibliographic instruction on an ''as requested basis'' (12 responses) and library orientation (18 responses) predominated. Fourteen libraries checked that they furnish various self-instructional materials. Eleven indicated a formalized program of one-on-one instruction as requested by students and five noted a credit course in library use. As one might expect, a broad range of library instructional activities were indicated and foreign students could participate as could any other student on campus.

In many universities, library instruction is also offered by areas other than the library. Such instruction could be within an academic department (English, Communications, etc.), or in the case of foreign students, it could be handled by those components of the university (International Programs, Foreign Student Office, Student Exchange Program, etc.) which are responsible for recruiting and/or providing academic and social services for foreign students. Of the responding libraries, twelve revealed that academic departments were responsible at their institutions for providing some form of library instruction for foreign students and eleven libraries declared that those areas accountable for foreign students furnished such assistance.

As to the type of instruction offered, library orientation (a physical tour of the library) tended to be most prevalent whether it be by the academic department or by those having oversight for foreign student programs. One library commented that an academic department did provide a credit course in library use that was exclusively for foreign students.

Interestingly, only five of the thirty-one different libraries which completed this survey marked ''No'' to all three questions asking whether some form of a specific program of library instruction was assisting foreign students at either the library, academic department, or area responsible for foreign students. Of course, there is always the potential that certain services available elsewhere on campus were not known to the librarians completing this questionnaire.

Coordination of Library Instruction

Another key concern is the extent of coordination that exists between the library and other areas of the university in providing library instruction. Lack of such coordination can mean either nonexistent or duplicative efforts that are wasteful to both students and faculty alike. Twenty respondents revealed that there was at least some form of coordination while fourteen respondents were not involved in any collaborating efforts. For those who did cooperate, the most usual form of coordination (16 checked this response) was between the library and those responsible for foreign student programs. Eight libraries indicated that such coordination existed between the library and academic departments and two explained that academic departments and those responsible for foreign students on campus teamed together in library instruction efforts. Coordination between both the library and academic departments as well as between the library and those in charge of foreign student activities was revealed by four of the responding libraries. One library wrote ''the librarians at the Undergraduate library instruct the instructors for the Intensive English Language Institute. These instructors then work with a small group of foreign students.'' Additional representative responses include the following:

> "Office for International students contacts User Education Coordinator before the beginning of each semester to request orientation classes and tours.

> "International programs has assisted library staff in the preparation of special orientation sessions."

> "The Reference Department . . . cooperates with the International Center in promoting tailored tours for foreign students."

> "All international students are required to take 18 quarter hours of ESL. During one of these classes, Library instruction is given in multiple (usually 3-4 one hour) sessions."

> "Staff of IELI (Intensive English Language Institute) assigns students in various disciplines to appropriate unit of University Libraries for orientation."

Another library listed a formalized program of coordination between the library and international student groups which included the following steps:

1. "International Students' Office invites the library to participate in its orientation."
2. "CELOP (Center for English Language Orientation Program) classes are regularly given classes on library use by the library staff."
3. "Liberal Arts English classes for foreign students have incorporated a multi-visit library instruction program into their curriculum."

Additional Comments

A questionnaire often has severe limitations as a method for obtaining information necessary to present a full view of the issue at hand. Checking answers that provide a brief and pre-defined statement often limits the respondent in communicating any unique situations that are relevant to their situation. Recognizing this as a potential concern, a cover letter was attached to this survey in which it was requested that more detailed comments be provided as it was thought necessary to convey the attitudes, problems, and methods of dealing with library instruction for foreign students. As already evidenced in this article, many observations were given on a variety of topics. Several respondents took the time to write personal statements on a number of concerns and their attempts to facilitate library use skills. Many of these responses were quite concise while others wrote a rather thorough description of present operations or their views on what programs should be implemented.

One university wrote that in addition to the usual printed guides and library tours that were available to all students, there had been developed a short library assignment for those foreign students at the intermediate level in the university's Applied English Center. In addition, an eight unit non-credit course in library skills had been designed. And although it was not originally structured specifically for foreign students, slightly over one-half of the students taking the course were foreigners.

Another library observed that although the Intensive English Language Institute on campus assigns students in various disciplines to the appropriate area of the library for orientation that there is a need for more detailed instruction. It was suggested that ''It would seem reasonable to provide foreign students doing graduate work with instruction in small groups arranged by subject field'' and ''It would be ideal to require foreign students to be in a program like IELI and that library instruction be a more structured part of it.''

As previously mentioned, situations from campus to campus and from library to library vary significantly. For while many libraries noted the difficulty they have with foreign students effectively using the library, one large university stated:

> the English fluency requirements at . . . are considerably more stringent than at most other institutions, and students not meeting those requirements are obliged to take the necessary course in the American Language Program before they can be admitted to regular University and professional school classes. As a result, we in the library are not particularly aware of foreign students as a group having exceptional difficulties in using the libraries.

In one university, nearly fifty percent of the student body is composed of foreign or bilingual students. Those students who cannot pass an English competency test are enrolled in intensive English courses where library instruction is offered. However, communication problems appear to be minimal since nearly one-half of the library professionals are also bilingual (Spanish).

SUMMATION

Clearly, there is the opinion held by most of the respondents that foreign students do have significantly greater problems in using the library than do most native born students. Unfamiliarity with American libraries, cultural differences, difficulties in oral communication, lack of an adequate vocabulary, and the inability to conceptualize and apply the English alphabet all combine to make the library a laborious place to accomplish research as well as making "the reference interview" a time consuming and potentially unsuccessful process. Nearly all the librarians questioned believed that a specific program of library instruction was needed to overcome these problems. A definite majority felt that such instruction should be offered as a separate program exclusively for foreign students in order that the weaker backgrounds could be more adequately compensated.

The type of instruction offered and the degree of coordination that exists between the library and other areas on campus differ markedly. Most library instruction assistance appears to comprise the traditional forms whereby a tour of the library is provided or the teaching faculty member requests bibliographic instruction for a particular topic on an "as requested basis." Librarians also mentioned many other services including non-credit classes in library use as well as one academic department which offers a credit course in library skills that is strictly for foreign students. Some degree of coordination does appear between the library and others at their university who have responsibilities for foreign students. However, this is not prevalent and differences as to the degree of such coordination, the amount of instruction, and how it is structured vary significantly.

There does not appear to be any single dominant trend in how library instruction is given to foreign students. As for the limited evidence available from this survey, it would appear that most of the respondents deemed that such instruction should be much more extensive than is presently the practice at most of their campuses. Nevertheless, certain institutions believe that they have openly recognized this need and have adequately organized to address this concern.

SOURCES OF ADDITIONAL IDEAS AND PROGRAMS

The desire to exchange ideas with others who have experienced similar needs has been an important factor for librarians whether the information obtained is in published research or gathered at organizational meetings. In order to further contribute to this process, the last question in the survey asked: "Does your Library have materials (handouts, slides/tapes, details of presently used programs, etc.) related to the library instruction of foreign students which you would be willing to share with others who contacted your institution?" Those libraries which indicated that they had such materials and would be willing to cooperate in this endeavor are listed below:

University Librarian
Boston University
Mugar Memorial Library
711 Commonwealth Ave.
Boston, MA 02215

Director of Libraries
Michigan State University
University Library
East Lansing, MI 48824

University Librarian
Lockwood Library or Undergraduate Library
SUNY, at Buffalo
Buffalo, NY 14260

Director of the Library
United States International University
University Library
10455 Pomerado Road
San Diego, CA 92131

Assistant Director of Public Services
The University of Houston
M D Anderson Memorial Library
4800 Calhoun Blvd.
Houston, TX 77004

Director of Libraries
University of Southern California
Edward L. Doheny Memorial Library
Los Angeles, CA 90007

An excellent book on this subject is titled *Guide to Academic Libraries in The United States: for students of English as a second language.*[18] It contains many examples of essential library research skills in a style readily understandable to foreign students but which could also be useful to all students with a limited background in the use of the library.

In addition, one should not forget to contact the following address: Director, LOEX Clearinghouse, Eastern Michigan University, Ypsilanti, MI 48197. LOEX has collected numerous samples from many academic library programs for teaching library skills to foreign students.

REFERENCES

1. *Open Doors, 1980/81.* New York: Institute of International Education, 1981, p. 4.

2. Scully, Malcolm. "1 Million Foreign Students at U.S. Colleges, Triple Present Number, Seen Likely by 1990." *Chronicle of Higher Education* 23 (21 October 1981): 1.

3. *Open Doors, 1980/81,* p. 11.

4. McLean, Dulce D. "Library User Education for the International Student: A Feasibility Study." Arlington, Va.: ERIC Document Reproduction Service, ED 197702, 1978.

5. Lewis, p. 271.

6. Sharma, Sarla. "A Study to Identify and Analyze Adjustment Problems Experienced by Foreign Non-European Graduate Students Enrolled in Selected Universities in the state of North Carolina." *California Journal of Educational Research* 24 (May 1973): 135-46.

7. Cable, John N. "Foreign Students in the United States." *Improving College and University Teaching* 22 (Winter 1974): 40-41.

8. Payind, Mohammad. "Academic Personnel and Social Problems of Afghan and Iranian Students in the United States." *Educational Research Quarterly* 4 (Summer 1979): 3-11.

9. Jameson, Sanford. "Advising Offices Overseas - Closing the Information Gap." *College and University* 47 (Summer 1974): 549-79.

10. Jameson, p. 566.

11. Sharma, p. 144.

12. Payind, p. 6.

13. Cable, p. 40.

14. Scully, p. 14.

15. Ibid., p. 14.

16. Shaugnessy, Thomas. "Library Services to Educationally Disadvantaged Students." *College & Research Libraries* 36 (November 1975): 443-48.

17. Open Doors, 1980/81, pp. 55-56.

18. Byrd, Patricia. *Guide to Academic Libraries in the United States: for students of English as a second language.* Englewood Cliffs, N.J.: Prentice-Hall, 1981.

No Royal Road

Melissa R. Watson

"There is no royal road to learning; no short cut to the acquirement of any valuable art."

Trollope, *Barchester Towers*

The reference librarian who ventures to address the subject of library use instruction does so at the considerable risk of alienating at least half of his or her readers. This is an issue fraught with controversy, and few librarians seem to be able to approach the subject with much equanimity. There are those who consider the library to be a center of education and librarians to be teachers, and so vehemently support library instruction programs as essential to the education process. Then there are others who insist that librarians are *not* teachers and that libraries, while still essential to the education process, are information centers and their librarians disseminators of information. Between these two camps the invective seems to flow with a steady force, with one side or the other scoring points with each new article that appears in the literature. It would seem that as there is no "royal road to learning," neither is there any easy solution to the library use instruction question. However, operating under the assumption that learning to use a library is a "valuable art" which should be acquired, this article will attempt to suggest a way in which this might be achieved.

The issue of library instruction is one that is often of great concern to reference librarians, usually because the reference librarian is the one who has to arrange a meeting between the users and the materials they desire. And while one can support the ideal of max-

Melissa R. Watson is Reference Librarian, Northeastern Oklahoma A. & M. College, Box 70, Miami, OK 74354.

imum service, (i.e., directly providing the user with the materials desired) when there are maximum amounts of users to be helped and a minimum of librarians to do the helping, educated library users can be a boon to all. This is particularly true in an academic library where waves of students flood into the reference section at the same time, all of them desperately in need of assistance. It has been this writer's experience that when there is a formal library instruction program in existence, those students who have participated in that program are more efficient library users and seem to experience less frustration in their use of the library than those who have not.

It is not the intent of this writer to address the question of whether or not librarians are teachers, that has been addressed elsewhere with great eloquence and erudition. Let it suffice for the moment that librarians involved with library instruction programs will of necessity employ teaching methods to carry out those programs, and leave the question of what that makes them for the time being. Instead, the library instruction program that is employed where this writer works will be explored because for us, it seems to work. Granted, this is an entirely subjective view, but then this is an issue that lends itself to subjectivity.

It has been pointed out in connection with library instruction that those programs which are undertaken by librarians alone are doomed to failure, primarily because a library cannot motivate due to the fact that it cannot reward. In order to succeed the library must tie in with someone that can. In an academic setting this means that unless one has the cooperation of the faculty, the best instruction program in the world will dwindle into obscurity. It was for this reason that at the junior college where this writer is employed that the library instruction program was designed in cooperation with faculty from the English department. The library instruction program is essentially a unit of Freshman Composition 1, with sections of that unit taught by the English instructors and others by library personnel. Because the students are graded on their mastery of library skills, they are more highly motivated to acquire those skills.

When this program was first designed, a booklet was created to serve as a guide. Both English instructors and library personnel were involved in the creation of the booklet, which would form the basis for the program. As this library is a learning resources center (LRC), the booklet was divided into four sections, each dealing with a different function of the LRC: card catalog, reference, periodicals, and audio-visual. There is also a page devoted to general policies and hours of operation, as well as another page with a general layout of the entire facility.

The card catalog section contains the simple rules for finding information in the card catalog, as well as examples of the author, title, and subject cards. There are pages given to examples of cross-references and actual locating of the book, as well as one with the simple headings for the Dewey Decimal System. The section concludes with several assignments meant to increase the user's skills in locating subjects.

The section on the reference collection was originally set up to give examples of the different types of reference books (atlases, handbooks, etc.), and was followed by a series of questions which were designed to acquaint the user with some of the more important resources in the area. A drawback to this feature was discovered after a few years when it was seen that the books in question would fall open to the answers as soon as they were removed from the shelf, and they also were becoming obsolete due to new editions. In a newer edition of the booklet these questions were replaced by a reiteration of the ten main sections of the Dewey System, a brief explanation of the types of works to be found in those sections, as well as several titles of reference books which might be helpful to the student. New sets of questions are now made up each school year and are supplied to the instructors who are free to assign as many as they might desire. This eliminates the problems with updated editions and helps to insure that the students are doing the work themselves.

The periodicals section explains the differences between magazines and journals (for some reason this is a problem with many students) and gives a detailed example of a *Reader's Guide* entry. There are brief explanations of the other indexes owned by the LRC and a list of topics which can be looked up as the instructor so assigns.

The final section is devoted to the LRC's audio-visual resources, which range from record albums to videocassettes. The various types of resources are explained, and an exercise for locating a program through the card catalog and carrying through to actual use of the program is included.

These booklets are handed to the students when they come to the LRC with their respective classes for the actual orientation section of the instruction program. Generally the classes are taken through two of the four divisions during one class period, then return for the remaining two the next time the class meets. Approximately twenty-five minutes are allowed for each section, each of which includes an introduction to the area by the appropriate member of the staff (cataloger for the card catalog section, reference librarian for the reference section, etc.), a tour of the area and a ten minute videotape. These videotapes are produced by the LRC staff in conjunction with AV personnel and are filmed on the premises. (The college has its own TV studio and equipment.) The object of the videotapes is twofold: they provide visual reinforcement of the materials being covered, and since they are somewhat humorous, they help to dispel the negative image some students have of libraries.

After orientation, the students return to their classrooms where they are tested, and various assignments concerning the different sections are given. Those students who complete all the assignments are then qualified to be more efficient users of the LRC during their stay at the college, and hopefully better library users wherever they may happen to go.

In addition to the library instruction program with the Freshman Composition classes, the LRC also conducts a number of specialized orientation tours as requested by faculty members. These have included sessions with Criminal Justice majors, Nursing students, Music, Theater, and Heating and Refrigeration classes. These tend to be as successful as the instructors involved.

Does all this then mean that our LRC has found the ultimate answer to the library instruction question? Of course not. One cannot learn all there is to know about reference works in two semester long courses, let alone learn everything there is to know about an entire LRC in just a few class sections. There are those who claim that programs such as this are detrimental. After completing this course some students may think they know all they need to find their way around the LRC and thus cut themselves off from other avenues which they might find through asking the reference librarian. This is a valid objection and sometimes it is unfortunately true. Naturally, all of the orientation sections stress the need to ask, ask, ASK questions when they don't understand, but the resistance upon the part of students to asking the very questions they need to ask is often high.

Another problem with this method is the very thing which makes it work in the first place, the link with the English instructors. While all instructors do send their classes to the orientation sessions, the instructors are under no obligation to follow up with further assignments, and some do not. The majority of the instructors are very cooperative and spend a great deal of time preparing their students for the orientation sessions, testing them and assigning the various exercises. The students who have these instructors usually become quite proficient in their ability to use the LRC's resources. Those students whose instructors do not make any of the assignments are usually little better off than if they had never come to the LRC in the first place. (At least they know where the LRC is, if nothing else!)

Even though this program is far from the ideal solution to a rather sticky problem, it does have another benefit which pays off for our particular LRC. Many of the students who attend this college have had very little experience with libraries of any sort and, unfortunately, sometimes that experience has been negative. Old stereotypes die hard, and many of the students envision going to the library as something akin to a session in Purgatory. Through the orientation program, with its emphasis that asking questions is not stupid and the rather gentle familiarization with the various resources, many students come to realize that the LRC is not such a horrible place to visit and, wonder of wonders, it might actually help them with their schoolwork! If we can cure some of these students of their library-phobia and help make them life-long library users, this is certainly worth the frustrations of working with an imperfect solution.

As far as this reference librarian is concerned, this particular program helps me because students at least have an idea where to start when they come to the LRC to do their research. For the complex research questions I still prefer that the students check with me so that I can help them find more resources than they know exist. I am committed to providing maximum service as the situation allows, but often the number that need help prevent me from giving each and every student as much help as I would like. In this event, those students who have had the library instruction sessions are able to get started on their own, which helps to lessen their frustration, as well as my own. This may not carry much weight with those who are categorically opposed to formal library instruction programs, but for my students and myself, it is enough.

BIBLIOGRAPHY

Budd, John. "Librarians are Teachers." *Library Journal,* October 15, 1982, pp. 1944-46.
Dickenson, Dennis W. "Library Literacy: Who? When? Where?" *Library Journal,* April 15, 1981, pp. 853-55.

Katz, William A. *Introduction to Reference Work, Vol. II: Reference Services and Reference Processes.* New York: McGraw-Hill Book Co., 1982, pp. 56-61.

Rosenblum, Joseph. ''The Future of Reference Service: Death by Complexity?'' *Wilson Library Bulletin,* December, 1977, pp. 300-301.

Schiller, Anita R. ''Reference Service: Instruction or Information.'' *Library Quarterly,* January, 1965, pp. 52-60.

Spencer, Robert C. ''The Teaching Library.'' *Library Journal,* May 15, 1978, pp. 1021-24.

Vuturo, Robert. ''Beyond the Library Tour: Those Who *Can,* Must Teach.'' *Wilson Library Bulletin,* May, 1977, pp. 736-40.

Wilson, Pauline. ''Librarians as Teachers: The Study of an Organization Fiction.'' *Library Quarterly,* April, 1979, pp. 146-62.

Betwixt and Between: Some Thoughts on the Technical Services Librarian Involved in Reference and Bibliographic Instruction

Amy Dykeman

It does not take long before the average librarian entering the profession fresh out of library school realizes that all the theory learned about the organization and dissemination of knowledge translates into the real world of most academic libraries as "us against them" or public services vs. technical services. One need only peruse the job ads to see that the "unity" of library science education is often reduced to various functions like "reference librarian," "acquisitions librarian," or "cataloger," to name a few. Job descriptions with overlapping functions are usually the exception.

The bibliographic instruction movement of the last decade was primarily developed by reference librarians who were in a position to notice a few things about most library patrons. First, they saw that users, especially students, did not know how individual libraries were arranged (hence orientation programs), and, second, they recognized that users lacked a research methodology (hence bibliographic instruction programs labeled "course-related" or "for-credit"). What I find interesting is that after years of discussion, evaluation, journal articles, and "agendas," bibliographic instruction is still perceived as the occupation of reference librarians only. There must be—and are—other people like me who work in technical services and perform reference and library instruction duties.

I wondered how prevalent it was for librarians to work in both public and technical services roles, if these librarians performed reference and bibliographic instruction differently from their col-

Amy Dykeman is Technical Services Librarian, Douglass Library, Rutgers University, New Brunswick, NJ.

233

leagues who devote full-time to reference, and what advantages or disadvantages the integration of these roles would have.

Given the plethora of literature on bibliographic instruction, I was surprised to find few organized studies on this subject. An article written by Lois Pausch and Jean Koch[1] presents the findings of a survey they sent to 219 academic libraries on the current status of technical services librarians in bibliographic instruction. They found that in 64% of the responding libraries these librarians were engaged in some aspect of library instruction. Of this total, 61% served as tour guides, 54% staffed the public catalog information desk, 49% were class instructors, 44% were consultants, 20% prepared lessons, 15% staffed the reference desk, 6% wrote study guides, and 3% were term paper clinic interviewers.

These percentages—obtained from primarily academic libraries—are higher than I would have expected, although it is not clear how often in a normal week these functions were performed nor what type of technical services person was involved. I suspect that in many organizations, bibliographers and collection development librarians are considered part of technical services; their subject expertise has long been valued for both library instruction and reference purposes and these duties are often a regular part of their job.

Anne Roberts' study[2] of library instruction programs at ten campuses of the State University of New York mentions more specifically that of the forty-five SUNY librarians at these institutions engaged in for-credit instruction courses, seven were also in technical services—four in collection development positions and three as catalogers.

Quantifiable studies on the type of librarians engaged in library instruction do seem to be lacking, and maybe in a field which, to me, often seems burdened in statistical data and "over-surveyed," this is not such a bad thing. The existing literature on bibliographic instruction emphasizes the product (i.e., the program) over the qualifications and background of the instructor engaged in it.

Nevertheless, librarians are the last ones to be deterred if numbers are lacking, since experience and theories on good library service are always available. Donald Kinney[3] offers suggestions on how technical services librarians, particularly catalogers, could aid in library instruction programs and at the same time gain insight into patrons' needs. Michael Gorman's essay, "On Doing Away with Technical Services Departments,"[4] repeats these sentiments, and while Gorman does not mention library instruction directly, he does hope for the integration of public and technical services so that "librarianship will regain its professional pride, will cease to suffer from splintering and functionalism, and will become more effective in economic and practical terms."

Many of the authors I have mentioned lament the untapped subject expertise of the cataloger or collection development librarian who is not involved in reference or bibliographic instruction. And yet those of us engaged in reference work often find, for instance, that our subject background in American literature is hardly relevant when we search for articles on edible protein in sludge for an environmental sciences student. We know intuitively that in bibliographic instruction programs that a person's willingness to teach and a good speaking ability can be more important than the appropriate subject background. Can technical services librarians who work in areas without a definite subject connection, like acquisitions, serials, and bindery, offer something of value to an instruction program? I think it can still be said that a generalist is a valuable commodity in reference service and in many introductory level instruction classes. I'm not suggesting that any old generalist be pulled off the street to conduct a class. Certain components—known to most librarians—are necessary for even the most rudimentary instruction classes. A basic knowledge of reference sources is, of course, essential, as is a familiarity with those methodologies and search strategies that best provide help to students. Other variables such as the librarian's attitude and teaching ability cannot be overlooked.

If a librarian has these components of bibliographic instruction completely mastered, can he or she teach the same content at different libraries? Probably not, since every library (even those within the same system) is different. Different collections exist due to the manner in which collection development librarians perceive library needs. These professionals are responsible for the continual addition and withdrawal of materials that over time change the nature of collections; their knowledge of collections is an important source of public service information.

Different internal systems result in different library practices. Catalogers are a good source of information on local options. It would seem that by now the shared cataloging systems used by libraries would have eradicated differences in call numbers and subject headings across member libraries. Then one needs only, for example, to look up on the RLIN terminal the title of a subject bibliography to see that some libraries use ''Z'' call numbers, and others use the subject classification numbers.

Serials are treated by individual libraries in more ways than can be imagined: some classified, some alphabetical by title; some circulating, some not; some in microforms, some not. Serials librarians may be of help in explaining these systems of organization. They should be able to explain exactly what a serial is, and the differences between those items called ''periodicals,'' ''journals,'' ''magazines,'' and ''newspapers.''

Inconsistencies among libraries in terms of the collections and the local systems of organization are unavoidable and explain how even the best library users must re-familiarize themselves or, better yet, be instructed in the use of an unfamiliar library. In addition, differences between libraries, however miniscule, point out the problems inherent in the profession's search for uniformity in library instruction materials. Clearinghouses of bibliographic instruction guides and hand-outs are useful starting points for every library; nevertheless, in many instances the wheel must be re-invented to explain local systems and to up-date an ever-changing collection.

The librarians who work with and develop internal systems like the few mentioned above and who determine the nature of a collection (and its maintenance) may have something to both offer and to learn by participating in reference and library instruction. It has been my experience that wearing both public and technical services hats is beneficial in all aspects of my work.

Many library procedures exist for historical reasons that now may be totally unrelated to the actual users' needs. To someone in technical services this can most easily be discovered by working in reference or on an instruction class, much more pleasantly than listening to the complaints of the reference staff. I think an instruction class, in particular, allows someone (for a pre-determined amount of time, away from their regular duties) to give a presentation to a group of patrons on a specified subject as it exists within their library setting. In a course-related session, discussion about frustrating aspects of using the library often occurs between the librarian, the teaching faculty member, and the class of students.

In the end, of course, most patrons simply want the library to easily allow them to find the materials they need. It is amazing how many barriers are created to thwart this. More interaction with the public can help the acquisitions librarians better understand the necessity of finding the most efficient means of procuring books and the cataloger better understand the problems posed in the assignation of subject headings.

For libraries involved in cataloging (and which one isn't?), there is probably a definite trade-off when doing reference and library instruction. In most libraries there is no one more qualified to explain Library of Congress subject headings, call numbers, and cross references than catalogers. (As a matter of fact, many reference librarians are reluctant to tackle these subjects.) On the other hand, it never hurts to be reminded that subject headings like "Moving Pictures" and "European War" are a problem for patrons. With the advent of on-line catalogs, it seem crucial that both technical services and public services librarians notice how the patron perceives the subject headings and uses them as well as how much bibliographic information is needed at each access point.

It is useful for the cataloger to be reminded that the card catalog (or its COM or on-line successor) is only indicative of a small amount of a library's holdings. As Jesse Shera wrote:

> I think it was Grace O. Kelley's study back in the 30's that showed that cataloging brought out only about 30 percent of the total resources of the library on any given subject. This varied somewhat from subject to subject, but there is always materials in encyclopedias, periodicals, and handbooks which is not analyzed in the catalog. The reference librarian has to build a bridge among all the tools of the library, using the handbooks, encyclopedias, the bibliographies and so on to bridge the gap.[5]

I would add to Shera's list of bridge builders the various on-line data bases that have revolutionized the way reference librarians work. It is equally important that, when applicable, these tools are in technical services. For instance, the on-line version of *Books in Print* is much more up-to-date than the printed copy and should be utilized by acquisitions librarians.

When the librarian involved in acquisitions, bindery, and gifts also works at the reference desk, there is an occasional advantage to the patron that I hesitate to mention, because it is not systematic: memory. I often know that the latest replacement book on resume-writing has just arrived (and still resides in the "back room"), or that a bindery shipment has just returned that will be ready for shelving tomorrow. To think that one can rely on memory is dangerous and naive; nevertheless, it amazes me how often ''pre-accessioned'' library items are asked for at the reference desk.

There are a number of articles in the literature devoted to burn-out among librarians, especially those involved in bibliographic instruction. In course-related sessions, it often difficult over time to enthusiastically meet another group of new faces who will then march out of your life an hour later, supposedly better versed in the use of the library. Fears about the effectiveness of bibliographic instruction contribute to burn-out, and are quite evident given the search for the perfect method of evaluation that is present in the literature of this field and that is needed by librarians seemingly to justify to others the value of what they do. Fresh approaches and attitudes about bibliographic instruction are important and could be aided by the addition of librarians from non-reference areas.

For the technical services librarian, whose interaction with the public is limited and who deals with subjects in an abstract way, reference work offers a variety of subjects in a concrete and, often, challenging form. The outcome of this for many librarians, might be greater job satisfaction. In addition, for those academic libraries with tenure requirements, contact with the public (especially with faculty members) and a willingness to try new professional duties are often worthwhile endeavors for promotion considerations.

Many readers will by now readily acknowledge that in my discusson of this matter I have left out something crucial. In my search for a ''unified'' profession, I have omitted the fact that many technical services librarians have no interest in or no time available to give to reference or library instruction. In addition, the organizational structures of many larger libraries would resist this integration. It is obvious that for a successful implementation of this kind that a great deal of planning is necessary. Input and support from library administrators would be essential. And to be honest, I have not discussed a reciprocal arrangement whereby public services librarians ''donate'' time to technical services departments—a lengthy and complex subject in itself.

What I have tried to do is open for discussion the advantages that might occur if both technical services and public services librarians were familiar with the way in which patrons use the library. In an ideal system, those responsible for the availability of materials should be encouraged to understand, through reference work, what kinds of demands are actually placed on those same materials.

REFERENCES

1. Lois Pausch and Jean Koch, "Technical Services Librarians in Library Instruction," *Libri* 31 (September 1981): 198-204.

2. Anne Roberts, *A Study of Ten SUNY Campuses Offering an Undergraduate Credit Course in Library Instruction* (Washington, D.C.: Council on Library Resources, 1978), ERIC Document 157129.

3. Donald Kinney, "Role of Technical Services Librarians in Library Instruction," *Southeastern Librarian* 31 (Spring 1981):11-13.

4. Michael Gorman, "On Doing Away with Technical Services Departments," *American Libraries* 10 (July/August 1979), p. 435.

5. Jesse Shera, "Foundations of a Theory of Reference Service," in *Knowing Books and Men; Knowing Computers, Too* (Littleton, Colorado: Libraries Unlimited, 1973), p. 201.

Library Instruction and the Advancement of Reference Service

Kathleen Coleman

Of the changes taking place in public services in college and university libraries during the past decade, none has created more controversy among academic reference librarians than the growth of library instruction programs. Those active in instruction make themselves very visible both on campus and in the profession (even referring to themselves as a "movement"[1]), leaving their non-teaching colleagues back on the desk, wondering whether or not the results are worth the effort. And when library instruction activists suggest that their programs are more relevant to the library's role in academia than reference desk work, the advocates of traditional services are understandably concerned.[2] Such overstatements do nothing, of course, to increase the spirit of cooperation between the two groups. Despite the well-publicized arguments between the advocates of library instruction and of one-on-one desk work,[3] the literature and practice of library instruction have much to offer to traditional reference service. This paper will discuss some of the major sources of conflict between teaching and non-teaching librarians, and will identify some theoretical and practical contributions of library instruction to reference service.

ARGUMENTS AGAINST LIBRARY INSTRUCTION

Over the years, several arguments opposing library instruction programs have been published. Katz[4] points out several of these, including: library use cannot be taught adequately in one lecture or even one course; most library users want information, not instruc-

Kathleen Coleman is Reference Librarian and Coordinator, Instructional Services, San Diego State University Library, San Diego, CA 92182.

241

tion; after a brief amount of instruction, students erroneously assume that they know all that is needed; and library instruction has not yet been proven effective. Wilson[5] describes the role of librarian-instructor as an "organization fiction" designed by librarians to improve their status. She sees this fiction as harmful because it causes dissension in the library profession. Indeed, "instruction" has a negative connotation to the tradition-minded reference librarian because of the information versus instruction controversy which has appeared in library literature for more than a generation. In this context, "information" represents maximum reference service, because the librarian supplies the user's need, while "instruction" represents minimum service, because the librarian merely shows the user how to find the information.[6]

Most of the above points are valid to some extent. It is probably impossible to teach the user all that he or she will ever need to know about libraries, yet many users assume that their one-hour freshman tour was the definitive experience. Many users would prefer being given their statistics in lieu of a lecture on how to find them (although just as many, in this writer's experience, and inveterate do-it-yourselfers.) Conclusive evaluation of the effects of library instruction has yet to be carried out; however, evaluation of traditional reference service has been just as inconclusive. Whether the teaching role of librarians is a fiction or a reality, it has definitely caused dissension in the profession. But the "instruction versus information" question is an artificial one, because the two alternatives are not mutually exclusive. In reality, reference librarians routinely dispense both information *and* instruction. Furthermore, formal library instruction programs make students more aware of the resources available and their potential use, as well as of the assistance available from reference librarians. Most students do not request individual reference assistance, and therefore underutilize the academic library. For example, at San Diego State University Library, the percentage of library users asking the staff any type of question ranged from 23% to 15% on a monthly basis between July, 1982 and January, 1983, and the percentage asking reference or research questions was between 11% and 6% during the same period.[7] Several writers have described the reluctance of most library users to ask questions.[8-10] Brian Nielsen, in describing the role of the traditional reference librarian, points out that service is actually offered only to a minority: "reference service as it is classically performed in an intermediary role model, of necessity, advocates providing information only to those who ask, and promises maximum service to that minority."[11] Indeed, one reason for the inception and growth of library instruction programs was the realization by concerned reference librarians that traditional one-on-one reference service was not doing the job.

Library instruction often breaks down the barrier between student and librarian. Every librarian who has given a successful class lecture has made himself or herself approachable to the students in that class, and can expect several office or desk visits from an otherwise "silent majority." The teaching which occurs in formal library instruction programs differs from the informal teaching offered at reference desks in several important respects. Library instruction programs are more likely to have stated objectives, planned curriculum, organized presentation, and evaluation by the users. Therefore, what is lost in personal relevance is likely to be gained in comprehensiveness and quality.

THEORETICAL INSIGHTS FROM LIBRARY INSTRUCTION

As library instruction programs have become more sophisticated and more integrated into college and university curricula, manuals and papers on library instruction have come to include theoretical insights as well as practical information. And because traditional reference service involves many of the same insights and skills which are required in library instruction, these concepts have validity on the desk. Two important areas in which library instruction has made contributions to reference theory are the bibliographic structure of disciplines and learning theory. Smalley and Plum[12] compare the goals of scholarship in the humanities fields and those of research in scientific disciplines. They find that the emphasis in the humanities is on valid interpretation of a work of art, but in the sciences it is on valid experiment to prove general laws. Most scholarship in the humanities is done by individuals, and two-thirds to three-quarters of the literature is monographic. Furthermore, scholarly literature in the humanities remains valid for a long time. In science fields, on the other hand, research is cooperative, and multiple authorships are common. Eighty percent of the significant literature appears in journals, because making and promptly reporting a discovery is important. In the sciences, knowledge is cumulative, and the most useful literature is the most recent. These generalizations make broad divisions; on closer analysis, of course, each discipline within the humanities, and each within the sciences, is seen as unique. Beaubien, Hogan, and George[13] analyze the research process and resulting literature in several social science and humanities fields, and show how to integrate their findings into the library instruction program. Hopkins[14] states that library instruction should teach students to find literature and information within the bibliographic network of a discipline. Furthermore, librarians should point out to students the differences in publishing patterns and in bibliographic control between related disciplines. McInnis[15] relates analysis of the structure of disciplines directly to the reference services of the academic library, with considerable emphasis on the teaching function. He states that the existence of reference works which give order to and control the literature of a discipline is not self-evident. Students must be told that they exist, and shown how to use them.[16] While most reference librarians are aware of research and publication patterns and their consequences for information retrieval in a general way, these elaborations in recent library instruction literature stimulate further thinking, and show how these insights can help our students with their library research.

Library applications of learning theory are another contribution of recent library instruction literature to reference librarianship. In an effort to make their programs more effective, library instruction librarians have turned to educational psychology's learning and development theories for guidance. Aluri[17] presents three learning models—cognitive, conditioning, and cybernetic—and points out applications in various modes of library instruction. The cognitive perspective is important in formal presentations. The teacher prepares the mind of the learner with "advance organizers," which give him/her a conceptual framework for new knowledge. The teacher then presents materials in a sequence designed to enhance learning. The conditioning perspective is relevant to programmed instruction. Here, behavior change is seen as central to learning. The conditioning perspective has influenced librarians to set concrete, specific objectives for their instructional programs.[18] The cybernetic perspective emphasizes knowledge of results, or feedback; it is important in computer-assisted instruction. The learner interacts with the program, and learns from his/her errors. Kobelski and Reichel[19] elaborate on the need for cognitive structure in library instruction. They identify six conceptual frameworks which can be used to organize presentations, including 1) type of reference tool, 2) systematic literature search (search strategy), 3) form of publication, 4) primary versus secondary sources, 5) publication sequence, and 6) citation patterns. Using such a framework, the authors believe, greatly improves student retention and learning.

Library instruction librarians have also explored developmental psychology for insights into how students at different stages of intellectual development can best learn. Mellon[20] has used William Perry's four stages of intellectual and ethical development to design library instruction appropriate for students at various stages in their academic careers. At the *dualism* stage, the difference between right and wrong is very important to the student, along with an emphasis on authority. Library instruction at this stage (generally freshman orientation) should be straightforward and easily understood. When the student reaches the *multiplicity* stage, he/she becomes less certain about right and wrong, and recognizes that there can be several approaches to a problem. Library instruction can become more complex at this stage, and search strategies for problem-solving presented. *Relativism,* the third stage, brings the realization that few things can be known absolutely, and that one's opinions must be backed up with supporting evidence. Students at this stage sense the need to gather and analyze data before forming opinions and making decisions. Library instruction reaches fertile ground in these students, with their keen information needs. *Commitment* is the stage at which students make a decision and take a stand, while still recognizing that nothing can be certain. As Mellon points out, these last two stages tend to blend into one another.

Development models such as this one have considerable value for the librarian at the reference desk. They help him/her to realize that students are still growing, that a naive or somewhat intolerantly phrased request often reflects immaturity, but not stupidity. Furthermore, the detailed search strategy which the student will find highly useful next year is now dismissed as overwhelming and irrelevant. Most librarians know about development theories in common-sense, general ways, but seeing them elucidated in detail makes them much more useful on the desk.

In an effort to show how students progress in their knowledge of libraries and information sources, Frick [21] has identified four levels of bibliographic awareness: 1) knowledge of specific titles which perform given functions, 2) knowledge of types of sources which can answer types of questions, 3) the knowledge that the nature of a given discipline determines the types of publications available, and 4) the knowledge that the structure of literature in a society informs, and is informed by, the society. Awareness of this more cognitive development model enables the reference librarian to assess the level of sophistication of the user. The librarian can then help the user to better understand information sources and their structure through reference assistance.

PRACTICAL BENEFITS OF LIBRARY INSTRUCTION

In addition to the theoretical models described above, library instruction offers several practical benefits to the reference librarian. The librarian preparing for a presentation needs to study the reference sources to be covered very carefully for scope, arrangement, time periods covered, and other characteristics.[22] Library instruction requires more detailed knowledge of sources and their interrelationships then does reference desk work, because the individual works must be presented to students in a meaningful cognitive structure. Also, students often ask very specific questions, so the librarian must be well-prepared. A request for instruction in a field relatively unfamiliar to the reference librarian is a splendid opportunity to grow professionally. While most of us know that we should increase our knowledge of unfamiliar subjects, the demands of other duties prevent us from following through until the necessity for an instructional presentation arises. Furthermore, by preparing instructional materials and presentations regularly, reference librarians become more aware of differences and similarities in the bibliographic structure of disciplines.[23] Inevitably, the instruction librarian comes to view reference desk service as another teaching situation. As Rader[24] points out, the librarian at the reference desk uses teaching techniques, counseling and interviewing methods, and knowledge of the information system to help the user.

Library instruction offers another benefit to the reference librarians by upgrading the quality and quantity of individual reference encounters. Students who have had some instruction are more aware of what the library can provide, and therefore ask better questions.[25] Koyama sees library instruction as a manifestation of consumerism—that is, effective library instruction enables students to be better consumers of library services, including reference assistance.[26]

Indeed, if the user comes to the reference desk knowing about publication patterns, the ways in which statistics are collected and reported, the general types of materials available in the library, and how they are organized, he/she will be able to make better use of the expertise of the librarian. McCarthy, in describing the benefits of library instruction, includes the positive attitude instilled in students:

> Let us now consider the good effects of library instruction, as observed from the reference desk. These are patience, adventurousness, and trust in—or at least respect for—reference librarians. Patience is a result of realistic expectations. Well-prepared library users know that time and effort will be required of them. They realize that their questions and problems may not have easy solutions, that the path of their research will probably not be a straight line.[27]

IMPROVING REFERENCE SERVICES

Library instruction also makes valuable contributions to the reference department as a whole, most notably in planning the public service program and in collection development. Librarians planning course-integrated instruction with teaching faculty gain detailed and current insight into the materials and methods used in the classroom. Too often, reference services are planned and materials ordered without regard to how disciplines are taught today. And changes are occurring. McInnis[28] shows how, discipline by discipline, innovative instructors are abandoning the traditional textbook/lecture/term paper/exam course organization. Instead, faculty give writing assignments which require field and library research, use of primary sources, and more active evaluation and analysis. Learning facts and ideas formulated by others becomes less important than learning how to find evidence and examine it. As McInnis points out, preparing students for this kind of research requires close cooperation between the instructor and the reference librarian:

> When a student research project is considered for a particular course—if it is expected to be a reasonably successful and rewarding experience—certain preparations should necessarily be made. Perhaps the biggest problem confronting classroom instructors and reference librarians alike is how to inform students rapidly of the reference sources they need to consult

in order to expose them to the required material related to their research topic.

Neither the classroom instructor nor the reference librarian can solve such problems satisfactorily when each is working separately. By working together, however, considerable success can be achieved. In addition to being well acquainted with the subject, the instructor provides the stimulation and motivation necessary to get most students seriously concerned about engaging in research. After the students' interest is developed, it becomes the task of the reference librarian to provide the means for students to effectively engage in research. Implementing such programs requires considerable preparation, especially on the part of the reference librarian.[29]

As librarians become more involved in formal instruction work, they become more aware of the teaching role of the reference department, and are more likely to evaluate the reference environment. Are the signs clear and easy to read? How hard is it to find the reference desk? Are the materials arranged logically? Instruction-oriented librarians demystify the library by designing self-guided tours, writing guides, bibliographies and pathfinders, and setting up point-of-use instruction. Rader[30] provides a fine summary of the teaching potential of reference departments. Library instruction activities often help with development of the reference collection as well. The librarian discovers gaps in the collection, outdated editions, and misplaced reference tools while preparing presentations and instructional materials.

CONFLICTS IN THE REFERENCE DEPARTMENT

Despite the benefits which library instruction can offer to reference librarians, the conflicts between teaching and non-teaching librarians remain very real. As Oberman-Soroka[31] points out, the myth of the outgoing, energetic instruction librarian has created a separate identity for the "teachers," and isolated them from their colleagues. Roberts[32] reinforces this idea, and adds that instruction librarians often establish programs without consulting with other professionals on the staff. As a consequence, the library may now be committed to delivering services in which some librarians do not believe. Instruction librarians sometimes make a cult of teaching, which causes dissent in the profession.[33] Unfortunately, some advocates of library instruction make statements which can only be deterimental to the relationship between teaching and non-teaching librarians. For example:

> investigations of the quality of traditional reference-desk service tend to support the suspicion that the privacy of the reference transaction, combined with low user expectation, fosters superficial work and protects incompetence. Classroom instruction exposes librarians' claims of bibliographic expertise to public scrutiny, a situation that motivates all but the most irresponsible to do their homework well.[34]

Overly zealous instruction librarians can alienate not only their colleagues, but reference service users as well. While some students are grateful for a description of the publishing activities of the Census Bureau, others would prefer that the librarian on duty provide them the demographics they need, minus the library lecture. Kenney, in an article entitled "Instruction Librarians: Barriers to Information?" points out the danger in trying to dispense universal library instruction from the reference desk.[35] Instruction librarians, like all reference librarians, must approach each desk encounter with sensitivity to the user's needs and wants.

THE FUTURE OF LIBRARY INSTRUCTION AND REFERENCE SERVICE

In the future, library instruction will very likely have a central place in the public service program of the academic library. Instructional activities of all kinds are on the increase, not only because librarians feel duty-bound to offer them, but also because faculty and students want them. And what will be the future of conventional reference desk service? A few library instruction advocates expect it to wane in importance,[36] but this is highly unlikely. With new information products and services entering our libraries constantly, thorough library research is certainly not becoming any less complicated. Furthermore, effective library instruction nearly always increases traffic at the reference desk. As Reichel points out, there is a place in the public service program both for library instruction and for individual reference work. Indeed, each activity offers an advantage not present in the other:

In bibliographic instruction presentations, emphasis must be placed on the overview; introduction of too many details simply loses the audience. At the reference desk, it is rarely desirable or possible to launch into a discussion of the literature of a field, while it is appropriate to teach the use of specific indexes or bibliographies.[37]

The public service librarian of the future will most likely be doing more library instruction and more individual reference service. He/she will also be more visible to campus administrators, faculty, and students than is the case in many colleges and universities at present. Daughterty has issued a warning to reference librarians concerned about erosion of their budgets and administrative support:

> Public service librarians must combine their skills and interests. They must take a broader view of public services to include bibliographic instruction, traditional reference, and data base services, all as important parts of an integrated information services program. Librarians must abandon the reference desk and heighten their profile within the academic community.[38]

Many reference departments have heeded this warning already. Those who have not would do well to stop feuding about library instruction and start reaping its benefits.

REFERENCES

1. Frances L. Hopkins, "User Instruction in the College Library: Origins, Prospects, and a Practical Program," in *College Librarianship,* ed. William Miller and D. Stephen Rockwood (Metuchen, N.J.: Scarecrow Press, 1981), p. 173.

2. David W. Lewis and C. Paul Vincent, "An Initial Response . . .," *Journal of Academic Librarianship* 9: 4-6 (March, 1983).

3. For a recent and stimulating view of several sides of the question, see "Reactions to the Think Tank Recommendations: a Symposium," ed. Joanne Euster, *Journal of Academic Librarianship* 9: 4-14 (March, 1983).

4. William A. Katz, *Introduction to Reference Work: Vol. II, Reference Services and Reference Processes* (4th ed., New York: McGraw-Hill, 1982), p. 56-60.

5. Pauline Wilson, "Librarians as Teachers: the Study of an Organization Fiction," *Library Quarterly* 49: 146-62 (April, 1979).

6. For an excellent presentation of this controversy, see Anita R. Schiller, "Reference Services: Instruction or Information," *Library Quarterly* 35: 52-60 (January, 1965).

7. The detailed statistics are given in this table. (Actual visitor statistics should undoubtedly be somewhat lower than the numbers given, to indicate some entrances by our staff

	Number of visitors	Total questions asked	Reference or research questions	Percentage all questions	Percentage reference or research questions
July 1982	50,085	11,644	5,149	23%	10%
August	49,228	10,919	4,917	22%	10%
September	272,893	49,821	20,832	18%	8%
October	261,025	51,073	28,088	20%	11%
November	305,811	46,617	22,810	15%	7%
December	175,196	29,311	14,512	17%	8%
January 1983	131,963	21,505	8,520	16%	6%

of approximately 130. However, these adjustments would not raise the percentage of question-askers appreciably.)

8. Mary Jane Swope and Jeffrey Katzer, "Why Don't They Ask Questions?" *RQ* 12: 161-66 (Winter, 1972). The authors report that 65% of their respondents with library questions were unwilling to ask a reference librarian for help.

9. Roger Horn, "Why They Don't Ask Questions," *RQ* 13: 225-33 (Spring, 1974).

10. Richard M. Daugherty, "Avoiding Burnout," *Journal of Academic Librarianship* 7: 333 (January, 1982).

11. Brian Nielsen, "Teacher or Intermediary: Alternative Professional Models in the Information Age," *College and Research Libraries* 43: 186-7 (May, 1982).

12. Topsy N. Smalley and Stephen H. Plum, "Teaching Library Researching in the Humanities and the Sciences: a Contextual Approach," in *Theories of Bibliographic Education: Designs for Teaching,* ed. Cerise Oberman and Katina Strauch (New York: Bowker, 1982), pp. 135-70.

13. Anne K. Beaubien, Sharon A. Hogan, and Mary W. George, *Learning the Library: Concepts and Methods for Effective Bibliographic Instruction* (New York: Bowker, 1982).

14. Hopkins, "User Instruction in the College Library," p. 188.

15. Raymond G. McInnis, *New Perspectives for Reference Service in Academic Libraries* (Westport, Conn.: Greenwood Press, 1978).

16. McInnis, *New Perspectives for Reference Service,* p. 123.

17. Rao Aluri, "Application of Learning Theories to Library-Use Instruction," *Libri* 31: 140-52 (August, 1981).

18. *The Bibliographic Instruction Handbook* (Chicago: Policy and Planning Committee, Bibliographic Instruction Section, Association of College and Research Libraries, 1979) places a strong emphasis on behavioral objectives for library instruction programs.

19. Pamela Kobelski and Mary Reichel, "Conceptual Frameworks for Bibliographic Instruction," *Journal of Academic Librarianship* 7: 73-77 (May, 1981).

20. Contance A. Mellon, "Information Problem-Solving: a Developmental Approach to Library Instruction," in *Theories of Bibliographic Education: Designs for Teaching,* ed. Cerise Oberman and Katina Strauch (New York: Bowker, 1982), pp. 75-89.

21. Elizabeth Frick, "Information Structure and Bibliographic Instruction," *Journal of Academic Librarianship* 1: 12-13 (September, 1975).

22. Beaubien, Hogan, and George, *Learning the Library,* p. 188.

23. Beaubien, Hogan, and George, *Learning the Library.*

24. Hannelore B. Rader, "Reference Services as a Teaching Function," *Library Trends* 29: 95-103 (Summer, 1980).

25. Lewis and Vincent, "An Initial Response," p. 5.

26. Janice T. Koyama, "Bibliographic Instruction and the Role of the Academic Librarian," *Journal of Academic Librarianship* 9: 12 (March, 1983).

27. Constance McCarthy, "Library Instruction: Observations from the Reference Desk," *RQ* 22: 37 (Fall, 1982).

28. McInnis, *New Perspective for Reference Service.*

29. McInnis, *New Perspective for Reference Service,* xx-xxi.

30. Rader, "Reference Services as a Teaching Function."

31. Cerise Oberman-Soroka, "Personality to Education: a Necessary Change," in *Directions for the Decade: Library Instruction in the 1980's, Papers Presented at the Tenth Annual Conference on Library Orientation for Academic Libraries, May 8-9, 1980,* ed. Carolyn Kirkendall (Ann Arbor, MI: Pierian Press, 1981), p. 34-6.

32. Anne Roberts, "The Politics of Library Instruction: Internal and External," in *Proceedings of the Second Southeastern Conference on Approaches to Bibliographic Instruction, March 22-23, 1979,* ed. Cerise Oberman-Soroka (Charleston, S.C.: College of Charleston, 1980), p. 1-9.

33. Nielsen, "Teacher or Intermediary," p. 188.

34. Hopkins, "User Instruction in the College Library," p. 184.

35. Donald J. Kenney, "Instruction Librarians: Barriers to Information?" in *Directions for the Decade: Library Instruction in the 1980's, Papers Presented at the Tenth Annual Conference on Library Orientation for Academic Libraries, May 8-9, 1980,* ed. Carolyn Kirkendall (Ann Arbor, MI: Pierian Press, 1981), p. 54-6.

36. For example, Hopkins makes the following statement: "Conventional reference-desk service, relatively passive and uneven in quality, will be seriously challenged. The bureaucratic work styles and clerical hours of traditional librarianship are already suffering comparison with the greater individual autonomy and more intense commitment of the instruction librarian." ("User Instruction in the College Library," p. 199).

37. Mary Reichel, "Bibliographic Instruction and the Reference Desk," *Journal of Academic Librarianship* 9: 10 (March, 1983).

38. Daugherty, "Avoiding Burnout," p. 333.

FORTHCOMING
IN THE REFERENCE LIBRARIAN

EVALUATING REFERENCE SERVICES AND COLLECTIONS

Theory and Practice in the Collection and Analysis of Data
  Descriptive of Reference Desk Service . . . . Margaret Joseph
Implementing the Evaluation Study . . . . Sam Rothstein
Statistics and Evaluation . . . . Juri and Jean Stratford
Evaluation of Methods of Evaluating
  Reference Services . . . . Sydney Pierce
Evaluating the Reference Librarian . . . . Bill Young
Why Not Accredit Reference Departments . . . . Bernard Vavrek
Factors Affecting the Performance of Question Answering
  Services in Libraries . . . . F. W. Lancaster
Reference Evaluation: What's the Use? . . . . Eleanor J. Rodger
Evaluating Heavily Illustrated Reference Materials
  for Selection and Use . . . . Charles Bunge
Tailoring Measures to Fit Your Service . . . . Douglas L. Zweizig
Evaluation of Reference Services and Personnel . . . Terry L. Weech
Unobstrusive Evaluation of Reference Services—A One-Sided View
  of the Multifaceted Activity . . . . Robert Harris
A Community Approach to Reference Evaluation
  in Public Libraries . . . . Mary Lee Bundy
So What Do You Mean When You Say "A Good Reference
  Librarian" . . . . Mignon Adams
Self-Diagnosis and Evaluation . . . . Charles R. McClure
Definitions for Planning and Evaluating
  Reference Services . . . . Katherine Emerson
The Whole Shebang—Comprehensive Evaluation
  of Reference Operations . . . . Ellsworth Mason
Developing Criteria for Database Evaluation:
  The Example of Women's Studies . . . . Sarah M. Pritchard

Qualitative Methods in the Evaluation
    of Reference Services ....David Shavit
Use of Citation Studies in Evaluation ....Alvin Schrader
Evaluating Bibliographic Instruction................Steve Falk

CONFLICTS IN REFERENCE SERVICES

Conflicts Between Interlibrary Loan
    and Reference Services ....Marcia L. Sprules
Help/We Need a Better Name for What We Do........Paul Wiener
Conflict Between Libraries
    in Same Geographical Area ....D. E. Davidson
Arbitrary Limits on the Public to Be Served ....Peggy Sullivan
Conflicts Between Reference Librarians and Faculty
    Concerning Bibliographic Instruction ....David Isaacson
Charging for Services: Then and Now ....Margaret Steig
The Reference Librarian as Middleperson:
    Potential Conflicts Between Catalogers
    and Reference Librarians ....Gillian M. McCombs
A Collection of Books: The College Professor
    vs the Reference Librarian ....Melissa R. Watson
The Provision of Health Information to the Public .....Robert Berk
The Role of the Reference Librarian as Viewed by Faculty
    and Administration in a College Library ....Eric Johnson
Paying Twice: The Philosophy and Reality of Fees as a Barrier
    to Information Access ....Dean Brugess
Between the Devil and the Deep Blue Sea-Reference:
    Some Conflicts and Dilemmas in Reference
    Service ....George R. Bauer and Joan Robb
Role Ambiguity and Conflict in Reference Service:
    A Direction for Research ....Henry R. Mendelsohn
Help Your Boss Support B.I. ....Robert E. Brundin
The Encapsulated Reference Librarian:
    Breaking Down Departmental Barriers ....Judith B. Quinlan
Reference Philosophy
    vs Service Reality...........Larry D. Benson and Julene Butler
Yours, Mine or Ours: Identifying Who
    and How We Serve...........Debbie Masters and Gail Flatness
The NASA Industrial Application Center: Fee Based
    vs Free Information Services ....Lynn Heer
Uneven Reference Desk Service......................Fred Batt